Praise for
Third Culture Kids

"As an adult TCK, I have long wrestled with how I fit into this world. This book is the 'bible' for anyone who wants to understand the blessings and the curses of growing up multiculturally."

> —Wm Paul Young, author of the #1 *New York Times* Best Seller *The Shack*

"Growing up as a TCK has been a gift and has significantly shaped my life and work. As I interact with world leaders one day and with those living in refugee camps the next, I continually draw upon my experience of living among different cultures. I am delighted to see the lessons learned from the traditional TCK experience live on in this new edition of *Third Culture Kids*."

> —Scott Gration, Maj Gen, USAF (Ret), President Obama's Special Envoy to Sudan

"I called the first edition of *Third Culture Kids* 'absolutely brilliant.' This revised edition continues to earn that acclaim. It's a powerhouse of a book through which readers growing up 'among worlds'—and their parents and the professionals responsible for their care and teaching—become able to take leadership of the challenges and opportunities presented by such a rich and complex childhood."

> —Barbara F. Schaetti, Ph.D., Transition Dynamics, second-generation
> dual-national Adult TCK and lead author of *Making a World of Difference.*
> *Personal Leadership: A Methodology of Two Principles and Six Practices*

"Because Third Culture Kids have been exposed to other cultures in significant ways and have experienced multiple transitions while growing up, it is in their DNA to thrive within the pace and nature of globalization. This book is a must to understand the challenges TCKs face and the unique skills they can leverage as global leaders."

> —Katrina Burrus, Ph.D., CEO of MKB Conseil & Coaching and
> author of *Global Nomadic Leaders: How to Identify, Attract, and Retain*

"In today's globalized and highly mobile world, the lessons to be learned from this new edition of *Third Culture Kids* transcend mere cultural enlightenment about a unique group of individuals growing up between worlds. This book is timelier than ever, and should be essential reading for parents anywhere in the world raising *cross-cultural* children."

> —Robin Pascoe, author of *Raising Global Nomads:*
> *Parenting Abroad in an On-Demand World*

"This revised edition of *Third Culture Kids* opens up the topic of cultural hybridization in new and exciting ways. By recognizing similarities between TCKs, children from bi/multicultural parentage, children of immigrants, those who live on or near borderlands, international adoptees and those forced into geographic and cultural transition through war and/or famine, the author puts her finger on one of the most interesting, complex and potentially most liberating aspects of our increasingly globalizing society. This book opens up hope for dialogue, empathy, mutual learning and ultimately the joyful acceptance of the diversity in us all."

> —Marc Levitt, storyteller, educator, and creator of www.thirdculturestories.com

For Betty Lou Pollock and David Van Reken, our lifelong partners and unfailing supporters throughout our journeys. And to our children, who have taught us so much—TCKs "for true."

Third Culture Kids

revised edition

Growing Up
Among Worlds

David C. Pollock

Ruth E. Van Reken

NICHOLAS BREALEY
PUBLISHING

BOSTON • LONDON

This trade edition first published by Nicholas Brealey Publishing in 2001. Revised in 2009.

20 Park Plaza, Suite 1115A	3-5 Spafield Street, Clerkenwell
Boston, MA 02116, USA	London, EC1R 4QB, UK
Tel: + 617-523-3801	Tel: +44-(0)-207-239-0360
Fax: + 617-523-3708	Fax: +44-(0)-207-239-0370
www.nicholasbrealey.com	

First published as *The Third Culture Kid Experience* by Intercultural Press in 1999.

Printed in the United States of America

15 14 13 12 11   3 4 5 6 7

Library of Congress Cataloging-in-Publication Data
Pollock, David C.
   Third culture kids : growing up among worlds / David C. Pollock,
Ruth E. Van Reken. — Rev. ed.
      p. cm.
   Includes bibliographical references.
   ISBN 978-1-85788-525-5
  1. Social interaction in children—Foreign countries. 2. Social skills in children—Foreign
countries. 3. Children—Travel—Foreign countries. 4. Children—Foreign countries—Attitudes.
5. Intercultural communication—Foreign countries. 6. Parents—Employment—Foreign
countries. I. Van Reken, Ruth E., 1945– II. Title.
   HQ784.S56P65 2009
   303.3'208209—dc22

                                                                            2009024639

Contents

Part III   Maximizing the Benefits   167

Appendices

Acknowledgments

WITHOUT LOIS STÜCK'S ORIGINAL ENCOURAGEMENT, transcriptions of seminar tapes, suggestions, and expert help throughout the initial creative process of this book, it would have remained only a dream. Without Professor Barbara Cambridge's original guidance in the writing process or Professor Jon Eller's most helpful ideas about organization, the manuscript would never have gotten back to Lois or our publishers. Thinking partner and artist Barb Knuckles has shaped this book with her ideas and art. Karen Allen, Kay Wilson, and mother Betty Frame have patiently read, corrected, and proofed this text. Anthropologist Ken Barger; friends Margie Becker, Lori Beuerman, Christine Dowdeswell, Janet Fischer, Stephanie Hock, Brenda Keck, Ann Kroeker, Erica Lipasti, Paul Pedersen, Paul Seaman, Alan Shea, Francisco West, and Elisabeth Wood; wife Betty Lou Pollock; and daughter Stephanie Van Reken Eriksen have all given most helpful suggestions while reading various drafts of the manuscript. Helen Fail's insights into international schooling have been invaluable. The list could go on and on.

Above all, without each TCK and ATCK who has shared his or her story with us through the years, without the honest dialogue we have witnessed among so many, there would have been no story to tell. In particular, we thank the Global Nomad chapter at Valparaiso University for the time they gave to engage in dialogue specifically designed to address issues we are raising in this book. And a huge thanks to "Erika" not only for letting us use her story, but also for helping in the early stages of writing it.

And many thanks to David Hoopes for having the vision that this is a topic whose time has come—to say nothing of his masterfully helping two people join their different thoughts and writing styles into one text. He did not have an easy job. Thanks also to Toby Frank for her further suggestions and Judy Carl-Hendrick for substantial help in the final editorial process of the first edition. Without each of them this book couldn't have been written in the readable form we trust it now is. And now thanks to Nicholas Brealey for having the vision to make this book more available to the public, to Trish O'Hare for her original encouragement to update and expand this book, to Nicholas Brealey and Chuck Dresner for agreeing, and to Erika Heilman and Rebecca Greenberg for their great help in the final editing process. We've decided it not only takes a village to raise a child, but it also takes one to birth a book. Last, but certainly not least, we thank God not only for life but for the richness of our lives. We have experienced much joy in our journeys as we have studied this topic and lived it as well.

Introduction

By Ruth E. Van Reken

IN 1999, DAVID POLLOCK BEGAN THE FIRST EDITION OF THIS book with the following words: "Third culture kids (TCKs) [children who spend a significant period of their developmental years in a culture outside their parents' passport culture(s)] are not new, and they are not few. They have been a part of the earth's population from the earliest migrations. They are normal people with the usual struggles and pleasures of life. But because they have grown up with different experiences from those who have lived primarily in one culture, TCKs are sometimes seen as slightly strange by the people around them." He went on to say that "since we are dealing with people, we are writing about process and progress, not a fixed entity. In the past two decades alone, dramatic changes related to the care of children and adults have occurred in the global nomad community, and undoubtedly new theories and practices will continue to evolve."

And that is why it is time for an update of this book. Many of those changes Dave predicted have happened or are happening. In our globalizing world, the degree of cultural complexity many now face within their families is staggering. Traditional assumptions of what it means to belong to a particular race, nationality, or ethnicity are constantly challenged by those whose identities have been formed among many cultural worlds. While diversity programs address the differences in the visible layers of culture such as race, ethnicity, and gender, the hidden diversity of those shaped in these larger arenas often goes unnoticed.

Consider what happened during the 2008 presidential campaign in the United States. Cable TV news commentators spent endless hours struggling to define then-candidate Barack Obama's cultural and racial identity. They seemed trapped by old definitions or categories of identity, none of which were sufficient to explain the complex intertwining of cultural worlds making up President Obama's life story, including his experience as a TCK. Ironically, these same commentators also never seemed to consider how the global upbringing of John McCain, the opposing presidential candidate, might have shaped his sense of identity and worldview. Neither did they discuss how the many other adult TCKs President Obama named to his administration, such as Valerie Jarrett, Timothy Geithner, James L. Jones, or (Ret.) Major General J. Scott Gration, might have been impacted by their internationally mobile childhoods.

Perhaps these attempts to define President Obama did lead to some awareness that these old categories of identity are no longer sufficient models for today's world. A few months after the election, a school board in the Washington, D.C., area said students could check more than one category of racial identity on the admission forms. While this change seeks to recognize the growing possibility of racial mixing, it continues to miss the potential of cultural mixing also possible for those who, like TCKs, grow up in multiple spheres of cultural influence. How, then, do we begin to find language to define these changes and consider the implications of these global shifts for both individuals and society?

Perhaps the answer is simpler than it seems. We need to keep building strong new structures on lessons learned from globally and culturally mobile families in the past so present and future generations of TCKs and others raised among a plethora of cultural worlds can continue to thrive.

In our last e-mails before Dave's untimely death in 2004, we talked of how, despite many changes in the world, the original TCK Profile had continued to generate the countless "a-ha!" moments we had watched over and over again in audiences everywhere. Dave often began his seminars by saying, "I'm probably not going to tell you something that you don't know, but I may well tell you something you don't know you already know." And that's what he did. Our files were filled with letters from TCKs and their families who had read our book or attended a seminar, thanking us for giving language and understanding to an experience lived but, to that point, unnamed for them.

We were, however, also increasingly aware of how much bigger this topic was growing. As mentioned earlier, the traditional TCK experience itself has become more complicated for many. We wondered: What is the same or different for TCKs who also happen to be part of a minority group in their passport culture? Are there differences for those who go to a new country with parents for reasons other than a career? What about bicultural or biracial TCKs? Are these increasingly complex experiences changing in some way the fundamental story of the more traditional TCK experience about which we have written?

In addition, new insights and questions developed as we began to connect with others around the world. We met Dr. Momo Kano Podolsky, an adult TCK and sociologist in Japan, and became aware that researchers in other countries were also studying this phenomenon under different names (see appendix B). Momo made the observation that our work focused primarily on the impact of this experience on the individual, while the Japanese research also considered how reintegrating TCKs back into their culture impacted the entire society. This difference in approach not only reflected how individualistic versus collectivistic societies might look at the same circumstances, but it also raised an intriguing question: How, in fact, has the presence of TCKs and adult TCKs changed or is changing societies in the West as well as the East? Perhaps it is only now when so many world leaders, including President Obama and many in his administration, are adult TCKs in public view that the answers to this previously unconsidered question might become apparent. We can also learn lessons from the Japanese experience on how a society moves from seeing the TCK experience as a negative for its culture or the individual to recognizing the positive nature of the experience for both.

While we saw the growing complexity for many TCKs and learned much from the larger group of people studying them, another phenomenon began as well. No matter where either of us went, people came up after seminars or wrote e-mails to say, "I am not a TCK as you talk about, but I related to nearly every-thing you mentioned as part of the TCK Profile. Why?" Some had grown up as immigrant children, or refugees, or in different cultural worlds in one country. Others were international adoptees or children of minorities. In our first edition, we mentioned why these types of experiences were different from the traditional TCK life we were writing about. But eventually we could not ignore the reality that *something* connects all of these journeys of children who grow up in a multi-plicity of cultural worlds, no matter how they happen. Yet we were also presented with the very challenge our dear and special colleague, the late Norma McCaig, wrote about in her Foreword for our first edition of this book. If every person who had grown up in some form of a cross-cultural childhood could be called a TCK, as we were already beginning to do, how could anyone research either traditional TCKs or these other types of experiences?

Although Dave died before we were able to complete our project, in our last discussions we agreed it was time to do an update and try to sort out some of these emerging matters. How would we start? We thought of two ways.

First, we looked seriously at Norma's injunction to find a way to look at all the experiences without confusing the research. It seemed if we created a new umbrella name for all children who grew up in any type of cross-cultural envi-ronment, we could look at what commonalities they shared and still leave room for the different details of each type of experience. In 2001 we added the term *cross-cultural kid (CCK)* to our lexicon to include all children who for any reason had grown up deeply interacting with two or more cultural worlds during child-hood. But the challenge remained. How would we compare and contrast these many different types of experiences?

This took us to our second step. In 1984, Dr. Ted Ward, then a sociologist at Michigan State University, predicted in a plenary talk at the International Con-ference for Missionary Kids (ICMK) in Manila that third culture kids were the prototype citizens of the future. In other words, a childhood lived in, among, and between various cultural worlds would one day be the norm rather than the exception. We realized from so many who told us their story that the time Dr. Ward saw had come. All sorts of CCKs were taking lessons learned from the TCK Profile and intuitively applying it to their own life story.

We began to wonder: Could we consider the work we have done with TCKs as a petri dish of sorts? Could our research be like scientists who first isolate a particular organism to grow in a petri dish to study its interactions with various drugs and then experiment to see if what works on the agar in that petri dish will work in more complicated hosts?

What is it we are studying in the traditional TCK "petri dish"? Bottom line: *it is here we can begin to see the first results of a great, but not yet fully explored, cultural shift of our changing world—the difference between being raised in a monocultural environment or a many layered cultural setting.* We believe the TCK experience is an area where certain factors related to growing up in a culturally mixed lifestyle already have been isolated and studied. The more we understand this experience for what it is, the better we can then apply this knowledge to other types of cross-cultural childhoods.

How did we accomplish both of these things in this revised edition?

First, we have updated the original TCK material to reflect the reality of changes globally nomadic children experience in today's world. Hopefully this will clarify even further what we see in our TCK petri dish. We consider such questions as: Does the presence of the Internet, Skype, instant messaging, new patterns of overseas assignments for their parents, multiple cultures in their international schools, or higher levels of security risk change the basic TCK Profile as previously described? What are some new insights we have learned from and about this population since our first edition?

We considered these questions in the hope of continuing to achieve our original goal: to help TCKs, adult TCKs (ATCKs), their families, and all who work with them understand how they can build well on the many gifts of this upbringing while dealing effectively with the challenges. That is the heart of our ongoing theme for all generations of TCKs, ATCKs, and their families.

While our main focus remains specifically on the traditional TCK experience, we also take a beginning look at other categories of CCKs, some implications of the global shifts occurring as countless children now grow up in the "new normal" of cultural complexity, and what some of the differences between specific types of CCKs might also be. For ease of writing, and because this is the specific population we have studied for years, most references in the book are to TCKs. We expect, however, that those of other culturally mixed backgrounds will be able to apply these insights to their specific experiences as well. We hope this expanded vision will help generate a new dialogue that can unite people of many backgrounds, nationalities, ethnicities, and social and economic groups as they recognize their commonalities, as well as where and how their experiences differ, and we hope that discussion will continue long after you close the last page.

Part I

Understanding the World of TCKs

THE FIRST PART of this book looks in detail at who a third culture kid (TCK) is and why the two major realities of this experience—growing up among many cultural worlds and high mobility—have such a significant effect on them. We will also consider how (and why) lessons learned from the TCK journey can be applied to other types of cross-cultural childhoods, even when the details of these other experiences may be quite different from the traditional TCK lifestyle.

CHAPTER 1

Where Is Home?
Erika's Story

As the Boeing 747 sped down the runway, Erika sat inside
with seat belt secure, her chin propped against a clenched
fist, staring out the window until the final sights of her beloved Singapore disappeared from view.

*How can it hurt this much to leave a country that isn't
even mine?* Erika closed her eyes and settled back in the
seat, too numb to cry the tears that begged to be shed. *Will I
ever come back?*

For nearly half of her twenty-three years, she had
thought of Singapore as home. Now she knew it wasn't—and
America hadn't felt like home since she was eight years old.

Isn't there anywhere in the world I belong? she wondered.

COUNTLESS PEOPLE of virtually every nationality and from a great variety of backgrounds identify with Erika's feeling of not fully belonging
anywhere in the world. Like her, they may be North Americans who grew
up in Singapore. But they may also be Japanese children growing up in Australia,
British kids raised in China, Turkish youth reared in Germany, African children
living in Canada, or the child of a Norwegian father and a Thai mother growing up in Argentina. All of them have one thing in common: like Erika, they are
spending, or have spent, at least part of their childhood in countries and cultures
other than their own. They are *third culture kids (TCKs)* or, by now, *adult TCKs
(ATCKs)*.

Children are TCKs for many reasons. Some have parents with careers in international business, the diplomatic corps, the military, or religious missions. Others have parents who studied abroad. Still other families live for a period of time outside their home culture because of civil unrest and wars.

TCKs are raised in a neither/nor world. It is neither fully the world of their parents' culture (or cultures) nor fully the world of the other culture (or cultures) in which they were raised. Contrary to popular misconceptions, however, this neither/nor world is *not* merely a personal amalgamation of the various cultures they have known. For reasons we will explore, in the process of living first in one dominant culture and then moving to another one (and maybe even two or three more and often back and forth between them all), TCKs develop their own life patterns different from those who are basically born and bred in one place. Most TCKs learn to live comfortably in this world, whether they stop to define it or not.

TCKs are not a new phenomenon. They've been around since the beginning of time, but, until now, they have been largely invisible. This has been changing, however, for at least three reasons.

1. *Their number has increased.* In the last half of the twentieth century, the number of people involved in international careers of all types grew dramatically. In her book *The Absentee American*, Carolyn Smith says,

> Since 1946, therefore, when it was unusual for Americans to live overseas unless they were missionaries or diplomats, it has become commonplace for American military and civilian employees and businesspeople to be stationed abroad, if only for a year. The 1990 Census counted 922,000 federal workers and their families living overseas, and the total number of Americans living abroad either permanently or temporarily is estimated at 3 million.[1]

By 2007, this estimated number had grown to more than four million, with no end in sight of how high this tally might rise.[2] That's a lot of people! But these figures only account for U.S. citizens. Australia has more than one million citizens living outside its borders on either a long- or short-term basis.[3] In 2006, Japan also disclosed that for the first time in history, more than one million Japanese were living for longer than three months as expatriates all over the world. Add to these figures the burgeoning number of citizens from every other country working and living outside their home cultures and we can only imagine the total number of expatriates worldwide.

Of course, as more adults have international careers or live abroad for whatever reason, there are more children accompanying parents into new lands. Many things have changed since the days of early explorers, traders, colonial governors, or pioneer missionaries when children often remained in the home country to avoid the rigors of travel and disease or for educational purposes. Traveling between home and a host country rarely takes more than one day, an easy trip compared to the three months it used to take on an ocean liner. International schools exist everywhere; advanced medical care is an airlift away (and even more immediate with telemedicine). It is now normal for children to accompany their parents overseas rather than to stay home.

2. *Their public voice has grown louder.* As these growing numbers of TCKs become adults, they are becoming more vocal. Through alumni associations or web chat rooms such as *www.tckid.com* and *www.facebook.com*, TCKs and ATCKs have formed visible, identifiable groups. The proliferation of blogspots has also brought their story forward. TCKs have become well-known politicians, newscasters, actors, actresses, sports figures, and authors. The election of President Barack Obama made the entire world aware that this type of childhood exists. Many of his first cabinet choices were also adult TCKs. Through politics, speaking out, or writing, their voices are beginning to be heard. As these TCKs and adult TCKs share their stories, they encourage others to do the same.

3. *Their significance has increased.* The TCK experience is a microcosm of what is fast becoming normal throughout the world. Few communities anywhere will remain culturally homogeneous in this age of easy international travel and instant global communication. Part of the discussion by TV pundits throughout the 2008 presidential campaign in the United States centered on how President Obama's background reflected a change happening around the world. Growing up among cultural differences is already, or soon will be, the rule rather than the exception—even for those who never physically leave their home country. In 1984, sociologist Ted Ward claimed that TCKs were "the prototype [citizens] of the future..."[4] We believe that time is now. Experts are trying to predict the outcome of this cultural juggling. Looking at the TCK world can help us prepare for the long-term consequences of this new pattern of global cultural mixing. We will look at these new trends in depth when we focus on the broader group of *cross-cultural kids (CCKs)* in chapter 3.

The benefits of the TCK lifestyle are enormous. Many TCKs and ATCKs are maximizing the potential of these benefits in their lives, both personally and professionally. This will become clearer in part II when we look in detail at what these benefits are. Unfortunately, for some TCKs and ATCKs, the challenges of their experience have seemingly canceled out the many benefits—a sad waste for both the TCKs and the world around them. It is our hope that a better understanding of some of these benefits and challenges will help TCKs and ATCKs everywhere use the gifts of their heritage well. That's why, throughout this book, we examine the paradoxical world of the TCK and other cross-cultural experiences during childhood from a variety of perspectives.

We begin by returning to Erika for a better look at one young woman's true story. Only the names and places have been changed.

Erika didn't notice that the captain had turned off the "Fasten your seat belt" sign until a flight attendant interrupted her reverie.

"Would you like something to drink?" he asked.

How many Cokes and miniature pretzels have I eaten on airplanes? she wondered. *Far too many to count.* But today her grief outweighed any thought of food or drink. She shook her head, and the attendant moved on.

Erika closed her eyes again. Unbidden memories flashed through her mind. She remembered being eight years old, when her family still lived in upstate New York, Erika's birthplace. One day her father entered the playroom as she and her younger sister, Sally, performed a puppet show for their assembled audience of stuffed animals.

"Wanna' watch, Dad?" Erika asked hopefully.

"In a few minutes, sweetie. First, I have something special to tell you."

Puppets forgotten, Sally and Erika ran to their dad, trying to guess what it could be.

"Are we gonna have a new baby?" Sally began jumping up and down in excited anticipation.

"Did you buy me a new bike?" Erika inquired.

Erika's dad shook his head and sat in the nearby rocking chair, gathering one daughter on each knee. "How would you like to take a long airplane ride?" he asked.

"Wow!"

"Sure."

"I love airplanes."

"Where, Daddy?"

He explained that his company had asked him to move from the United States to Ecuador to start a new branch office. The family would be moving as soon as school ended that June.

A flurry of activity began—shopping, packing, and saying good-bye to relatives and friends. It all seemed so exciting until the day Erika asked, "Mom, how is Spotty going to get there?"

"Honey, it's not easy to take a dog. Grandma's going to take care of him 'til we get home again."

"Mom, we can't leave Spotty! He's part of our family!"

No amount of pleading worked. Spotty was sent to his new home, and finally, with a mixture of eagerness for the adventures ahead and sadness for the people and things they were leaving, Erika and her family flew off to their new world.

Wanting to stop this flood of memories, Erika opened her eyes, trying to focus on her fellow passengers. The diversion didn't work. As soon as she had adjusted her cramped legs and resettled in a more comfortable position, the flashbacks continued. It was almost as if every few seconds a virtual click inside her brain advanced her mental PowerPoint show. Pictures of Ecuador replaced those of New York. She had been so scared the first time her family flew into Quito. How would the airplane wiggle its way between the mountain ranges and find a flat place to land? Yet Erika remembered how, in time, those same Andes mountains gave her a deep sense of security each morning when she woke to see their towering peaks looming over the city, keeping watch as they had for centuries past.

But what did these memories matter now? She put on her headset, hoping that music would divert her thoughts. Unfortunately, the second channel she switched to played the haunting music of the hollow-reed flute pipes that always evoked a twinge of melancholy whenever she heard it. The sound brought instant memories of going to fiestas with her Ecuadorian friends and dancing with them while the pipers played. Certainly, listening to this music wouldn't help her now. She took the earphones off, letting them dangle around her neck.

By now the images of an in-flight movie were on the monitor in front of her, but Erika never saw them. Her own internal picture show continued with its competing images— the scene changing from towering mountains to the towering skyscrapers of Singapore. After two years in Ecuador, her father had been transferred once more, and for the thirteen years since then—including the four years she attended university in Wisconsin—Erika had considered Singapore her home. Now she knew Singapore would never truly be home. But the question continued to haunt her: Where was home?

Still refusing to dwell on that topic, her mind searched for a new show to look at. Pictures of countless scenes from other places she had visited with her family through the years appeared—the Kathmandu Valley in Nepal at the beginning of the rainy season, the monkey cup plants in the Malaysian rain forest, the Karen tribal people in the hills of northern Thailand, winter on the South Island of New Zealand, the water-derrick wells of the Hortobágy in Hungary. One after another the images flashed in her mind's eye. Even to herself, it seemed incredible how much she had done, seen, and experienced in her first twenty-three years of life. The richness and depth of the world she knew was beyond measure—but what good did that do her today?

Finally, the other pictures ran out and Erika was left with the visions of life in Singapore that kept returning, insisting on a paramount spot in the show. Now instead of places, however, she saw people—her amazing collection of friends from the International School in Singapore: Ravi, Fatu, Sam, Kim Su, Trevor, Hilary, Mustapha, Dolores, Joe. One after another they came to her memory. How many races, nationalities, styles of dress, cultures, and religions did these friends represent? With diversity as their hallmark, who could say what was "normal"?

Erika never stopped to wonder that others might be surprised to know that this diversity among her friends reflected the norm rather than the exception of her life. Instead, she reminisced on how she hated parting from them each summer when her family returned to the States for vacation. (It was never America or the United States—simply "the States.") Somehow, she always felt much more like a fish out of water with her Stateside peers than she did in Singapore.

For the first time since the airplane had lifted off, a wry smile came to Erika's face. She remembered how strange she had felt the first time her American cousins had asked her to go "cruising." She presumed they meant some type of boat ride—like when she and her friends in Singapore rented a junk and sailed to a small island for a day of sunbathing, swimming, and picnicking. She was eager to go.

To her amazement, cruising for her cousins had nothing to do with boats and water. Instead, it meant endless driving about town with no apparent purpose. Eventually, they parked at a shopping mall and simply stood around. As far as Erika could see, it seemed their purpose was to block aisles rather than purchase any goods. What was the point?

For Erika, "going home" meant something entirely different than it did for her parents. When her parents spoke of "going home," they meant returning to the States each summer. For her, "going home" meant returning to Singapore at the end of summer. But where was home now? The nagging question returned.

Temperatures dropped inside the airplane as the short night descended. Erika stood up to get a blanket and pillow from the overhead compartment, hoping for the comfort of sleep. But would sleep ever come on this journey? Not yet. Another set of pictures pushed their way into the muddle of her mind—now with scenes of the time she left Singapore to attend university in the States.

"Don't worry, darling. You'll be fine. I'm sure you'll get a wonderful roommate. You've always made friends so easily. I know you'll have no trouble at all," her parents had reassured her as she faced that transition.

But somehow it hadn't been that easy. Fellow students would ask, "Where are you from?" At first, Erika automatically answered, "Singapore." The universal reply was, "Really? You don't look like it," with the expectation of some explanation of how she was from Singapore.

Soon, Erika decided she would be from New York—where her grandparents lived. She hoped that would simplify these complicated introductions.

Eventually, as she adapted outwardly, picking up the current lingo and attire, others accepted her as one of them. By the end of her first year, however, she felt angry, confused, and depressed. How could anyone care so much about who won last week's football game and so little about the political unrest and violence in Sudan or Tibet? Didn't they know people actually died in wars? Perhaps they never read the global news that crawled across their TV screens while supposedly erudite "news" commentators went on endlessly about the latest celebrity scandal. They couldn't comprehend her world; she couldn't understand theirs.

As time went on, Erika found a way to cope. Once she realized most of her peers simply couldn't relate to what her life had been, she no longer discussed it. Her relatives were happy to tell everyone she was "doing fine."

Just before graduating from university, however, she lost the last internal vestige of home. Her father was transferred back to the States and her family settled in Dayton,

Ohio. For school vacations, she no longer returned to Singapore. Erika closed that chapter of her life. The pain of longing for the past was just too much.

As she stared at the rhythmic, almost hypnotic, flashing red lights on the jet's wings, Erika continued her reflections. That chapter on Singapore didn't stay closed for very long. *When did I reopen it? Why did I reopen it?*

After graduation, she had decided to get a master's degree in history. Thinking about that now while flying somewhere over the Pacific Ocean, she wondered why she had chosen that particular field. *Was I subconsciously trying to escape to a world that paralleled my own—a world that was once exciting but is now gone forever?*

Who could know? All Erika knew was that her restlessness increased in graduate school, and she finally dropped out. At that point, Erika decided only a return to Singapore would stop this chronic unsettledness, this sense of always looking for something that might be just around the corner but never was. But also, she couldn't define what she wanted. Was it to belong somewhere? Anywhere?

Although her family no longer lived in Singapore, she still had many Singaporean friends who had often invited her to stay with them. Why not live her own life overseas? Surely it would be far better to live in a place where she belonged than to wander forever in this inner limbo.

Erika went online and booked a flight to Singapore. The next step was to call one of her former classmates still living in Singapore. "Dolores, I want to come home. Can you help me find a job? I'm coming as soon as I get my visa, and I'll need a way to support myself once I'm back."

"That's wonderful! I'm sure we can find some kind of job for you," came the reply. "You can stay with me and my family until you get everything lined up." Erika was ecstatic! It felt so familiar, so normal to be planning a trip overseas again. She couldn't wait to return to the world in which she so obviously belonged.

When she arrived in Singapore, her dream seemed to have come true. What airport in the world could compare to the beauty of Changi? Graceful banners hung on the walls, welcoming weary travelers in their own languages. Brilliantly colored flowers cascaded down the sides of the built-in garden beds throughout the terminals. Trees grew beside waterfalls that tumbled over rocks to a pond below.

The piped-in sounds of chirping birds completed her sense of entering a garden in paradise. How could anyone not love this place?

As she walked out of the terminal, she took a deep breath. How wonderfully familiar were the smells: tropical flowers and leaded petrol fumes—what a paradox! Living, life-giving plants and dead, polluting, fuel—intermingled. Was it possible her whole life was a paradox? A life full of rich experiences in totally diverse cultures and places, each experience filled with a special vibrancy that made her want to dance and celebrate the joy of life. And yet, a life in which she always felt a bit like an observer, playing the part for the current scene, but forever watching to see how she was doing.

Erika quickly brushed these thoughts aside. Those times of being an outsider were gone now because she knew where she belonged—in Singapore. How wonderful finally to be home!

As the days progressed, however, life seemed less familiar. She discovered that many things she had taken for granted as a child in the expatriate business community of Singapore were no longer hers to enjoy as a young, single, foreign woman living with a Singaporean family. No maid, no expensive restaurants, no car, fewer friends. Instead, she had to wash her clothes by hand, grab cheap rice dishes from street vendors, and get around the city by walking blocks in the hot sun to take a crowded bus.

While growing up, her family might not have been classified as wealthy, but there had always been enough money for them to be comfortable and not worry about paying the bills, to take little side trips or splurge on a particularly nice outfit. Now she had to consider seriously such mundane questions as how much lunch cost and how she could pay for her barest living expenses.

Finding a job was harder than she had imagined it would be. Jobs that paid enough for her to rent a reasonably modest apartment and buy food and clothes had to be contracted with international companies before entering the country. Now she realized that was what her father had done. To make matters worse, she learned that available jobs were next to impossible for a noncitizen to get. Because the government wanted to save jobs for Singaporeans, it rarely issued a work permit for local jobs to a foreigner. Besides, the jobs for local hires that she could find would not pay enough for her to live safely, let alone well. Because a young white woman was so obvious in a cheaper rent district with higher crime rates, Erika feared she would present a far too easy target for someone bent on robbery or assault.

Here, in the world she had always thought of as home, Erika realized she was seen as a foreigner—an outsider. There was no such thing as an international passport.

The sad day came when she finally had to admit that she didn't fit in this country either. Sitting in her friend's tiny apartment in a world she had thought was home, despair swept over her. She was lost. The promises of big dreams seemed foolish and childish. She belonged nowhere. With a muffled sob she picked up her cell phone and called her parents.

"Mom, I can't make it here, but I don't know what to do. I don't fit in Dayton, but I don't fit here either. Somehow I seem to have grown up between two totally different worlds, and now I've found out I don't belong to either one."

With infinite sorrow this time, she made one last airline reservation, and now she was here, 40,000 feet in the air, going—home?

Erika's story is only one of thousands we have heard from TCKs all over the world. The particulars of each tale are different, yet in a sense so many are the same. They are the stories of lives filled with rich diversity but conflicted by the underlying question of where they really fit in. What are some of the reasons for this common thread among TCKs? Who, indeed, are these TCKs and what are some of the benefits and challenges inherent in the experience they have had? How does this relate to those who have grown up among various cultures for many reasons besides moving physically or internationally? These are the questions we will address in the chapters that follow.

CHAPTER 2

Who Are "Third Culture Kids"?

WHO OR WHAT EXACTLY IS A THIRD CULTURE KID? Coauthor David Pollock developed the following definition:

> A Third Culture Kid (TCK) is a person who has spent a significant part of his or her developmental years outside the parents' culture. The TCK frequently builds relationships to all of the cultures, while not having full ownership in any. Although elements from each culture may be assimilated into the TCK's life experience, the sense of belonging is in relationship to others of similar background.[1]

Let's look at this definition in detail.

"A Third Culture Kid (TCK)..."

Some of the most vigorous discussions about TCKs start with a debate over the term itself. People often ask, "How can you possibly say people with such incredibly diverse cultural backgrounds and experience can make up a "culture," when the word *culture*, by definition, means a group of people who have something in common?"

This is one of the strange paradoxes about TCKs. Looking at the differences among them—of race, nationality, sponsoring organizations, and places where they are growing (or have grown) up—you would think TCKs could have little in common. But if you have attended a conference sponsored by Global Nomads International[2] or Families in Global Transition[3] and have watched the animated, nonstop conversation of the participants throughout the weekend, you wouldn't question the powerful connection between them. Norma McCaig, founder of Global Nomads, called it a "reunion of strangers." What is this almost magical bond? Why have they been called third *culture* kids?

THE THIRD CULTURE AS ORIGINALLY DEFINED

A common misconception about third culture kids is that they have been raised in what is often called the "Third World." While this might be true for some TCKs, the Third World has no specific relationship to the concept of the third culture. TCKs have grown up everywhere, including such places as Abu Dhabi, Accra, Amsterdam, Bangkok, Caracas, Kunming, London, New York, Singapore, Sydney, Timbuktu, and Vienna. Where, then, did this term develop? Two social scientists, Ruth Hill Useem and John Useem, coined the phrase *third culture* in the 1950s when they went to India for a year to study Americans who lived and worked there as foreign service officers, missionaries, technical aid workers, businesspeople, educators, and media representatives.[4] While in India, the Useems also met expatriates from other countries and soon discovered that "each of these subcultures [communities of expatriates] generated by colonial administrators, missionaries, businessmen, and military personnel—had its own peculiarities, slightly different origins, distinctive styles and stratification systems, but all were closely interlocked."[5] They realized the expatriates had formed a lifestyle that was different from either their home or their host culture, but it was one they shared in that setting.

To best describe this expatriate world, the Useems defined the home culture from which the adults came as the *first culture*. They called the host culture where the family lived (in that case, India) the *second culture*. They then identified the shared lifestyle of the expatriate community as an *interstitial culture* or "culture between cultures" and named it the *third culture*. Figure 2-1 illustrates this concept.

The Third Culture Model

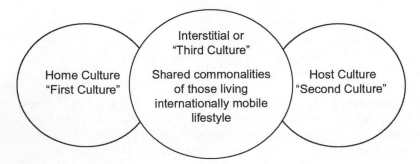

Figure 2-1 The Third Culture model
(© 1996 Ruth E. Van Reken)

As time went on, Dr. John Useem continued to focus on how the expatriate adults interacted with those from the local culture, while Dr. Ruth Hill Useem became fascinated with common characteristics she noticed among those growing up in this third culture. She called the children raised in that interstitial culture *third culture kids (TCKs)*. Although Ruth Useem defined TCKs simply as "Children who accompany their parents into another society,"[6] the TCKs she initially studied had all traveled overseas with parents working in international careers. The model in Figure 2-2 represents the traditional expatriate groups from which the TCKs came during those early days of her studies.

It's important to remember that the Useems' research wasn't in one expatriate subculture or "sector," such as corporate or military, but included them all. Because of that, as Dr. Ruth Useem studied TCKs of all backgrounds and did not isolate them into sector-specific groups, she was able to see the common threads that linked them. At that time, most were also in what she called *representational roles*; these TCKs were seen as "little ambassadors," "little missionaries," or "little soldiers." People around them (including parents) expected the children's behavior to be consistent with the goals and values of the organizational system for which the parents worked. If it wasn't, the children could jeopardize a parent's career. Dr. Useem felt this reality was part of what made the TCK experience distinctive from other ways children might grow up cross-culturally, such as children of immigrants or bicultural parents.[7]

The Third Culture Kid (TCK) Model

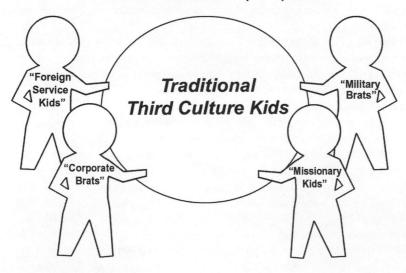

Figure 2-2 The Third Culture Kid Model
(© 1996 Ruth E. Van Reken)

THE THIRD CULTURE AS CURRENTLY DEFINED

The world has changed dramatically since the days when the Useems first defined the TCK term. Communities all over the world are becoming more culturally mixed. Many TCKs choose to blend into the world around them. They, and others, no longer believe it is their duty to represent a parent's company, country, or organization as children of the past might have done. On the other hand, some TCKs in the military, foreign service, or mission sectors may still feel pressure to meet various social or behavioral expectations of the organizational system.

When the Useems did their research, most Western expatriates lived in specific communal systems such as military bases, missionary compounds, or business enclaves. Identifying a visible, local expatriate community was relatively easy. Although there remain army bases and missionary and diplomatic compounds around the world, many expatriates no longer live in such physically defined communities. Many non-Westerners now live "abroad." For example, the Japanese families who live in Kokomo, Indiana, and work for a large multinational corporation don't live in a compound but throughout neighborhoods in that city. While their children may attend "Japanese school" on Saturdays, most of them attend local rather than international schools during the school year. Few, if any, go off to boarding schools as TCKs often used to do.

Because there are frequently no well-marked expatriate enclaves anymore, some argue that the terms *third culture* and *third culture kid* are now misnomers. How can there be a culture if people don't live together? Based on traditional understandings of *culture* as something people experience communally, how can we say that people from all these different races, cultures, creeds, ethnicities, or nationalities can actually share enough to be considered a "culture"? Is it still a valid term when the world has changed so much from the days in which it was first introduced?

When we asked Dr. Ruth Hill Useem what she thought about this, she said, "Because I am a sociologist/anthropologist I think no concept is ever locked up permanently.... Concepts change as we get to know more; other times concepts change because what happens in the world is changing."[8]

In her survey of adult TCKs, Dr. Useem herself defined the third culture as a generic term to discuss the *lifestyle* "created, shared, and learned" by those who are from one culture and in the process of relating to another one. These larger definitions are justifiable because if culture in its broadest sense is a way of life shared with others, there's no question that, in spite of their differences, TCKs of all stripes and persuasions from countless countries share remarkably important and similar life experiences through the very process of living in, and among, different cultures—whether or not they grew up in a specific local expatriate community. Further, the kinds of experiences they share tend to affect the deeper rather than more superficial parts of their personal or cultural being. Japanese researchers have developed their own terms for this experience: children of

Japanese temporarily living as overseas residents are called *kaigai-shijo* and those who formerly lived overseas and have now returned to Japan are *kikoku-shijo.*[9] (Appendix B talks about the Japanese research in this area.)

In 2000, anthropology student Ximena Vidal wrote, "Third Culture Kids [are] an example of a people whose experience and cultural identity cannot be understood within the limiting [traditional] frameworks of culture."[10] She goes on to say that TCKs are an example of a new way to define culture that is emerging in our post-modern world. Vidal claims that culture can be what we share experientially as well as the more traditional ways we have defined it.

So what is it that all TCKs share simply because they have accompanied parents into other societies and grown up in a world outside the one that their passports would define as "home"?

Like a double rainbow, two realities arch over the TCK experience that shape the formation of a TCK's life:

1. *Being raised in a genuinely cross-cultural world.* Instead of simply watching, studying, or analyzing other cultures, TCKs actually live in different cultural worlds as they travel back and forth between their passport and host cultures. Some TCKs who have gone through multiple moves or whose parents are in an intercultural marriage have interacted closely with four or more cultures.
2. *Being raised in a highly mobile world.* Mobility is normal in the third culture experience. Either the TCKs themselves, or those around them, are constantly coming or going. The people in their lives are always changing and the backdrop of physical surroundings may often fluctuate as well.

Members of this broad third culture community often have other characteristics in common, including:

1. *Distinct differences.* Many TCKs are raised where being physically different from those around them is a major aspect of their identity. Even when external appearances are similar to either their host or home culture, TCKs often have a substantially different perspective on the world than do their peers.
2. *Expected repatriation.* Unlike immigrants, third culture families usually expect at some point to return permanently to live in their home country. Not all do, but that is the general presumption when they first leave their home countries, and this expectation shapes countless decisions along the way that affect their children, such as educational choices or making efforts to learn or not learn the local language.

The following characteristics are more dependent on "why" and "where" the families are living outside their culture but are still the reality for many third culture experiences.

3. *Privileged lifestyle.* Historically, employees of international businesses and members of missions, the military, and the diplomatic corps have been part of an elitist community—one with special privileges bestowed on its members by the sponsoring organization, the host culture, or both. Often, there are systems of logistical support or "perks": those in the military can use the commissary or PX; embassy or missionary compounds may employ home repair or domestic service personnel; diplomatic families may have chauffeurs to drive the children to school or around town. Even without the perks, there are entitlements such as worldwide travel to and from their post—all at the expense of the sponsoring agency, or "supporters" in the case of missions.

4. *System identity.* Members of specific third culture communities may be more directly conscious than peers at home of representing something greater than themselves—be it their government, their company, or God. Jobs can hinge on how well the adults' behavior, or that of their children, positively reflects the values and standards of the sponsoring agency. This is the reason Dr. Ruth Hill Useem talked about the "representational roles" of many TCKs.

The first two characteristics of living in a culturally diverse and highly mobile world are true for virtually every third culture person. The degree to which TCKs may differ from their host culture, expect to repatriate, enjoy a privileged lifestyle, or identify with the organizational system varies a bit more depending on where (and why) their families are living outside the home culture, but they are still the reality for many third culture experiences.

The magical connection, however, that happens when TCKs meet is more than a sharing of these facts alone. There is something about growing up in and among many cultures that creates an emotional experience and bond that transcends the details. What is that?

A SAMPLE SLICE OF THE "NEITHER/NOR" THIRD CULTURE

ATCKs Rob and Heather are citizens of different countries who grew up on opposite sides of the globe. The only thing they share is the fact they were both raised outside their parents' home cultures. They met at a lecture on the *third culture* term at a Families in Global Transition conference and began chatting during a break.

> Rob spoke first. "I felt pretty skeptical before coming to this conference, but maybe there is something to this third culture bit. It never occurred to me that the military lifestyle I grew up in had a culture that was different from my home or host cultures. I just thought of myself as an American in Japan."
>
> "Why?" Heather asked.

"I was nine when my family moved from Oregon to the 'American Bubble' in Japan—that's what everyone called our military base. It seemed completely American. Through the commissary or PX we could get Cheerios for breakfast, Nikes to run in, and even Pringles for snacks. The movies in our base theater were the same ones being shown in the States. Man, we even had tennis courts and a swimming pool just like I did at my YMCA in Portland!"

Heather looked at Rob with amazement. "I can't believe it!" she said. "I'm at least twenty years older than you, I've never been to Japan, my dad worked for the British government in Nigeria, but I can relate to what you're saying!"

"How come?" asked Rob.

"Well, I really don't know. I guess I never thought about it before. Maybe because we lived in a 'British Bubble'? We just didn't call it that. Although we didn't have a PX or commissary, we did have Kingsway stores in every major city. They imported all those wonderful British things like Marmite, Weetabix, and Jacob's Cream Crackers. We also had a swimming pool and tennis courts at the local British club. It all seemed very British and very normal."

Rob responded, "Yeah, well, I don't know about you, but for me, even with so many American trappings, life in Japan still wasn't like living in Portland. When I left the base and took the train to town, I suddenly felt isolated because I couldn't understand the people chattering around me or read most of the signs."

"I know what you mean," Heather responded. "With all our British stuff around, it still wasn't like living in England. I had a Nigerian nanny who taught me how to speak Hausa and how to *chiniki*, or bargain, for things as I grew up. I wouldn't have done that in England. But I probably got more into the local culture than you did since we moved to Nigeria when I was two."

"Well, I got into the local culture too," Rob said, a bit defensively. "I mean, after a few months I found Japanese friends who taught me how to eat sushi, use chopsticks, bathe in an *ofuro*, and sleep on a futon. But my life wasn't like theirs any more than it was like life back in Portland. For one thing, I went to the local international school, where I studied in English instead of Japanese."

"I understand that, too!" Heather exclaimed. "My life wasn't the same as my Nigerian friends' lives either—even if I could speak their language. I had a driver who took me back and forth from school each day while most of my friends had to walk long distances in the heat of the day to attend their schools."

"So did your life overseas seem strange?" Rob and Heather looked up in surprise to see that someone had joined them.

Both shook their heads at the same time in response to the stranger's question.

"Nope, not to me," said Rob.

"Me either," interjected Heather.

The newcomer persisted. "But how could you feel normal when you lived so differently from people in either your own countries or Japan or Nigeria? Seems to me that would make you feel somewhat odd."

Rob thought for a quick moment. "Well, I suppose it's because all the other American kids I knew were growing up in that same neither/nor world the speaker talked about today. All my Army and international friends had moved as often as I had. We were used to saying good-bye to old friends and hello to new ones. No big deal. That's life. Nothing unusual since we were all doing it. I don't know—it just seemed like a normal way to live, didn't it, Heather?"

"Exactly. I lived the same way all my other British and expatriate friends did. They had house help. So did we. They flew from one continent to another regularly. So did I. When we went out to play, all of us wore the same kind of pith helmets so we wouldn't get sunstroke. To me, it's just how life was."

While both Rob and Heather happened to grow up in an easily identifiable expatriate community, expatriate families who live in less defined communities still find ways to keep some expression of their home culture. In Indiana, the Japanese community has organized special swimming classes at the local YMCA for their TCKs because they want to maintain their traditionally more disciplined approach to training children than is expected of most American children. They also conduct Saturday classes when all academic subjects are taught in Japanese so their TCKs maintain both written and verbal language skills. A similar thing is happening in Slovakia. The Koreans working for international businesses send their children to the international schools during the week but have Saturday school there to make sure they can fit back into Korean schools when they repatriate.

But all this talk about the third culture should not distract us from understanding the most crucial part of the TCK definition, the fact that a TCK:

"...is a person..."

Why are these words critical to all further discussion on third culture kids? Because we must never forget that, above all else, a TCK is a person. Sometimes TCKs spend so much time feeling different from people in the dominant culture around them that they (or those who notice these differences) begin to feel TCKs are, in fact, intrinsically different—some sort of special breed of being. While their experiences may be different from other people's, TCKs were created with the same need that non-TCKs have for building relationships in which they love and are loved, ones in which they know others and are known by them. They need a sense of purpose and meaning in their lives and have the same capacities to think, learn, create, and make choices as others do. The characteristics, benefits, and challenges that we describe later in this book arise from the interactions of the various aspects of mobility and the cross-cultural nature of this upbringing and how they do or don't help meet these most fundamental needs, not from some difference in them as persons.

"...who has spent a significant part..."

Time by itself doesn't determine how deep an impact the third culture experience has on the development of a particular child. Other variables such as the child's age, personality, and participation in the local culture have an important effect. For example, living overseas between the ages of one and four will affect a child differently than if that same experience occurs between the ages of eleven and fourteen.

While we can't say precisely how long a child must live outside the home culture to develop the classic TCK characteristics, we can say it is more than a two-week or even a two-month vacation to see the sights. Some people are identifiable TCKs or ATCKs after spending as little as one year outside their parents' culture. Of course, other factors such as the parents' attitudes and behavior or the policies of the sponsoring agency add to how significant the period spent as a TCK is—or was—in shaping a child's life.

"...of his or her developmental years..."

Although the length of time needed for someone to become a true TCK can't be precisely defined, the time *when* it happens can. It must occur during the developmental years—from birth to eighteen years of age. We recognize that a cross-cultural experience affects adults as well as children. In 2000, during the Families in Global Transition conference in Indianapolis, Paulette Bethel, Joanna Parfitt, and Christine Dowdeswell convened a group of interested attendees to look at what they called *third culture adults (TCAs):* those who go overseas for the first time after growing up in a more traditional "monocultural" environment of their passport culture. The difference for a TCK, however, is that this cross-cultural experience occurs during the years when that child's sense of identity, relationships with others, and view of the world are being formed in the most basic ways. While parents may change careers and become former international businesspeople, former missionaries, former military personnel, or former foreign service officers, no one is ever a former third culture kid. TCKs simply move on to being adult third culture kids because their lives grow out of the roots planted in and watered by the third culture experience.

" . . . outside the parents' culture."

The home culture is defined in terms of the parents' culture, because often TCKs have a different sense of "home" than their parents might. For that reason, we will generally use the terms *passport country* or *passport culture* to mean the parental country or culture. Most often, TCKs grow up outside their passport country as well as culture, and the stories throughout our book predominantly feature this more typical TCK experience. It's important to recognize, however, that children can have a TCK-like experience who never leave their parents' country but are still raised among different cultural worlds. We will look at this reality in chapter 3.

" . . . The TCK frequently builds relationships to all of the cultures, while not having full ownership in any."

This brings us back to Erika.

> As she flew back to the United States, Erika wondered how it could be that life felt like such a rich dance in and through so many cultures, while at the same time that very richness made it seem impossible to stop the dance. To land in Singapore would mean she could celebrate the hustle and bustle of that wonderful city she loved so much, but then she would miss the mountains of Ecuador and the joy of touching and seeing the beautiful weavings in the Otavalo Indian markets. To end the dance in Ecuador meant she would never again see the magnificent colors of fall in upstate New York or taste her grandmother's special Sunday pot roast, but to stop in New York or Dayton, where her parents now lived, meant she would miss not only Singapore and Ecuador, but

all the other places she had been and seen. Erika wished for
just one moment she could bring together the many worlds
she had known and embrace them all at the same time, but
she knew it could never happen.

This is at the heart of the issues of rootlessness and restlessness we will discuss
later. This lack of full ownership is what gives that sense of simultaneously belonging "everywhere and nowhere."

"...Although elements from each culture may be assimilated into the TCK's life experience..."

Obviously, there are specific ways each home and host culture shapes each TCK.
(Rob loves peanut butter and jelly, but Heather prefers Marmite; Rob eats his
Cheerios and speaks Japanese, while Heather eats Weetabix and speaks Hausa.)
But it's not only food and language that shape them. Cultural rules do as well.

- After living in London where his dad served as an ambassador for six years,
  Musa had trouble with how people dealt with time when he returned to
  Guinea. Instead of relaxing as others from his home culture could when
  meetings did not begin and end as scheduled, he felt the same frustration
  many expatriates experienced. Musa had exchanged his home culture's more
  relational worldview for a time-oriented worldview during his time abroad.
- At his summer job in Canada, Gordon's boss thought he was dishonest and
  lazy because Gordon never looked anyone in the eye. But where Gordon had
  grown up in Africa, children always kept their eyes to the ground when talking with adults.

Certainly cultural practices are incorporated from the unique aspects of
both host and home cultures, but the third culture is more than the sum total of
the parts of home and host culture. If it were only that, each TCK would remain
alone in his or her experience.

"...the sense of belonging is in relationship to others of similar background."

Erika returned to Dayton, Ohio, after her long, final flight
back from Singapore. She began teaching high school French
and Spanish during the day, and tutoring international business people in English filled her evenings. Once more she
tried to accept the reality that her past was gone. Life must

go on, and she couldn't expect anyone else to understand her when she didn't understand herself.

Then a remarkable thing occurred. Erika met Judy.

One evening Erika went to see a play and got there a few minutes early. After settling in her seat, she opened her program to see what to expect.

Before she could finish scanning the first page, a middle-aged woman with curly, graying hair squeezed past her, settling on the next seat.

Why couldn't she have a ticket for the row in front? That's wide open. Erika rolled her eyes to the ceiling. *All I wanted was a little space tonight.*

Then it got worse. This woman was one of those friendly types.

"Hi, there. I'm Judy. What's your name?"

Oh, brother, lady. I'm not into this kind of chit chat. "I'm Erika. It's nice to meet you."

There, she thought. *That's over with.* And she turned her eyes back to study the program again.

"Well, I'm glad to meet you too."

Why won't she leave me alone? Erika wondered.

The lady went on. "I come for the plays every month but I haven't seen you before. Are you new here? Where are you from?"

C'mon, lady. Erika was becoming more internally agitated by the moment. *This is the theater, not a witness stand. Besides, you don't really want to know anyway.* "I live here in Dayton," Erika replied, with cool politeness. *That ought to end it.*

But Judy continued. "Have you always lived here?"

Why does she care? Erika was definitely losing composure at this point. "No, I've only lived here for two years." *Now shut up, lady.*

"Oh, really? Where did you come from before that?"

With a sigh, Erika half turned to look at this pesky woman and said, "I've lived in lots of different places." *So there.*

"Hey, that's great. So have I! Where have you lived?"

For the first time, Erika looked Judy in the eye. She couldn't believe it. This lady genuinely wanted to know. Erika hesitated. "I lived in Ecuador and Singapore."

"How long?"

"Oh, about ten years between the two places, if you're talking about actually living and going to school there full time."

"You're kidding! I grew up in Venezuela. I'd love to talk to you about it. It's not always easy to find someone here in Dayton who understands what it's like to grow up in another country."

Just then the curtain went up for the play so they stopped talking. Afterward they went for coffee and Erika found herself amazed. Here they were, two women from two totally different backgrounds and generations—Judy's parents had been in the foreign service while Erika's were in business; Judy had lived in Venezuela and Erika had lived in Ecuador and Singapore; Judy was forty-seven, married, and the mother of four grown children, while Erika was twenty-six, single, with no children. Yet they were soon talking and laughing together like long-lost friends.

"I remember when the CEO's wife first came to our house for dinner," Erika said with a chuckle. "She had just arrived in Singapore and kept talking about how awful everything was. My sister and I made up all sorts of stories about how big the roaches were and how poisonous the spiders were just to scare her."

Judy laughed. "I know how you felt. I hated it when new people came out and complained about everything. I always felt so protective for what seemed like my personal Venezuela."

"Well, I guess it was kind of mean," Erika said, "but we didn't like her barging into our world without trying to understand the parts we loved so much. We thought she was arrogant and narrow-minded and didn't deserve to be there—and she probably thought we were the same!"

They laughed together and continued talking for three hours. Erika couldn't believe it. For the first time in years she could speak the language of her soul without needing a translator. A space inside that had almost dried up suddenly began filling and then overflowing with the joy of being understood in a way that needed no explanation.

TCKs around the world instinctively feel this connection when they meet each other. But why? How can someone from Australia who grew up in Brazil understand that inner experience of someone from Switzerland who grew up in Hong Kong?

A video of TCKs meeting at Cornell University clearly demonstrates this bond.[11] Among the TCK panelists are:

- Kelvin—born in Hong Kong, raised in Nigeria and England;
- Marianne, a Danish citizen who grew up in the United States;
- Kamal, an Indian who lived in Japan as a child;
- a young Turkish man who spent his childhood in Germany, England, and the United States;
- one North American who grew up in the Philippines; and
- another North American reared in France.

Although each person in the video has differing points of identification with his or her host culture (e.g., the Turkish man feels he is extremely punctual as a result of living in Germany for many years), throughout the discussion it is obvious that their commonalities of feelings and experiences far outweigh their differences. It is equally obvious how delighted they are finally to find a forum where simply naming how they have felt in various circumstances brings instant understanding. No further explanation is needed to elicit a sympathetic laugh or tear from their peers.

But the question remains: What is it about growing up in multiple cultures and with high mobility that creates such instant recognition of each other's experiences and feelings? We'll continue to explore this and other questions about TCKs, but first we'll look at who (and why) others are claiming to relate to the TCK experience even though they haven't grown up in the traditional model of the third culture as initially described by the Useems.

CHAPTER 3

Who Are "Cross-Cultural Kids"?

My name is Brice Royer and I'm from Ottawa, Canada. Actually, that's a lie, but that's the answer I give to acquaintances.

So where am I really from? You be the judge. My father is a half-French and half-Vietnamese peacekeeper and my mother is Ethiopian. It was an unlikely love story that transcends race, culture, and values, but they found love across barriers. I'm grateful for the diversity of my heritage.

And where do I belong? I'm not French, Vietnamese, Ethiopian, or Canadian, and I certainly don't belong everywhere and nowhere. I belong to a group of multicultural people—cross-cultural kids. I've always been the "Foreigner." I look different and feel different. I even sound different—including among family members. I eat French food for breakfast, Ethiopian food for lunch, and my own special multicultural recipe for dinner. The truth is, I order Chinese take-out more often than I would like to admit, because let's face it, it's convenient and I can be lazy.[1]

—Brice Royer, developer of *TCKID.com*

SO WHO IS BRICE? Certainly he is a TCK because his father had an international career and Brice traveled the globe with him. But what do we do with the rest of his story? It seems far more complicated than those we have looked at so far.

All over the world, we meet people like Brice whose stories defy simple categorization based on traditional definitions. Consider the angst of news broadcasters as they tried to define the 44th U.S. president, Barack Obama, during the

2008 campaign. Should they call him an African American? Half-white? Half-black? Mixed? While the pundits worked hard to define President Obama by race and ethnicity, few seemed to understand one of the most basic facts about his life story: President Obama is not only racially mixed, but, as Brice describes himself, he is *culturally mixed* as well.[2] He fits none of those groups exactly. Like Brice, Obama grew up as a TCK during the childhood years he spent in Indonesia, and he is also the son of a bicultural/biracial union. As a minority, Obama found himself moving, sometimes daily, between dominant and minority cultural worlds even when living in his passport country.

This experience of growing up in a profoundly culturally mixed environment is becoming increasingly common, not only for TCKs but for many others as well. These people may have grown up as children of immigrants or refugees, or may have been international adoptees or minorities. Some simply grew up in an environment where they commonly interacted deeply between and among various cultural worlds around them, rather than moving to other cultures with parents who were engaged in international careers. Although their experiences differ markedly from those of the traditional TCKs first described by Ruth Hill Useem, people who grew up amid this wide variety of cross-cultural experiences tell us how much they relate to the common characteristics for TCKs. They want to know: Am I a TCK or not? Pravin was one who asked this question.

> Pravin began life in normal fashion—being born in his parents' homeland, India. From the moment of his birth, Pravin's parents wanted one thing: to give him every opportunity they could to be successful in a changing, internationalizing world. Part of their dream included helping him develop proficiency in English. With this goal in mind, they sent him to a British boarding school high on a mountainside in the north of India, which required students to speak and write only in English.
>
> Because his parents lived quite far away, they were not able to see Pravin during the school holidays. Finally the end of term came, and the day six-year-old Pravin had waited for all year: his parents were coming to pick him up for summer vacation. He could hardly contain his excitement! Yet he did have a slight fear—what if he didn't recognize his parents? How would he find them?
>
> Finally, he saw them. He did know them after all! He ran to his parents, they picked him up, and then the unthinkable happened. Pravin couldn't understand what they were saying. Their words sounded vaguely familiar, but he could not respond even to the few words he understood. During that year away from home, he had forgotten his mother tongue, and his parents didn't know English. When they

took him back to their village for summer vacation that
year and each year thereafter, he could no longer communicate with his former playmates. From that day to this, he
has lived in and among many cultural worlds without feeling totally at home in any.

Stories abound of those who have grown up in a multiplicity of cultural
worlds for many different reasons. This raises the legitimate question: Can all
who grow or grew up among many cultures for whatever reasons be considered
TCKs or ATCKs per se?

Some who work with or know about TCKs say no. They believe there are so
many differences between these types of experiences that none can be properly
researched if all are included under one umbrella. The problem then is that there
seems to be little effort to understand why there exists such a commonality of
response from those with greatly assorted cross-cultural backgrounds. Instead,
each group is left on its own to understand from scratch its collective story.

Conversely, those who see themselves or others relating to the TCK profile,
even if they never lived as traditional TCKs, say, "Yes, include everyone." They
believe any child who has grown up among various cultural worlds is a bona fide
TCK. But then how do we make allowances for the vastly different experiences
of a child who grows up outside a parent's culture in a refugee camp and one
who grows up in many different lands living in embassy housing with swimming
pools and tennis courts available on the grounds? Surely these are not the same
story?

Yet, amazingly, there are some major connections even between these
experiences.

In 1997, Ruth and her husband traveled to Ghana and
learned that many friends from their nine years spent in
Liberia lived in a nearby refugee camp.

Ruth wanted to see her friends, but what would she say?
Their experiences since they last met were beyond belief.
How did anything in her life relate to the horrors of war
and displacement they had known?

In the first moments of meeting, it seemed like old
times. The familiar sounds of Liberian English rang like
music in her ears. They all chatted to catch up on news of
family and friends. But soon the conversation began to include the sadder stories of the many friends who had died in
the war and the atrocities so many had been through. Ruth
could only grieve for them. How could anything in her life
relate to theirs?

One friend finally asked what she had been doing since
their last meeting. To Ruth, all she had done seemed rather
irrelevant in this situation. Her fairly routine activities

paled in comparison to their dramatic and sad stories. Yet in sharing her life story and also her work regarding TCK topics, her Liberian friends began telling her their stories— what it felt like for them to realize their children had no idea about the Liberia they as parents had known. How their children were now caught in a world between worlds, neither fully Liberian nor fully Ghanaian.

There they were: a white ATCK woman with enough means to travel to Ghana for a family visit, and her friends—black men, women, and children, victims of a terrible civil war, living on the rations given by the U.N. Still, in that moment of talking about the impact of living and growing up outside the environment defined as "home," they connected in a shared experience that transcended all the differences in their outer circumstances.

So are these children of refugees TCKs or not? If not, why do they relate? What are their points of commonality and contrast?

As the cultural mixing of today's world increases, these questions regarding who can or cannot be included as an "official TCK" are important ones to address. Historically, we assumed the difference between the TCK experience and that of immigrant children was simple: immigrants moved to a land to stay and many never took even one trip back to the homeland after arriving in the new country. TCKs moved with the expectation of one day returning to their original country. But in today's highly mobile world, immigrant children go back and forth, often with great regularity, between their country of origin and their adopted land, just as TCKs do. How do we factor all of these changes into our understanding of how we define and describe the many "new normals" we are seeing in our changing world?

Somehow we need to better understand both the commonalities these groups share as well as understand their differences so we can use what we have learned for the good of all. But how can we do that?

We believe there is a way.

Just as we have included children from the various communities of those who work internationally (corporate, military, missionary, foreign service) under the broader language of *third culture kid*, so we can enlarge our language and make room under one umbrella for all types of cross-cultural childhoods. In doing so, we can use the TCK experience as a lens for viewing common themes children express when raised among many cultural worlds for any reason. By seeing what is shared, we can also see what is specific to each particular type of cross-cultural experience as well. We propose using the term *cross-cultural kid* to help us carry this topic forward.

IDENTIFYING CROSS-CULTURAL KIDS

Coauthor Ruth Van Reken developed the following definition of cross-cultural kids:

- A *cross-cultural kid (CCK)* is a person who is living or has lived in—or meaningfully interacted with—two or more cultural environments for a significant period of time during childhood (up to age 18).
- An *adult CCK (ACCK)* is a person who has grown up as a CCK.

Figure 3-1 illustrates some of the many types of CCKs. We define these particular groups of CCKs in the following way:

- *Traditional TCKs:* Children who move into another culture with parents due to a parent's career choice.
- *Children from bi/multicultural homes:* Children born to parents from at least two cultures. May or may not be of the same race.

The Cross-Cultural Kid (CCK) Model

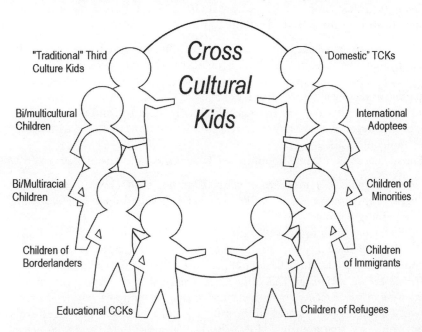

Figure 3-1 The Cross-Cultural Kid Model
(© 2002 Ruth E. Van Reken)

- *Children from bi/multiracial homes:* Children born to parents from at least two races. May or may not be of the same culture.
- *Children of immigrants:* Children whose parents have made a permanent move to a new country where they were not originally citizens.
- *Educational CCKs:* Children who may remain in their home or passport country but are sent to a school (e.g., an international school) with a different cultural base and student mix than the traditional home culture or its schools.
- *Children of refugees:* Children whose parents are living outside their original country or place due to circumstances they did not choose, such as war, violence, famine, or natural disasters.
- *Children of borderlanders:* Children who cross borders frequently, even daily, as they go to school, or whose parents work across national borders.
- *Children of minorities:* Children whose parents are from a racial or ethnic group that is not part of the majority race or ethnicity of the country in which they live.
- *International adoptees:* Children adopted by parents from another country other than the one of that child's birth.
- *Domestic TCKs:* Children whose parents have moved in or among various subcultures within that child's home country.

These groups represent only a few of many other possible inclusions, such as foreign exchange students. We have been asked whether children of divorce who spend half their time in one parent's home and half in the other's house can be regarded as having a cross-cultural experience. Considering such questions is part of the current discovery process. Undoubtedly there are, and will continue to be, more categories than those named here. But for now, we begin with these few examples of CCKs.

Please note several things about the CCK definition and our model:

- *The traditional TCKs discussed in this book are also CCKs.* Just as a corporate "brat" or missionary kid is a TCK, so are TCKs a subgroup of CCKs, as our new paradigm shows.
- *Each category listed under CCKs could have additional subsets, just as TCKs do.* This enables continued study in each of the subgroups as we further compare and contrast the specific experiences.
- *Unlike the definition for TCKs, the CCK definition is not dependent on the question of where CCKs grow up, such as outside the passport culture or overseas.* This definition focuses on the multiple and varied layering of cultural environments that are impacting a child's life rather than the actual place where the events occur.
- *CCKs are not merely living side by side with those from other cultures, but are interacting with more than one culture in ways that have meaningful or relational involvement.*

- *CCKs and adult CCKs represent any and all nationalities, ethnicities, and economic groups.* Our focus is not on the traditional ways of defining diversity but rather to look at the shared commonalities of the experience that transcend our usual ways of categorizing people.

Like Brice and President Obama, many CCKs grow up in more than one of these cross-cultural environments. Looking through this expanded lens helps us see how the layers of cultural mixing and matching in today's changing world are becoming increasingly complex for many children and families.

> The Ngujos laughed when they saw the CCK model. "We never stopped to think of how many of these groups our kids are in." When asked to explain, Mrs. Ngujo said, "Well, I came from one region in Kenya; my husband came from another. We both spoke Swahili and English, but neither of us spoke each other's mother tongue. I guess that makes my kids members of the bicultural group. My husband took a job with a large international bank, so our family immigrated to the States. There we became part of a minority population for the first time, but soon his bank began sending us on assignments all over the world. At that point, our kids became traditional TCKs. I'm glad to know there is a term to describe all four experiences at the same time!"

President Obama himself is in six of our categories: *biracial, bicultural, TCK, minority*, and then *educational CCK* because he attended a local school where he studied in a different language from his home culture during his four years as a TCK in Indonesia. He is also a *domestic TCK*. When he grew up in Hawaii, he lived with his white grandparents in an environment where many others were also of mixed race and cultural backgrounds. When he moved to the mainland, others defined him as primarily "African American." His autobiography, *Dreams from My Father*, describes his struggles to come to terms with his identity during that time in a way TCKs of all backgrounds understand.

Even for many TCKs of one primary ethnic/racial background, life is getting more complicated. No longer do they navigate primarily between one host culture and their passport culture as they did in the days when Ruth Hill Useem first named them. Instead, many live in four or five (and sometimes more!) different countries while growing up. The layering of cultural influences in their lives grows exponentially as well.

The question, however, remains: While it may be good to find a common term to describe children who grow up among many cultures, how does that help us begin to compare and contrast these experiences with all of the obvious differences between them?

Lessons from the TCK "Petri Dish"

Before Ruth Hill Useem gave unifying language to this experience, those who lived in these various third culture communities assumed the issues they and their children faced were specific to their group (or sector) alone. Why were missionary kids so strange when they returned to their passport country for high school or college? Why were military kids such "brats"? And on and on the wonderings went. Each group looked at sector-specific phenomena they saw occurring among children being raised in their particular system. There was no assumption of commonality between the groups because there were so many different details in how or why the families had gone to another country

Understanding that virtually every child in each of these sectors grew up with similar experiences—such as a cross-cultural upbringing, high mobility, expected repatriation, and often a system identity as we mentioned in chapter 2—expedited the discussion for everyone. Each group no longer had to look only at the specific details of the basic phenomenon they saw; understanding and resources could be shared among all the sectors.

By looking at the shared whole, however, issues that applied specifically to each sector became more visible as well. For example, how did the long and often multiple separations from at least one parent, coupled with the fear (for those in a war zone) that this parent might never return, play out specifically for military kids? How did the sense that they and their families represented an entire nation affect children growing up in the foreign service? How did the "God" piece of growing up in a religious system impact the missionary kid? How did watching decisions made by a parent's corporation based on the "bottom line" that might adversely influence the local economy shape a business kid? Figure 3-2 illustrates these influences.

In other words, it's not entirely God's fault that a missionary kid might carry unresolved grief; that is a common characteristic for TCKs of all sectors. At the same time, dealing with separating a view of God from the religious subculture they have known may be a challenge unique to TCKs in the mission sector. Neither is the military to blame for a person who has "itchy feet" and is always looking to move after two years. But the fear of a black limousine pulling up to the front door to announce a parent's death may be specific to a child raised in this subset of the TCK experience. Once universals are defined, other specific issues can be discussed.

These same lessons apply to understanding CCKs. Figure 3-3 gives us examples of what CCKs of all backgrounds share and what issues may be specific for each particular type of experience.

Third Culture Kids:
Potential Commonalities and Differences

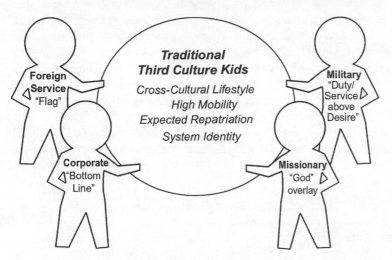

Figure 3-2 Third Cultural Kids: Potential Commonalities and Differences
(© 1996 Ruth E. Van Reken)

Cross-Cultural Kids:
Potential Commonalities and Differences

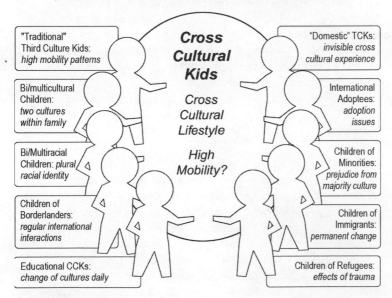

Figure 3-3 Cross-Cultural Kids: Potential Commonalities and Differences
(© 2008 Ruth E. Van Reken)

While the idea of CCKs is a growing concept, there is one thing we know for sure that virtually all CCKs share: by definition, each of them grows up in some sort of cross-cultural lifestyle or environment, no matter the particular circumstance. One friend who has worked with the refugees of Darfur looked at the CCK model and said, "This is the first time I see my friends at Darfur being invited back to the human race. We are so used to thinking of all their issues as a result of the violence, which is indeed terrible. But we have been forgetting that in addition to that, they have lost their cultural world as well and feel that loss as all others do when it happens to them for whatever reason. Thanks for letting them be part of yours."

Some of the most invisible CCKs, however, may be domestic TCKs—those who have moved in and among various cultures right within their homeland. Jennifer is one.

> Both of Jennifer's parents grew up in the upper-middle-class suburbs of Toronto. When Jennifer was nine, they became teachers for five years on a First Nation (Native American) reservation near Vancouver. Jennifer went to school, played, ate, and visited with her First Nation playmates almost exclusively during those years—yet her lifestyle was not the same as their lifestyle. For example, there were celebratory rituals in the First Nation culture that Jennifer's family never practiced. Her parents had rules for curfew and study hours that many of her friends didn't have, but Jennifer accepted these differences between herself and her friends.
>
> When she was 14, Jennifer's parents returned to Toronto. They wanted her to have a more "normal" high school experience. Unfortunately, it wasn't as normal as they had hoped. For one thing, Jennifer's new classmates seemed to judge one another far more critically by clothing styles than she had ever before experienced. Far worse, however, was that Jennifer saw this emphasis on apparent superficiality as stemming from a lack of concern for what she considered the *real* issues of life.
>
> When newspapers reported the ongoing conflict of land issues between the First Nation people and the Canadian government, she read the accounts with keen interest. She personally knew friends whose futures were directly affected by these political decisions. But when she tried to discuss such things with fellow classmates or their parents, their response was almost dismissive: "I don't know what those people are complaining about. Look at all we've already done for them." The more she tried to explain why this topic needed attention, the more they labeled her as

radical, and the more she labeled them as uncaring. Jennifer sobbed herself to sleep many nights, wishing for the comfortable familiarity of the world and friends she'd known before.

Although she had never left Canada, Jennifer had become a domestic TCK—someone raised in that world between worlds—within her own country.

The military is another place where domestic TCKs often develop, even though the family may never have gone overseas. Because the military subculture is quite different from that of the civilian population around it, a particular lifestyle develops (see Mary Edwards Wertsch's book *Military Brats*). When military parents return to civilian life, their children often experience many of the same feelings that internationally mobile TCKs describe when they return to their passport countries, despite the fact that they may have lived their entire lives on homeland soil.

Raised on U.S. Navy bases in California and Washington, D.C., Bernadette was fourteen when her father retired from the Navy and her family settled in the midwestern town of Terre Haute, Indiana. Bernadette later described the experience as one of total alienation from her peers, whose life experience was completely foreign to her. "They had no idea what the PX was, how much life on a base is governed by the security issues surrounding it, or how normal it was to mix with those of different races on a daily basis because our parents were all working as peers in their various assignments. And I had no idea what it felt like to grow up in one town in the Midwest with little interaction with others who were not from your presumed social group or race."

This is where the idea of TCKs as prototypes for others becomes reality. As we consider why a cross-cultural childhood matters in a TCK's life, we can begin to see what lessons learned there can be applied to other CCKs as well. For example, although the way cultural interactions occurred and the degree of mobility were different in all of these other types of CCK experiences from the traditional TCK's world, all shared the same common emotional experience: when they tried to relate to those who "should" be their own, none of them felt as if they fit or belonged to that group any longer. This is the "like experience" described in the TCK definition—one of the new places of connection in our changing world. As we continue to find the common points that CCKs of all backgrounds share, we can see more clearly what, in fact, are unique issues to consider for those various subgroups as well.

We will continue to focus *primarily* on the specifics of the traditional TCK experience as we proceed through this book. We do so for two reasons.

1. *This is the experience we know in detail.* We want to continue giving TCKs and ATCKs language and understanding for the depth and unique aspects of their own cross-cultural journey. We have seen for many years how important that is.
2. *As we do so, we invite all readers to consider common themes for the larger cohort of CCKs.* What are the principles and basic understandings from the TCK experience that we can apply to other experiences as well? This book will not finish that discussion, but we trust it will start it, and expedite that ongoing discussion.

With that in mind, we move on to why a cross-cultural childhood matters for TCKs and for others as well.

CHAPTER 4

Why a Cross-Cultural Childhood Matters

I am
a confusion of cultures.
Uniquely me.
I think this is good
because I can
understand
the traveller, sojourner, foreigner,
the homesickness
that comes.
I think this is also bad
because I cannot
be understood
by the person who has sown and grown in one place.
They know not
the real meaning of homesickness
that hits me
now and then.
Sometimes I despair of
understanding them.
I am
an island
and
a United Nations.
Who can recognise either in me
but God?[1]

—"Uniquely Me" by Alex Graham James

Who Am I?

This poem by Alex, an Australian TCK who grew up in India, captures the paradoxical nature of the TCK experience—the sense of being so profoundly connected yet simultaneously disconnected to people and places around the world. Again, the question is this: What makes Alex, like Erika and many other TCKs, feel this way?

Before we can answer that question, we need to take a closer look at the world in which TCKs grow up, a world filled with cross-cultural transitions and high mobility. These two related but distinct forces play a large role in shaping a TCK's life. Through this lens, we can later see how some of what we learn can be applied to CCKs as well.

One other note: We realize many adults also experience cross-cultural transitions and high mobility as they embark on international careers, and their lives inevitably are changed in the process. By looking into the impact of culture and mobility on their children, it is our hope that it will give them language and concepts to better understand their own journey. But we also believe it is important for these third culture adults to understand some distinct differences between making a cross-cultural move for the first time as an adult and *growing up* cross-culturally. People who initially go to another culture as adults undoubtedly experience culture shock and need a period of adjustment. They, too, have lifelong shifts in their worldview after a major cross-cultural move, but their basic value system, sense of identity, and establishment of core relationships with family and friends have already developed in the home culture. Most often, they clearly see themselves as Koreans, Americans, Australians, Kenyans, or Indonesians who happen to be living in another place or culture. Their basic sense of who they are and where they are from in this fundamental place is intact, even though they also may initially feel like strangers in their home country if they return after being gone for a long time.

Unlike third culture adults, TCKs move back and forth from one culture to another *before* they have completed the critical developmental task of forming a sense of their own personal or cultural identity. A British child taking toddling steps on foreign soil or speaking his or her first words in Chinese with an *amah* (nanny) has no idea what it means to be a human being let alone "British" yet. He or she simply responds to what is happening in the moment.

To have a meaningful discussion about TCKs, it is essential to remember that it is an *interplay* of these factors—living in both a culturally changing *and* highly mobile world during the *formative* years—rather than any single factor alone, that leads to the evolution of both the benefits and challenges we describe as well as the personal characteristics. To better understand how the interplay of these factors works, we need to look at each one separately. We will begin this chapter by taking a look at the cross-cultural nature of the TCK's childhood. Then, in chapter 5, we will move on to high mobility.

The Significance of Culture

All children, including TCKs, face a myriad of developmental tasks as they grow from helpless infants into healthy adults. Among them is the need to develop a strong sense of personal identity as well as group identity, answering the questions *Who am I?* and *Where do I belong?* Traditionally, the family and community mirror back the answers and the child sees his or her image reflected in them. Hans Christian Andersen's fable *The Ugly Duckling* reflects how this process of finding personal and group identity works.

> When a baby swan emerges from its shell in the midst of a nest of ducklings, mother duck is shocked and the other ducklings laugh at the clumsy, overgrown, freakish supposed-specimen of a duck. In the story, the presumed duck siblings bully and mercilessly tease the odd creature. Soon the baby swan accepts the judgment of his community, believes he is ugly and runs away. Not until much later does he see himself differently. He finally meets other swans and realizes they reflect his own image in a beautiful way. At last this little ugly duckling understands both his personal identity in being a swan and that he does, in fact, belong to a community.[2]

Through the ages, this process of learning identity and culture has occurred so naturally that it's been like breathing. It happens all the time, but until someone chokes and can't catch a breath, no one notices what's going on. Because it is such an unconscious process, however, we need to take time to dissect it so that we can find some important keys to unlock the mystery of *why* common TCK characteristics occur later on. We begin by looking in general at what culture is, how it's learned, and why it's important. Then we will compare how the process of cultural learning is the same or different for those who grow up among many cultures from children born and bred in the more traditional monocultural experience.

What Is Culture?

When we think of the word *culture*, obvious representations such as how to dress, eat, speak, and act like those around us come to mind. But learning culture is more than learning conformity to external patterns of behavior. Culture is also a system of shared concepts, beliefs, and values.[3] It is the framework from which we interpret and make sense of life and the world around us. As cultural anthropologist Paul Hiebert emphasized, culture is learned rather than instinctive— something caught from, as well as taught by, the surrounding environment and passed on from one generation to the next.[4]

In other words, young mothers don't buy books on *How to Teach Your Child Culture*. From the moment of birth, children are learning the ways of their community. Parents speak a particular language to them. They are clothed and carried in ways defined by that community as "right." *Pink is for girls, blue is for boys. Tie the baby on your back. Put the baby in a safe car seat.* As the children grow, extended family members reinforce the concepts of how life is approached and lived. "What do you say?" asks grandma after handing her grandchild a cookie. Later, teachers, peers, and others in the community reflect and teach how life is to be lived "properly" in this place.

The Role of the Visible and Invisible Layers of Culture

Anthropologist Gary Weaver suggested looking at culture as a kind of iceberg: one portion is clearly visible above the surface of the water, while the much larger chunk of ice is hidden below. The part above the water can be considered *surface culture*—what we can physically see or hear, including behavior, words, customs, language, and traditions. Underneath the water, invisible to all, is the *deep culture*.[5] This place includes our beliefs, values, assumptions, worldview, and thought processes. Figure 4-1 depicts the cultural iceberg Weaver envisioned.

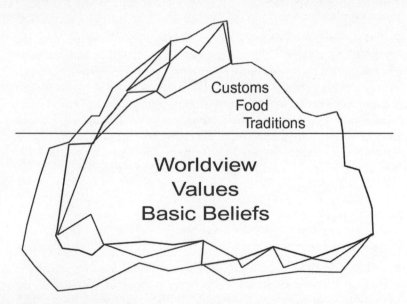

Figure 4-1 The Weaver Cultural Iceberg
(© Dr. Gary Weaver. Used with permission.)

The basic thesis behind this model is that the elements on the surface, or visible, layer of culture traditionally have been used to identify what is in the deeper, or invisible, layer. Conversely, the visible is where the invisible is expressed. Thus, what we see becomes our shorthand method to make early assessments and expectations of others. Is this person an "us" or a "them"? Will we relate from "likeness" or "difference"? The following are two examples of how this works.

- In some places, tribal markings make it clear whether strangers will interact as fellow tribespersons or foreigners from the first moment of their meeting. Because of these symbols, they know immediately whether they can use their tribal dialect or must speak in a more universal language before either has said one word.
- When we watch a sporting event, we cheer or boo the players based solely on the color of their uniform. We look around the grandstands and assume those who wear the blue jerseys or bandanas like us share our hopes for a home team victory. We are equally confident that those with red jerseys have come to root for the opposing team. In each case, without knowing one other thing about the people surrounding us, we have made decisions about who they are and what they want based on something we can see.

Stereotypes and racism can form easily when we make assumptions about who another person is based on appearances alone. On the other hand, these assumptions based on the visible expressions of culture also help us create order and structure in our lives and social relationships. Imagine the chaos teams would face if they had no uniforms. What would happen if every time a basketball player wanted to pass the ball to a teammate, that player had to stop and ask the intended receiver what team he wanted to win?

Another danger lurks within the iceberg. The *Titanic* didn't sink because it hit the visible portion of the iceberg. Disaster struck when the ship's captain assumed he knew where the iceberg lay because of what he saw. He had no idea of its mammoth size below the surface. The same can happen with cultural clashes. We can make many allowances for differences we recognize, but when our values, beliefs, or worldviews are at odds with others in ways we haven't stopped to consider and cannot see, our relationships can sink as the *Titanic* did without our knowing what we hit.[6]

Though the iceberg model explains many historical clashes as well as present-day situations, Weaver pointed out new challenges in our globalizing world. The advent of the Internet as well as TV, movies, and mass media of all kinds has made the visible layer of culture for people and groups around the world appear more similar than in previous eras. Because we initially base our expectations of likeness or difference on what we see, cultural clashes may increase, according to Weaver. He pointed out that we will assume we have commonality of thought, worldview, and beliefs when we look at another who appears very similar to ourselves in dress, manner, and even language. The reality is, however, that people change external cues of culture, such as dress and food, far more quickly than they alter their core values, manner of thinking, and belief system. Weaver stated that this developing discrepancy between who we *expect* others to be based on appearance and who they *are* in their invisible spaces will create more cultural clashes unless we find new ways to recognize and address this issue.[7]

The Importance of Cultural Balance

As mentioned earlier, understanding who we are and where we belong is a developmental task that takes place in the context of the surrounding community. It is there, while we are children, that we learn the basic rules and values by which our particular culture operates. As teenagers, we begin to test and challenge some of these assumptions and practices in the quest to establish our sense of individual identity as well. Ultimately, we internalize the practices and principles we have learned, challenged, and accepted. Then we can grow with confidence into adulthood because we know what is expected of us. Not only do we understand how the game is played, but we have had role models to watch in the age group just ahead of us and can follow in their paths.

At that point we experience what is called *cultural balance*—that almost unconscious knowledge of how things are and work in a particular community. Why is achieving this developmental state so important in establishing a sense of confidence and belonging?

When we are in cultural balance, we are like a concert pianist who, after practicing for years to master the basics, no longer thinks about how to touch the piano keys or do scales and trills. Those functions have become automatic responses to notations in the music score, and this freedom from *conscious* attention to details allows the pianist to use these very skills to create and express richer, fuller music for us all.

A sense of cultural balance allows that same freedom. Once we have stayed in a culture long enough to internalize its customs and underlying assumptions, we have an intuitive sense of what is right, humorous, appropriate, or offensive in any particular situation. Instead of spending excessive time worrying whether we are dressed appropriately for a business appointment, we concentrate on developing a new business plan. Being "in the know" gives us a sense of stability, deep security, and belonging, for we have been entrusted with the "secrets" of our tribe. We may not understand *why* cultural rules work as they do, but we know *how* our culture works.

In the days when most people lived in a basically monocultural environment and community, members shared essentially the same values, assumptions, behavioral styles, and traditional practices with one another. Achieving cultural balance wasn't hard because everyone reinforced what lay in the deeper layer of culture as well as the seen layer. Patterns of the past were repeated for generations and change came slowly enough to be absorbed without rocking the cultural boat too wildly.

Perhaps one of the best illustrations of this type of traditional cultural community is seen in *Fiddler on the Roof*, the musical about a farmer named Tevye and his Russian Jewish village of Anatevka. For years Tevye's culture had remained basically the same. Everyone knew where he or she fit, both in relating to one another and to God. There had been no major outside influences. The way things had always been was the way things still worked—with the milkman, matchmaker, farmer, and all others clearly aware of their assigned roles within the village. Roles assigned by whom? By *tradition*—another word for how cultural beliefs are worked out in practice. As Tevye says,

> Because of our traditions, we've kept our balance for many,
> many years. Here in Anatevka we have traditions for
> everything—how to eat, how to sleep, how to wear clothes.
> For instance, we always keep our heads covered and always
> wear a little prayer shawl. This shows our constant devotion
> to God. You may ask, how did this tradition start? I'll tell
> you—I don't know! But it's a tradition. Because of our tradi-
> tions, everyone knows who he is and what God expects him
> to do.... Without our traditions, our lives would be as shaky
> as—as a fiddler on the roof![8]

Tevye then laments that tradition is breaking down. As the old ways he knew rapidly begin to change, he loses his former sense of balance. His grip on life slips and his comfortable world is shattered. Mentally and emotionally, Tevye can't keep up and he becomes disoriented and alienated, even from his own children.

This story serves as a great metaphor for what is happening in our world at an ever quickening pace. The ways we have known and taken for granted as defining and "doing" life, complete with their neat little boxes of race, nationality, or ethnicity, are quickly breaking down. Cultural mixing and matching in every country is happening faster than we can understand. The normal feeling of many is to retrench and, like Tevye, long for the good old days when things seemed more in our control. We feel more comfortable and safer when we understand what's going on based on how things have always been.

A World of Changing Cultures

Now that we've looked at cultural balance and how important it is, we must admit one thing: most TCKs often feel quite out of cultural balance. Why? Because for many, the world of rapid cultural change has been their norm as they exchange complete sets of worldviews, expectations of behavior, and even languages with an overnight airplane ride. Before they know how they are to behave, they must figure out where they are. Through the years, many have wondered what is wrong with them because they never seem to "get it." Consider this story one ATCK told us:

> The Edleys had lived and worked in a remote village in Africa for ten years. The parents wanted to make sure their children would fit back into their passport culture with little notice when it came time to return. They bought the latest fashions they could find, dressed their four children carefully, and flew back to New York. The family collected its luggage and the parents led the family procession to the line for customs.
>
> Suddenly they realized people throughout the baggage claim area were looking at them. They wondered why when they had worked so hard to make their children appear "normal." They turned and then understood the stares. There, behind them in perfect single file, walked each of their children carrying a suitcase on their heads. A perfectly common, sensible way to transport things in their village, but not a common sight at JFK airport in New York.

In countless stories we've heard similar to this one, TCKs and ATCKs tell us that no matter what situation they are in or how hard they try, they often find themselves making what others see as a dumb remark or mistake. They unknowingly transgress standard cultural procedures at the very time they think they are doing exactly the appropriate thing, such as carrying suitcases on their heads because the suitcases are heavy. How were these kids to know this isn't the way people did it in the United States? Everyone they knew had been carrying heavy loads like this wherever they went. Those around the TCKs wonder at their apparent stupidity, and the TCKs and ATCKs are left with feeling shame that once more they are somehow so "out of sync" socially. Like the Ugly Duckling, they have accepted the judgment of the community that something is wrong with them and they definitely don't belong.

Perhaps ironically, the struggle many TCKs face in trying to find a sense of cultural balance and identity is not because they learn culture differently from the way others do. In fact, the real challenge comes *because* they learn culture as everyone does—by "catching it" from their environment rather than by reading a book or getting a master's degree in cultural anthropology. The point isn't the process of how they learn cultural balance, but the environment in which they are trying to learn it—a world filled with many cultures. In addition, the truth is that while many TCKs do, indeed, find a deep sense of belonging and cultural balance in a culturally mixed setting, they and others may invalidate that since it doesn't match our traditional expectations of how people find personal and group identity.

What TCKs and those who know them seem to forget is that their very life experiences have been different from those who grow up in a basically stable, traditional, monocultural community such as Tevye's. As TCKs move with their parents from place to place, the cultural values and practices of the communities they live in often change radically. What was acceptable behavior and thinking in one place is seen as crude or ridiculous in the next. Which culture are they supposed to catch? Do they belong to all of them, none of them, or some of each of them? And, as we said, the world they do fit in—the world of a global lifestyle—is so ephemeral no one validates it. Where in the world (literally) do they fit?

Another challenge for TCKs as they seek to find a sense of cultural balance is that not only do the overall cultural rules often change overnight, but equally often the various individuals around them may hold markedly different world and life views from one another. Norma McCaig, founder of Global Nomads, designed the model in Figure 4-2 to express this multiplicity of communities in which TCKs (aka global nomads) learn culture.[9]

The following sections look at how the normal process of learning cultural balance may be complicated by all of these cultural groups in a TCK's life.

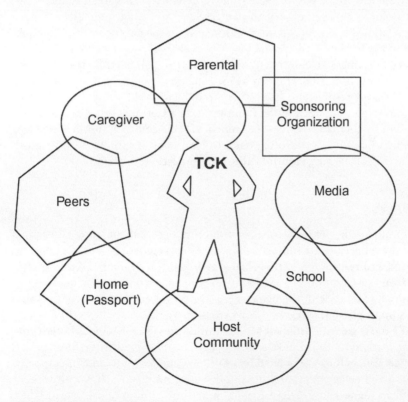

Figure 4-2 Possible Multiple Cultures in a TCK's World
(© 1998 Norma McCaig adapted. Used with permission.)

PARENTS

Parents communicate both the "above water" and "below water" cultural norms in various ways. They do it by example, dressing differently for a business meeting than for a tennis match, or when speaking respectfully of others. They do it by correction: "Don't chew with your mouth open." "If you don't stop hitting your brother, you'll have to take a time-out." Or they do it by praise: "What a good boy you are to share your toys with your sister!"

Wherever TCKs are being raised, their families' cultural practices and values are usually rooted in the parents' home culture or cultures and may be markedly different from the practices of the surrounding culture. This includes something as simple as the style of clothing. Girls from the Middle East may continue wearing a head covering no matter which country they live in. Dutch children wear Western dress in the forests of Brazil. Of course, it's more than that as well. Telling the truth at all costs may be a prime value at home, while shading the truth to avoid shaming another person may be the paramount value in the host culture.

As we noted in chapter 3, increasing numbers of TCKs like President Barack Obama are also being born to parents who are in an intercultural marriage or relationship. This is another reason why looking at the multiplicity and layering of the CCK experiences mentioned in chapter 3 is important. In 1960, one-quarter of American children living overseas had parents from two cultures, according to Ruth Hill Useem.[10] In 1995, Helen Fail found that 42 percent of her ATCK survey respondents had grown up in bicultural families.[11] One young man, for example, was born in the Philippines to a German father married to a Cambodian mother, and they speak French as their common family language. That's a lot of cultures for a young child to learn, and it complicates this most elemental step of learning cultural rules and practices from parents.

COMMUNITY

In a community like Tevye's, other adults reinforce what the parents teach at home because the rules are uniform. The same characteristics—such as honesty, hard work, and respect for adults—bring approval (or, in their absence, disapproval) from the community as well as from parents. No one stops to question by whose standards some cultural behaviors and customs are defined as proper and others as improper. But everyone knows what they are.

TCKs interface with different local communities, each having different cultural expectations, from the moment they begin their odyssey in the third culture experience. Unless they are isolated in a military, embassy, mission, or company compound and never go into the surrounding community, the host culture certainly affects them. They learn to drop in on friends without calling ahead. They call adults by their first names. When TCKs return to their passport culture, they usually have to switch to a different set of cultural customs and practices. Now an unexpected visit becomes an intrusion. Addressing a playmate's mother or father by her or his first name is rude enough to be a punishable offense. Woe to the TCK who forgets where he or she is.

But their community also includes this expat subculture the Useems first noted. It is here where they learn the norms of the third culture lifestyle, just as people in the past have learned their cultural norms in a community like Tevye's. When TCKs live in this third culture lifestyle, their peers also understand what it is to jet from place to place. They know what it is to say good-bye over and over. Just think of the powerful song written by one military ATCK, John Denver. "I'm leaving on a jet plane. Don't know when I'll be back again. Oh, babe, I hate to go...."[12]

How many TCKs and ATCKs claim this as their theme song? A lot we know do! The truth is TCKs do have a community, an "interstitial culture" that is there, but because it is not defined by place, nor is it understood by many who have not lived it, many TCKs have never recognized it as, in fact, their "tribe."

SCHOOL

Although culture isn't taught from a book, no educational system develops in a cultural vacuum. Teachers learn a particular style of teaching based on the philosophy of how that culture believes children should be taught. A curriculum, along with the teaching method, is a direct reflection of the cultural values and beliefs of the society. Those who believe in the curriculum do so because they feel the values and practices it emphasizes are correct. In a traditional monocultural community, both school and home reinforce what the other is unconsciously teaching at the "under water" level of culture.

For many TCKs, however, what and how things are taught at school may be vastly different as they shift from school to school while moving from one place to another. In addition, in an international community the individual teachers themselves often come from many different cultures. This can add significant complexity to a TCK's cultural development—let alone his or her academic achievement. Joe's story is an excellent example.

> My siblings and I found ourselves the only Americans in
> an Anglo-Argentine culture and we went to British schools.
> But the Argentines also thought their education was pretty
> good, so Peron mandated an Argentine curriculum for every
> private school and, with what time was left over, the school
> could do what it wanted. We went to school from 8:00 to
> 4:00 with four hours in Spanish in the morning and four
> hours in an English public school in the afternoon.

> Meanwhile, our parents fought desperately to keep some
> semblance of Americanism at home. They lost the battle of
> the crossed 7s. They lost the spelling battle. Worse, when
> they were told that in a given year there would be a focus
> on North American history, geography, and literature, they
> discovered, to their dismay, North America meant Canada.[13]

It isn't only Americans going to British-oriented schools who struggle. Some of
the most difficult situations are those of children who are from non-English-
speaking countries who go to American or other English-oriented schools. One
Norwegian girl who attended such a school writes,

> Norway became my well-kept secret. I was a fiercely patri-
> otic little girl, and every May 17 I would insist on celebrat-
> ing Norway's independence day. My American classmates
> had their Thanksgiving and Halloween parties. I was never
> invited, except for once, when I left the party in tears be-
> cause I didn't understand the English in the video they were
> watching. Little did it help that we had a teacher from Texas
> who taught us U.S. history that year. When I put Florida
> on the wrong side of the map she scolded me for it. That
> memory is still very vivid in my mind. I was forced to hear
> about the wonders of America, and no one cared to hear
> about Norway. No one seemed to care that English wasn't
> my first language, and the school wouldn't give us time to
> learn Norwegian during school hours—we had to study Nor-
> wegian during our vacations. I used to think that was really
> unfair.[14]

If school is a place for learning the values as well as the behavior of culture,
what happens when children attend a school with completely different customs,
values, or religious orientation from that of their parents? What happens when
the basic educational needs (e.g., "correct" spelling, penmanship, math processes, language) required for success in their passport cultures aren't taught in
the school they attend? This often occurs for globally nomadic families when the
choices for schools that teach the academic curriculum of their home country
may be limited to schools based on a belief system or in a language that doesn't
match their own. Even something like the style of teaching—such as rote versus
inductive methods—can add to the stress of learning.

TCKs who go to boarding school experience another distinct subculture
twenty-four hours a day rather than only during school. Without question, different rules are needed to organize scores of children in a dormitory environment rather than two or three in a home. Some TCKs talk of being raised by
their peers more than by adults in such a setting. Some consider this the most
positive thing about boarding school; others say it was the most difficult. Either

way, it is a different experience from going to a day school and returning to parents each night.

PEERS

When children play together, they instinctively parrot the cultural rules they have been taught: "You're cheating!" "Don't be a sissy!" "You made a great play!" They reflect what is considered to be, or not to be, in style. "Why are you wearing that ugly shirt?" "Wow! I really like your coat." Children enforce the cultural norms of a community as they shame or praise one another in this way.

Most TCKs attend school and play with peers from many cultures—each culture valuing different things. Some friends practically live and die for soccer and cricket; others love American football and baseball. Some children are raised to believe that academic success is the highest priority; others value peer relationships over high grades. Styles of relationship can be very different. Males holding hands in one culture is a common expression of friendship. In another, it may have connotations related to sexual preference. How does a child decide which is "correct"?

While virtually all children learn culture from their parents, community, school, and peers, TCKS often have two additional sources of cultural input: caregivers and sponsoring agencies.

CAREGIVERS

Like children all over the world, some TCKs are left with a caregiver while their parents work or socialize. While caregivers in the home culture generally share the parents' basic language and cultural outlook, TCKs are often cared for by members of the host culture who may only speak their national language. A German child being cared for by a Scottish nanny in Aberdeen will likely hear no German during the time they spend together.

Methods of child care in various cultures can be radically different. Instead of being pushed in a pram, Russian children raised in Niger will be carried on their African nanny's back until they can walk. Shaming may be the main method of training a child in the host culture rather than a more praise-based type of approach in the home culture or vice versa.

Caregivers, like all of us, inevitably reflect their culture's attitude toward children and life. The story goes that when Pearl Buck was a child in China, someone asked how she compared her mother to her Chinese *amah*. Buck replied, "If I want to have a story read, I go to my mother. But if I fall down and need to be comforted, I go to my amah." Her mother's culture valued teaching and learning, while her amah's placed a greater value on nurture. Even as a child, Buck instinctively knew the difference.

SPONSORING AGENCIES

In addition to the home and host cultures, many TCKs are also shaped not only by the overall expatriate community, but also by the subcommunity—missionary, business, military, diplomatic corps—in which they grow. Each of these groups also has its own subculture and clear expectations of behavior. In *Military Brats,* Mary Edwards Wertsch writes,

> Certainly by the time a military child is five years old, the values and rules of military life have been thoroughly internalized, the military identity forged, and the child has already assumed an active stage presence as an understudy of the Fortress theater company.[15]

Whatever the rules are in any TCK's given subculture—be they matters of correct dress, correct faith, or correct political views—TCKs know that to be an accepted member of that group, they must conform to those standards.

Many of these sponsoring agencies have, or have had in the past, special behavioral or philosophical expectations of not only their employees but the employees' families as well. This may result in situations that wouldn't happen to friends living in traditional settings in the passport culture. Two examples follow.

- A child's indiscretions (such as spraying graffiti on the wall of a public building) in a foreign service community might cause a major diplomatic rift with the host culture and force the parent to be re-assigned to another country, while that same behavior wouldn't cause a ripple in a parent's career if it happened in a suburban community in the home country.
- In the military, if a parent doesn't come in for a teacher-parent conference, the teacher can speak with the parent's officer-in-charge and the officer will require the parent to come in. If a military child does something as serious as getting drunk in school or setting off a firecracker, for example, he or she might be sent back to the home country, the parent won't be promoted that year, and the incident goes on the parent's permanent record.

One more point about organizational subcultures: often we forget to look at how the underlying dominant or national culture of the sponsoring agency itself may affect TCKs, particularly those who come from a different culture. If a corporation's CEO and high-level managers who make the decisions on policies that affect an employee's family (such as how often or how long leave time is) are all from England, they often unthinkingly base their decisions on plans that coincide with the British school year, without taking into account the realities for an employee who comes from the United States, for instance. Look at Ilpö's story to see what a major effect one factor alone—schooling options—can have on a TCK's life.

Ruth Van Reken met Ilpö, a Finnish TCK who had grown up
in Taiwan, while he was finishing his medical residency program at the University of Chicago. He had completed all his
post-secondary school education in the United States, including medical school. She asked why he had chosen to come to
the United States rather than returning to school in Finland.

"Well, it sort of just happened," Ilpö replied. "My folks
taught in a seminary in Taiwan, but the other missionaries
were from America and Norway. Even though the curriculum for our little mission school was supposedly an international one, we had an American teacher, so all our classes
were in English." Ilpö went on to explain how at age twelve
he had gone to the American boarding school in Taichung
and had lived in a small dorm run by the Finnish mission.
Although he spoke Finnish in the dorm, his classes and interactions with fellow students took place in English.

It was about this time that Ilpö faced his first cultural
crisis. If he had been in Finland, after ninth grade he would
have competed with all other Finnish students in a special
test to decide who could continue their academic schooling
and who would go to a trade or vocational school. When the
time came for Ilpö to take that exam, he encountered a major problem. His education had been in English and the exam
was in Finnish. Although he spoke Finnish fluently with his
family, his written language skills in that language and his
knowledge of the curriculum content from which the tests
came were deficient. Ilpö knew he wanted to be a doctor, but
if he went back and competed with students who had been
studying in Finnish schools, the chances of his scoring high
enough to attend university were slim.

Ultimately, he felt his only option was to attend university in the United States within the educational system
he knew. But that also meant he had to stay in the U.S.
for medical training, because in Finland medical training
is combined with what would be considered undergraduate
studies in the United States.

When Ruth asked Ilpö where he expected to live after
his training, he said it would be very difficult to go back to
Finland. Not only was their system different, but he didn't
know medical vocabulary in Finnish. Even if he learned
that, fellow physicians would look down on him because he
had trained somewhere else. When asked how he felt about

that, Ilpö said, "That's what I'm coming to grips with now. I didn't realize before how nearly impossible it would be ever to return to Finland. It's a choice that slipped out of my hands. I feel like my world slipped away."

TCKs in Relationship to Surrounding Dominant Culture

Because we learn our sense of personal and cultural identity in relationship to the world around us, there is another aspect of cross-cultural living that has a significant influence on a TCK's life—the changing nature of how he or she fundamentally relates to the surrounding dominant or majority culture, be that the home or host culture.

TCKs not only experience many cultural worlds in their developmental years, but they also physically move from place to place where the dominant cultures may be quite different. Thus, their identity is constantly being redefined in contrast or comparison to whichever world they are currently in. This is one of the key things we must understand in order to recognize how some of the "new normals" created by our globalizing world impact not only TCKs but children and families everywhere.

In the early 1990s, Barb Knuckles, a non-TCK friend of Ruth's, planted a vital seed in her mind. In a discussion of TCKs, Barb said, "I think there's a simple reason they have so many problems on reentry to their passport culture. In the host country, they are often seen as different. They can always console themselves that, yes, they are different, but it's because they aren't from this place. They see themselves as members of their passport country. The problem is when they go back to their passport country and still don't fit, what is their excuse?"

That seed grew after Ruth met two TCKs who were having almost classic reentry experiences—but they were having them in their host cultures! On wondering why this was so, she realized the only common factor for both of them was that in their host cultures they physically looked like members of the dominant culture. After sharing her thoughts with Dave, they batted these ideas back and forth and wound up with the model shown in Figure 4-3.

- *Foreigner—look different, think different.* In the early days of international mobility, most TCKs related to their host culture as foreigners, and many still do today. They differ from those in the dominant culture around them in both appearance and worldview. They know, and others know, they are not from this place. The visible layer of culture accurately reflects the invisible. *What you expect is what you get.*

The PolVan Cultural Identity Model
Cultural Identity in Relationship to Surrounding Culture

Foreigner Look *different* Think *different*	Hidden Immigrant Look alike Think *different*
Adopted Look *different* Think alike	Mirror Look alike Think alike

Figure 4-3 PolVan Cultural Identity Box

(© 1996 David C. Pollock/Ruth E. Van Reken)

- *Hidden immigrant—look alike, think different.* Norma McCaig and Dave began using the term in the mid-1980s to describe the experience of TCKs returning to their passport culture. TCKs can also be hidden immigrants when they are growing up in host countries where they physically resemble most of the citizens of that country. Internally, however, these TCKs—whether in the passport culture or host culture—view life through a lens that is as different from the dominant or majority culture as any obvious foreigner. People around them, of course, presume they share similar worldviews and cultural awareness because, from outward appearances, they look as if they belong to the group. No one makes the same allowances for the TCKs' lack of cultural knowledge or miscues as they would an obvious immigrant or recognized foreigner. *What you expect is not what you get.*
- *Adopted—look different, think alike.* This category can literally relate to international adoptees and other immigrants who may not physically resemble members of the dominant culture but have lived there long enough to assimilate culturally to that place. This is, however, another common pattern of relationship for TCKs. Sometimes they appear physically different from members of the surrounding dominant host culture, but they have lived there so long and immersed themselves so deeply in this environment that their behavior and worldview are virtually the same as members of that culture. The TCKs may feel very comfortable and often more "at home" in this situation than in their passport country, and they feel wounded when others treat them as foreigners. This sense of being misperceived can also happen when ATCKs return to visit the place where they grew up. Suddenly they realize for the first

time how "foreign" others see them to be when they feel this is, indeed, the world of their heart. Again, *what you expect is not what you get.*
- *Mirror—look alike, think alike.* This is the traditional pattern of those raised in a monocultural situation. While many TCKs feel there is nowhere in the world they fit as "mirrors," the truth is some TCKs grow up where they physically resemble the members of the dominant culture in the host culture. At times, they have lived there so long that they have adopted the deeper levels of that culture as well. No one would realize they aren't from this place unless they show their passports. TCKs who return to their home culture after spending only a year or two away or who were away only at a very young age may also fit in this category. Although they have lived abroad, their deeper levels of culture have remained rooted solidly in the home culture and they identify with it completely. And one other slight irony: perhaps in an international school where there is no standard of "look alike," TCKs find that they are mirrors to one another in the deeper places of culture where they reflect back to one another a shared understanding of what it is to grow up globally. At any rate, this is a comfortable box to be in. *What you expect is what you get.*

Non-TCK children and adults also may fall into one or another of these boxes at any given time, but the difference for TCKs is that throughout childhood they are constantly changing boxes depending on where they happen to be. They may be obvious foreigners one day and hidden immigrants the next. Many TCKs do not make a simple move from one culture to another; instead, they are in a repetitive cycle of traveling back and forth between home and host cultures throughout childhood. But why does that matter? Because as they move in and out of various cultures, TCKs not only have to learn new cultural rules, but more fundamentally, they must understand who they *are* in relationship to the surrounding culture. Each move is also a question of identity: *How do I fit in? Where do I belong?* As they see themselves constantly changing in relationship to others, it can be difficult to develop a true sense of a core identity.

There is one other interesting question to raise here. In appendix B, Japanese researcher and ATCK herself, Momo Kano Podolsky, makes some interesting observations comparing how the Japanese have studied children who have been raised globally and how those in the Western world have done the same. In Japan, this experience has been a well-known phenomenon almost from the earliest days when Japanese businesspeople began taking their families overseas. This traditionally monocultural society didn't know what to do with these children when they returned from abroad because they no longer fit easily in the prescribed boxes. The government itself became involved as they had to make changes in the school structures so these returnees could better fit back into Japanese society.

During one of their first conversations, Momo asked Ruth how the increasing number of TCKs had impacted the culture of the United States. Frankly, Ruth had never thought about that before and she told Momo she couldn't imagine this had ever been a topic high on any governmental agenda in the U.S. Momo then said, "I noticed one thing. In Japan we studied this topic to see what it had done to our culture. In the United States, you studied it to see what it had done to the individual." While they both laughed in realizing how even an approach to studying the impact of the global experiences of children had been shaped by their basic collectivistic versus individualistic worldviews, it raises a question to ponder. In her essay, Momo relates how originally *kikoku-shijo,* returned Japanese TCKs, were seen as a threat to the culture. Now they are valued. It would be interesting to see how the fact that their experience is far more visible and valued by the surrounding dominant culture plays out in terms of the way they do or don't relate to these patterns of cultural identity we discussed here.

At any rate, there are three common reactions we see from TCKs as they try to sort out their identity issues, particularly when they are in the hidden immigrant or adopted boxes:

- *Chameleons—those who try to find a "same as" identity.* They hide their time lived in other places and try to conform externally through clothes, language, or attitudes to whatever environment they are in
- *Screamers—those who try to find a "different from" identity.* They will let other people around them know that they are not like them and don't plan to be.
- *Wallflowers—those who try to find a "nonidentity."* Rather than risk being exposed as someone who doesn't know the local cultural rules, they prefer to sit on the sidelines and watch, at least for an extended period, rather than to engage in the activities at hand.

In later chapters we will give examples of each of these types of responses. In the end, however, TCKs and their parents don't always share a common sense of national identity or a similar sense of "home." This can be distressing for some parents. In addition, throughout life TCKs and ATCKs may encounter other unexpected or unrecognized cultural misunderstandings with teachers, peers at school or in the workplace, and their spouses or significant others. Why? Because, once more, what they appear to be outside, or by passport, isn't who they are in the invisible places within. We see in this experience what Weaver warned us would happen—more confusion when what we expect of each other is not what we get.

While cultural identity is far more complex than the simple model in Figure 4-3 depicts, we have seen in the many years since our initial conversation that formed this model what a great starting point this concept is for many TCKs, ATCKs, and countless others of many backgrounds to understand their stories.

Lessons from the TCK "Petri Dish"

If, indeed, Dr. Ted Ward declared that TCKs were the prototype citizen of the future back in 1984, what are the lessons learned from their experience in this cross-cultural piece that we can apply to others in today's world, beginning with other types of CCKs? The following are some of the kinds of stories we hear.

International adoptee Crystal Chappell writes in "American, Korean, or Both? Politics of Identity Reach Personal Levels":

> Because of their appearance, Korean American adoptees
> face assumptions that, as Asian Americans, they are for-
> eigners. "They always expect a story explaining why you're
> here, why you're so acculturated," Chappell says. "I've been
> complimented on how well I speak English! Duh! That's the
> final clincher."[16]

Crystal, and many others, are literally in the adopted box of our cultural identity grid. She may look quite different from her adoptive family, but she has grown up in that family's cultural world. Those from the dominant culture of her adopted land see her and presume "difference" at the deeper layers of culture when, in reality, she is far more like them than different from them.

But it can get even more complicated for some children in today's world.

> Kenny's parents moved to the United States from China
> when he was four years old. They worked hard to give him
> the best education possible, enrolling him in a rigorous
> private school in their area. As a high school senior, Kenny
> had to do primary research for one of his classes. He won-
> dered what topic to pursue. "Suddenly," he said, "it occurred
> to me for the first time that I probably live a very different
> lifestyle than most of my friends. At school they see me as
> an American but don't realize that every day when I leave,
> I become Chinese. Neither my grandmother, who lives with
> us, nor my mother speak English. Inside the walls of my
> home is an all-Chinese world." He then added, "I'm sure
> they don't realize that every time I go to China to visit our
> family, I become Chinese. The minute I get off the airplane,
> I change my clothes, my language, and my mannerisms
> completely, and they don't know I'm from America. I do the
> reverse when I come back to the States."

Kenny, like the children of many immigrants, attends school in the domi-nant culture but goes home each evening to an entirely different culture. Minori-ties or biracial/bicultural kids can have similar experiences. They may grow up in the same city but daily go back and forth between various cultural worlds as Kenny did. Is it possible ethnic communities of immigrants were, and are, in some ways, interstitial cultures similar to that of the "third culture"? Think of what post-integration school busing in the U.S. has done for years in terms of moving children across cultural borders on a daily basis. In the early days of busing, Paulette Bethel, an African American of Creole descent, was bused to a former all-white school in New Orleans. She says of that experience, "Each morning I left a black world to enter a completely different white culture. Each evening when I returned home, my parents expected me to be black again."

For many across the world, political realities also cause social upheavals. When the Berlin Wall fell, the cultural milieu of those who had never ventured beyond the confines of life within those walls changed remarkably. Suddenly previously unseen vistas opened to them. New architecture, new thinking patterns, new governmental structures altered their world completely without them ever moving to a new town or country. Practically overnight, parents shaped in one cultural world found themselves raising children in an entirely different reality, with no guidance from their own experience on how to accomplish such a task. Consequently, these children had no role models in the older generation to watch and learn how life was to be. Tea is one of these children:

> "I was born in Belgrade, the former Yugoslavia, and my mom's side of the family is from Croatia. The war started, and then I had to ask if I am Serbian or Croatian, because there was no more Yugoslavia. We never experienced the war, thankfully, just the economic effects—terrible inflation, my mom receiving her salary in flour and sugar bags instead of money."
>
> When Tea was 10, her family moved to Taiwan. After her parents divorced, Tea, her brother, Branko, and their mother moved to Switzerland to live with her new stepfather. Of that time she says, "My first five years in Switzerland were bad because I couldn't speak German and because I didn't like my new high school."
>
> Although she is enjoying her college days better, when asked where she belongs, Tea says, "Nowhere, really. I used to belong in Belgrade (Serbia) and in Taiwan, but I don't anymore. And I don't really fit in here in Switzerland even though I've lived here for seven years. Right now I have the most sense of belonging here at the university."

Our drawers and hearts are filled with these stories. None of the examples cited here lived their cross-cultural experience in the traditional TCK mode—a parent with a career going overseas to one country, staying for awhile, and then repatriating. Yet, over and over, they tell us they relate to much of the TCK characteristics described in Part II of this book. So what is the common thread of connection for all these stories?

One main theme many CCKs of all backgrounds seem to share with traditional TCKs is trying to develop a sense of personal and cultural identity when the world around them mirrors back changing definitions of who they are. Like

TCKs, their lives are also filled with multiple cultural worlds, even though an ethnic community may be substituted for a host culture and so on. Think of the various cultural identity boxes Kenny fits. At school, where the majority culture is white, past generations might have considered him to be a foreigner. In today's world, he is probably assumed to be "one of the gang." Others looking at him and at our grid might assume he is in the adopted box. He doesn't look like the majority population, but because he speaks with the same accent, likes the same entertainment, and wears similar clothes, most fellow students and teachers presume his life parallels theirs in the deeper levels of culture too. Yet none of them go home to a Chinese world. And what cultural identity box is Kenny in at home? A mirror? His grandmother speaks no English so how can she mirror his experience? A hidden immigrant—assumed to be the same but inwardly different? What about when he goes to China? Perhaps he is simply a true bicultural person? Maybe our grid itself needs to grow. The fact is for countless children, sorting out their basic sense of cultural identity is becoming very complicated. When asked if he felt his ultimate identity was Chinese or American, Kenny himself had to think for a moment and said, "I guess I'd have to say I feel more American than Chinese."

What about Tea? She, too, could be in any cultural identity box at any time, depending on her surroundings and circumstances. Many CCKs we know seem to live perpetually in the hidden immigrant or adopted categories. Because, like traditional TCKs, their lives also have been shaped by many cultural worlds, their visible and invisible layers often do not match.

A few years ago, Ruth and cross-cultural consultant Paulette Bethel began to use the term *hidden diversity* to describe and expand the basic concept contained in the idea of the hidden immigrant and adopted boxes—the idea that *what you see is not what you get*. They define hidden diversity as "a diversity of experience that shapes a person's life and worldview but is not readily apparent on the outside, unlike the usual diversity markers such as race, ethnicity, nationality, and so on."[17]

Our philosopher friend Barb Knuckles wonders if this hidden diversity so many CCKs experience creates another shared experience:

> Maybe the great commonality is that the children often are different than their parents' generation in cultural and identity ways, so they can't really "go home" to their parents world... is that the commonality with TCKs, too? That is true for people who come from noncollege families and communities, and then go off to college and end up jumping a couple social/educational levels. They never can really go home the same way again... I wonder whether it is an in-betweenness. [These] children do grow up in a different world than their parents, but in the same world as their

own generation. Those whose family's culture and expectations shape them enough to not be at-home with peers and... enough to not be at-home with parents, are at-home with others who are equally home-less... Maybe that is the commonality, an identity that is not unified internally.[18]

Is this so? We invite further discussion, but we believe there is a bottom line: Any time children grow up among many cultural environments where they are true participants rather than just looking at the "other" from a distance, the deeper layers of their cultural selves and identities are being formed in nontraditional ways. These are important factors to consider as our world continues to increase the degree of cultural mixing in years to come.

As we said earlier, there are two major overarching realities of a TCK's life. This cross-cultural lifestyle is one. Now we look at the second one—mobility.

CHAPTER 5

Why High Mobility Matters

I had adored the nomadic life. I had loved gallivanting from
Japan to Taiwan to America to Holland and onward. In
many ways, I had adapted well. I had learned to love new
smells and vistas and the mysteries inherent to new cultures.... I had conquered the language of internationalists,
both the polite exchange of conversation in formal settings and the easy intimacy of globetrotters. I was used to
country-hopping. To move every couple of years was in my
blood. In spite of the fact that foreign service life is one long
continuous meal of loss—loss of friends and beloved places—
I loved it. The warp of my life was the fact of moving on.[1]

—Sara Mansfield Tabor

SARA HAS WRITTEN ABOUT ONE OF THE GREAT BENEFITS
countless TCKs mention when they reflect on their lives: a wealth of experience where traversing time zones and date lines while skipping from
one airport to another is part of normal life. The amazing places they have seen
and cultures they have witnessed are almost beyond belief for those who have not
lived this way. There is no question that this is a great gift.

Yet, as we have looked at the cross-cultural nature of the TCK experience in
some detail, we have seen how the very richness of the first overlay—growing up
in a culturally diverse world—can still result in some real challenges along the
way. What about the second main overlay of the TCK experience—high mobility? Are there equally significant paradoxes for TCKs that rise from this part of
their lives as well?

We believe so. Did you notice the phrase that Sara almost off-handedly tucks into her account of the joys of mobility? She acknowledges that this wonderful, highly mobile lifestyle is also "one long continuous meal of loss." Why?

As we will soon see in our discussion of the Third Culture Kid Profile in Part II of this book, the benefits from both the cross-cultural and highly mobile nature of life for TCKs are great. But for TCKs to use them well and with joy, we must understand the underlying dynamics and fundamental challenges of growing up with high mobility as well as those of a cross-cultural upbringing. Again, remember a challenge isn't necessarily a liability. It can spur us on to greater things. But it *is* something we have to figure out how to work with, and work through, to succeed in reaching our goal. So let's take a look at why high mobility is such a significant factor for many TCKs.

When someone asks us what, despite the many benefits, we see as the *main* challenges TCKs and ATCKs face, we answer, "Finding a sense of personal and cultural identity and dealing with *unresolved grief.*" While the two distinct forces of cross-cultural living and high mobility intertwine to create the overall picture of the TCK Profile, the reality is that the matters related to identity are primarily embedded in the cross-cultural overlay, and the issue of unresolved grief is connected most closely with the mobile nature of this experience. To understand why, we'll first define what we mean by high mobility and see what normally happens during any cycle of mobility. Then we'll consider what extra factors may intensify "normal mobility" for TCKs and how, when not recognized, they can lead to special challenges.

Defining High Mobility

People often ask how we can say that high mobility is one of the two main characteristics of life for most TCKs when it's obvious mobility patterns vary so widely among them. Some move to a different country every two or three years with parents who are in the military or diplomatic corps. We can see that their lives are highly mobile. Others stay in one country from birth to university, so mobility wouldn't appear to be an issue for them. The advent of short-term assignments for the employee often means the family stays home. How can this be a life impacted by high mobility?

All TCKs, however, deal with mobility issues at one level or another. Children of parents in business like Erika or those with parents in the foreign service usually take a month of home leave each summer. Missionary children may only return to their passport country every two to four years, but they usually stay away from the host country for a longer period of time than other TCKs might, sometimes up to a year. Each leave means saying good-bye to friends in the host country, hello to relatives and friends at home, good-bye to those people a short time later, and hello again to the host country friends—if those friends are still there. When a parent takes a short-term assignment overseas, there are frequent and repeated cycles of mobility within the home itself as this parent travels while the remainder of the family stays in one place. Military families have known this type of mobility for generations. In today's world, more and more families living overseas have known the unplanned mobility of having to evacuate due to violence in the host country. TCKs who attend boarding school have other major patterns of mobility: Whether they go home once or twice a year or spend three months at school followed by one month at home, each coming and going involves more greetings and farewells—and more adjustments. Paul Seaman describes this pattern of mobility well.

> Like nomads, we moved with the seasons. Four times a year we packed up and moved to, or back to, another temporary home. As with the seasons, each move offered something to look forward to while something had to be given up.... We learned early that "home" was an ambiguous concept, and wherever we lived, some essential part of our lives was always someplace else. So we were always of two minds. We learned to be happy and sad at the same time. We learned to be independent and [accept] that things were out of our control.... We had the security and the consolation that whenever we left one place we were returning to another, already familiar one.[2]

Besides a TCK's personal mobility, every third culture community is filled with people who continually come and go. Short-term volunteers arrive to assist in a project for several weeks and then they are gone. A favorite teacher accepts another position a continent away. Best friends leave because their parents transfer to a new post. Older siblings depart for boarding school or university at home. The totality of all these comings and goings—of others as well as the TCKs themselves—is what we mean when we use the term *high mobility* throughout this book.

Why Mobility Affects Us

Any time there is mobility—ours or someone else's—everyone involved goes through some type of transition experience as well. In actuality, life for everyone, TCK or not, is a series of transitions: a "passage from one state, stage, subject, or place to another."[3] Each transition changes something in our lives. Some transitions are normal and progressive—we expect them, as in the transition from infancy to childhood or from middle age to old age. Sometimes these life transitions include physical moves from one place to another, such as when a young person goes off to university in another state. In most cases, we know these transitions are coming and have time to prepare for them.

Other transitions, however, are sudden and disruptive—such as the unexpected loss of a job, a serious injury, or the untimely death of a loved one. Life after these transitions is drastically different from what it was before. The abruptness of the change disorients us and we wonder, "What am I ever going to do?"

The transition we choose to focus on here, however, is to see what happens when we physically move from one place to another. Obviously, that is particularly relevant to TCKs. We view it from the lens of those making the move, but we realize those left behind are also affected—and they don't even have the excitement of a new adventure looming ahead. TCKs, of course, know what it is to be on all sides of the transition experience.

First we'll describe the common stages of transition and see how the TCK lifestyle may add complexity to that normal process. Then we will look at how all of this can lead to the unresolved grief we mentioned, and after that we will consider what lessons might apply to CCKs as well. Later chapters will include strategies for dealing successfully with transitions.

The Transition Experience

Coauthor David Pollock developed his classic model of the normal transition cycle in the early 1980s and noted the following five predictable stages:

1. *Involvement*
2. *Leaving*
3. *Transition*
4. *Entering*
5. *Reinvolvement*

Let's take a look at the normal ways we process transitions.

INVOLVEMENT STAGE

Our Response
We barely recognize this first stage of transition because life seems too normal to be a "stage." We feel settled and comfortable, knowing where we belong and how we fit in. Under ideal circumstances, we recognize we are an *intimate* part of our community and are careful to follow its customs and abide by its traditions so that we can maintain our position as a valued member. We feel a responsibility to be involved in the issues that concern and interest our community, and we're focused on the present and our immediate relationships rather than thinking primarily about the past or worrying about the future.

Community's Response

Involvement is a comfortable stage for those around us as well. People hear our name and instantly picture our face and form. They know our reputation, history, talents, tastes, interests, and where we fit in the political and social network.

LEAVING STAGE

Our Response

One day, life begins to change. We learn we will be leaving, and deep inside we begin to prepare. At first we may not realize what's going on—especially if our departure date is more than six months away. With shorter warning, however, the mostly unconscious leaving process starts immediately. We begin loosening emotional ties, backing away from the relationships and responsibilities we have had. We call friends less frequently. We don't start new projects at work. During the last year before graduation from high school or university, this leaning away is called "senioritis."

While it may be normal—and perhaps necessary—to begin detaching at some level during this stage, it is often confusing as well to both our friends and ourselves. This detachment can produce anger and frustration in relationships that have been close or in the way we handle our job responsibilities.

> During one transition seminar, Dave Pollock talked about this loosening of ties as part of the leaving stage. Soon he noticed a general buzz in the room. One gentleman sat off to the side, blushing rather profusely as others began to laugh. When Dave stopped to ask what was happening, the blushing gentleman said, "Well, I guess I better confess. I'm the manager here, and just yesterday those working under me asked to meet with me. They complained about my recent job performance and told me I don't seem to care; I take far too much time off; I'm unavailable when they need me, and so on. As you've been talking, I just realized what's been happening. Last month, my CEO told me I would be transferred to a new assignment, so mentally I've already checked out."
>
> "That's pretty normal," Dave said rather sympathetically.
>
> "I know," he replied. "The only problem is I'm not due to leave for two more years. Maybe I'd better check back in again!"

We may not upset an entire office staff as this man did, but unless we consciously choose to maintain and enjoy relationships and roles as long as possible, at some point all of us will back away in one form or another. It's part of the state of denial that comes during the leaving stage as we unconsciously try to make the leaving as painless as we can. Other forms of self-protective denials surface as well.

Denial of feelings of sadness or grief. Instead of acknowledging sadness, we begin to think, "I don't really like these people very much anyway. Susie takes way too much of my time with all her problems. I'll be glad when I'm out of here and she can't call me every day." We can also deny our sadness at leaving by focusing only on what is anticipated. We talk about the wonderful things to do, eat, and see in the next location and seemingly make a mental leap over the process of getting there.

> One Canadian ATCK began to weep at this point in a transition seminar. Later he said, "Dave, I feel terrible. I grew up in a remote tribe in Papua New Guinea. When I left to return home for university, I could only think about how much I'd enjoy having Big Macs, TV, and electricity. I looked forward to new friends. When my PNG friends came to say good-bye, they started to cry, but I just walked away. Now all I can think about is them standing there as my little plane took off. They thought I didn't care. I want to go back and hug them one last time. What should I do?"

Of course, there was nothing wrong with this TCK developing a positive view of the coming move, but when he didn't acknowledge the losses involved in the leaving, he had no way to deal with them. Denying our feelings may get us through an otherwise painful moment, but the grief doesn't go away, and we simply hold on to it into the next stage of transition.

Denial of feelings of rejection. As friends plan for future events (e.g., next year's school play or the annual neighborhood barbecue night), we suddenly realize they are talking around us. No one asks what we would like to do or what we think about the plans. We have become invisible. Of course, we understand. Why should they include us? We'll be gone. In spite of what we know, however, we can still feel rejection and resentment. If we deny those feelings and push them aside as ridiculous and immature behavior (obviously we *shouldn't* feel like this), then that underlying sense of rejection and resentment easily produces a seething anger, which results in almost unbelievable conflicts—especially with those who have been close friends and colleagues. Failing to acknowledge that we are beginning to feel like outsiders (and that it hurts) only increases the chances that we will act inappropriately during this stage.

Denial of "unfinished business." The closer we come to separation, the less likely we are to reconcile conflicts with others. We talk ourselves out of mending the relationship, unrealistically hoping that time and distance will heal it—or at least produce amnesia. Once more, the unfortunate reality is that we arrive at our next destination with this unfinished business clinging to us and influencing new relationships. Bitterness in one area of our lives almost always seeps out in another, and we sow the seeds of bitterness in others as well.

Denial of expectations. To prevent disappointment or fear, we may deny anything we secretly hope for. "It doesn't matter what kind of house I get; I can live anywhere." We deny we would like people to give us a nice farewell. We presume that if we have no expectations, we can't be disappointed. In reality, however, we all have expectations for every event in our lives. When they are too high, we're disappointed. When they're too low, we create fear, anxiety, or dread for ourselves.

Community's Response

We may not consciously realize it, but as we're loosening our ties to the community, it's loosening its ties to us. Not only do people forget to ask our opinion about future events, they begin giving our jobs to others. TCKs discover that school administrators have already chosen their replacements as soccer team captain or editor of the coming yearbook. The same types of denials we use are being used by them. Suddenly our flaws as friends or coworkers seem glaringly obvious and they secretly wonder why they've maintained this relationship for so long in the first place.

One thing, however, helps save the day for everyone. This is the time when communities also give us special attention. There are ceremonies of recognition—a watch presented for years of faithful service or a plaque given to say thanks for being part of a team. Graduation ceremonies remind us this school will never be the same without our shining presence. This special attention and recognition help us forget for a moment that even though we are promising never to forget each other, already there is a distance developing between us and those we will soon leave behind.

TRANSITION STAGE

At the heart of the transition process is the transition stage itself. It begins the moment we leave one place and ends when we not only arrive at our destination but make the decision, consciously or unconsciously, to settle in and become part of it. It's a stage marked by one word—*chaos!* Schedules change, new people have new expectations, living involves new responsibilities, but we haven't yet learned how everything is supposed to work. Norma McCaig, founder of Global Nomads, always said the transition stage is a time when families moving overseas become at least temporarily dysfunctional. This dysfunctionality doesn't last (we hope), but it can be painfully discomfiting at the time.

Our Response

First, we and all family members making the move with us lose our normal moorings and support systems at this point. Suddenly we aren't relinquishing roles and relationships—they're gone! We've lost the comfort they gave but haven't formed new ones yet. We're not sure where we fit in or what we're expected to do.

Second, this sense of chaos makes us more self-centered than normal. We worry about our health, finances, relationships, and personal safety to a far greater degree than usual. Problems that aren't generally a big deal are exaggerated.

Headaches become brain tumors and sneezes become pneumonia. The loss of a favorite pen causes despair. We know we'll never find it again because the usual places we would look for it are gone.

Third, parents who are focusing on their own survival often forget to take time to read their children stories, stop to pick them up, or sit on the floor with them for a few minutes as they did in the past. Children wonder what's happening. The insecurity of each family member contributes to the chaos for everyone. Family conflicts seem to occur for the smallest reason and over issues that never mattered before.

The enormous change between how the old and new communities take care of the everyday aspects of life—banking, buying food, cooking—can create intense stress. To make matters worse, we may be scolded for doing something in the new place that was routine in the old one.

> TCK Hanna grew up in an area of chronic drought. The local adage for flushing the toilet was "If it's brown, flush it down. If it's yellow, let it mellow." Breaking that rule meant serious censure from her parents or anyone else around.
>
> Unfortunately, Hanna's grandma in the United States had never heard this wonderful rule. At age thirteen, Hanna visited her grandma. Imagine Hanna's chagrin and embarrassment when grandma pulled her aside and scolded her for not flushing the toilet.

A severe loss of self-esteem may set in during this transition stage. Even if we physically look like adults, emotionally we feel like children again. Not only are we getting scolded for things about which we "should have known better," but, particularly in cross-cultural moves, it seems we have to learn life over practically from scratch. As teenagers and adults, probably nothing strikes at our sense of self-esteem with greater force than learning language and culture, for these are the tasks of children. Suddenly, no matter how many decibels we raise our voices, people around don't understand what we're trying to say. We discover gestures we have used all our lives—like pointing someone out in a crowd using our index finger—have completely opposite meanings now. (In some cultures, it's a curse.) Our cultural and linguistic mistakes not only embarrass us but also make us feel anxious and ashamed of being so stupid. Often anger erupts over little things. We feel upset with ourselves for our responses, and we may make bargains with those in the family for how we plan to do better, but all of that can turn to depressive moods as the enormity of the change hits us.

Community's Response

Initially the community may welcome us warmly—even overwhelmingly. But in every culture the newcomer is still exactly that—and newcomers by definition don't yet fit in. Our basic position in the new community is one of *statuslessness*.

We carry knowledge from past experiences—often including special knowledge of people, places, and processes—but none of that knowledge has use in this new place. No one knows about our history, abilities, talents, normal responses, accomplishments, or areas of expertise. Sometimes it seems they don't care. For TCKs entering a new school, it can be particularly devastating when their teacher makes an inaccurate comment about a country they've lived in and won't listen when the TCKs try to give their perspective. Soon we question whether our achievements in the previous setting were as significant as we thought.

People may now see us as boring or arrogant because we talk about things, places, and people they have never heard mentioned before. We feel the same way toward them because they talk about local people and events about which *we* know nothing.

Even with an initial warm welcome, we may discover it's not as easy as we thought it would be to make close friends. Circles of relationships among our new acquaintances are already well defined and most people aren't looking to fill a vacant spot in such a circle. It's easy to become resentful and begin to withdraw. *Fine,* we say inside, *if they don't need me, I don't need them.*

Sadly, this type of withdrawal results in more feelings of isolation and alienation, for it continues to cut us off from any hope of making new friends. This increasing sense of loneliness can lead to more anger—which makes us want to withdraw even more.

The transition stage itself is a tough time because we often feel keenly disappointed. The difference between what we expected and what we're experiencing can trigger a sense of panic. All connection and continuity with the past seem gone, and the present isn't what we had hoped it would be. How can we relate the different parts of our lives into a cohesive whole? Is the orderliness of the past gone forever? We look longingly to the future—hoping that somehow, sometime, life will return to normal.

ENTERING STAGE

> Standing on the edge of the Quad at Houghton College, TCK Ramona quietly said to no one in particular, "I think I'll go to my dorm and unpack my suitcase... and my mind."
>
> Ramona had graduated from an international school more than a year before. For fifteen months she'd been traveling and visiting relatives while working at short-term jobs. Without her own place to nest, Ramona could never finish the transition stage. Finally, with her arrival at school and the decision to settle in, she began the entering stage of the overall transition process.

Our Response

During this stage, life is no longer totally chaotic. We begin to accept that this is where we are and have made the decision that it is time to become part of this new community—we just have to figure out how to do it. Although we very much want to move toward people in this new place, we still feel rather vulnerable and a bit tentative. What if we make a serious social faux pas? Will others accept us? Will they take advantage of us? We often deal with these fears through an exaggeration of our normal personality traits as we begin to interact with others in our new location. People who are usually shy, introverted, or quiet may become more so. Normally gregarious or outgoing individuals may become loud, overbearing, and aggressive. Then, of course, we're mad at ourselves for acting so "dumb" and worry even more that people won't like us.

This stage is also when we feel a lot of ambivalence. We start to learn the new job or the rules at school, feel successful on a given day, and think, "I'm glad I'm here. This is going to be all right." Next day, someone asks us a question we can't answer and we wish we were back where we knew at least most of the answers. Our emotions can fluctuate widely between the excitement of the new discoveries we're making and the homesickness that weighs us down. When we say *boot* and *bonnet* instead of *trunk* and *hood* (or vice versa), everyone laughs and tells us we're so funny. We laugh with them, but inside there is that feeling that nobody thought this was strange in our last place. There we were "normal," not different. On the other hand, tomorrow we catch ourselves just before we say the wrong word and use the local term instead. When it passes without a flicker from those around us (in spite of how strange it sounds to our ears!), we realize we are actually beginning to learn how life works here.

Entering is the stage, more than any other, when we need a good mentor, someone who can show us how to function effectively in this new world (mentoring is discussed later in this book). Eventually, we go to the grocery store and actually recognize someone from our new community and can call that person by name. We drive to the other side of town, down quiet unmarked streets, without anyone telling us where to turn—and we find the house we are looking for! Someone calls with a procedural question at work and this time we *do* know the answer. Hope begins to grow that we will, in fact, one day have a sense of belonging to this community.

Community's Response

Of course, we must not forget that this entry stage is a bit uncomfortable for members of our new community as well, although they may have been eagerly anticipating our arrival. Before we came, everyone's roles were clear. Relationships—whether positive or negative—were established. Life functioned without explanation. We show up, and life changes for them too. Now *everything* seems to need an explanation. They also have to adjust their social order at least slightly to help us find our way in. In the end, however, people in the community begin to remember our names, include us in the events going on, realize we are here to stay rather than simply visit, and start to make room for us in their world.

REINVOLVEMENT STAGE

Our Response

And then the day finally comes. The light at the end of the proverbial tunnel is that in any transition, cross-cultural or not, a final, recognized stage of reinvolvement is possible. Although there have been moments of wondering if it will ever happen, given enough time and a genuine willingness to adapt, we will once again become part of the permanent community. We accept our new place, role, and community. We may not be native to that community, but we can ultimately belong. We have a sense of intimacy, a feeling that our presence matters to this group. We feel secure. Time again feels present and permanent as we focus on the here and now rather than hoping for the future or constantly reminiscing about the past.

Community Response

Others in the community again see us as part of the group. Once more, people hear our name and instantly picture our face and form. They know our reputation, history, talents, tastes, interests, and where we fit in the political and social network. They let us in on the news of the day, ask our opinion, and count on us for community events. Yes, it's a great place to be!

This is the normal process of transition. Knowing about the various stages doesn't keep them from happening, but it does help us to not be surprised by what happens at each stage, to recognize we are normal, and to be in a position to make the choices that allow us to gain from the new experiences we encounter while dealing productively with the inevitable losses of any transition experience.

Why the TCK Experience Increases Intensity of Normal Transition

Just as TCKs learn culture in the same ways others do, they are also as capable as anyone else of navigating their way through these stages of transition and being enriched by them. Some seem to almost soar through these cycles, no matter how frequently they occur. Other TCKs and ATCKs appear to lose their bearings in the midst of so much mobility. So what makes this such a varying experience for TCKs? We believe there are several factors that intensify the various normal dynamics of the transition experience when they occur in the context of the third culture lifestyle.

Psychologist Frances White says, "Because of the nature of their work, [third culture families] are particularly vulnerable to separations. They experience not only the . . . usual share of situational separations faced by the world at large but also a number of partings idiosyncratic to their profession."[4] In other words, because of the very nature of international living, TCKs undergo chronic cycles of mobility far more often than the population at large. That means they also go through the transition cycle with greater frequency. Some globally nomadic families make international moves every two years or less, and their TCKs may chronically move from entry to leaving stages without knowing the physical or emotional comfort and stability of involvement, let alone reinvolvement.

The reality is that with every transition, there is loss even when there is ultimate gain. No matter how much we anticipate the future as good, we almost always leave something of value behind as well. In loss, there is grief. An important thing to remember is that *grief during transition is not a negation of the past.* It is actually an affirmation of where we have been, geographically or relationally, because we do not grieve for things or people we don't love. The more we have loved, the deeper the sense of loss. Grief doesn't mean that we shouldn't move ahead to the new or that the next stage won't be great. It simply means that leaving things we have enjoyed—the people and places we have loved, the stages of life that have been good—is hard.

Any grief, both big and small, begins a well-defined process described by the late Dr. Elisabeth Kübler-Ross. She explained how we express grief through denial, anger, bargaining, depression, and acceptance.[5] In a way, it's a transition process within the overall transition experience. The intensity of this process is, of course, related to the intensity of the loss. What it also means for TCKs and their families is that there are multiple and repetitive cycles of loss and grief.

Notice that we don't always go through these stages in a linear fashion. Pam Davis, a counselor who works extensively with third culture families, developed the model shown in Figure 5-1 to demonstrate the often circular patterns of the grief cycle. The grieving process doesn't follow a clean path from one stage to the next. That's one reason transition can become quite complicated for families. Not only is everyone in the family going through the overall transition process at different rates, but each person may also be at a different stage of this grief cycle within that larger journey on any given day. One day it seems everyone is finally "well-adjusted," while the next day anger erupts at the slightest provocation. This uneven process can leave us wondering if we will ever make it through or what is wrong with us or those around us.

Second, TCKs not only go through the transition process more often than most people, but usually their moves mean changing cultures as well as places. This increases the degree of impact from that experience as the issues related to what is commonly referred to as *culture shock* or *culture stress* are piled on top of the normal stress of any transition.

When we consider these two factors alone, it's not hard to see why repeated cycles of mobility can lead to repetitive losses and the normal, ensuing grief those losses generate. It's not hard to imagine that changing cultures and cultural rules can make it more difficult or take longer to go through the transition phase to the true entry and reinvolvement stages. But why is *unresolved grief* such a major challenge for so many TCKS and ATCKs we have met?

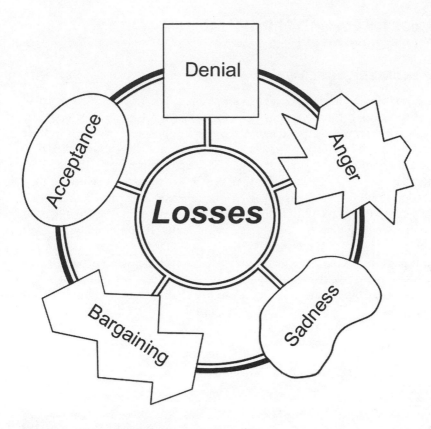

Figure 5-1 The Grief Wheel

(© 2003 Pamela Davis. Used by permission.)

Ironically, while there is no single reason unresolved grief is a major—and often unrecognized—factor for countless TCKs and ATCKs, many of them experience this grief *because* of the very richness of their lives. As we said earlier, we only grieve when we lose people or things we love or that matter greatly to us, and most TCKs have a great deal they love about their experience of growing up among worlds. They have not only seen so many places, but often they have made countless friends in each of these places who come from a wide variety of backgrounds and are living the life common to them all. For all the cultural complexity many have experienced, this very way of being part of the "many" is a fact they love.

Reasons for Unresolved Grief

FEAR OF DENYING THE GOOD

It seems that some TCKs believe that acknowledging any pain in their past will negate the many joys they have known. To admit how sad it was to leave Grandma in the home country feels like a denial of how glad they were to return to their friends in the host country. To say it was hard to leave the village where they grew up might mean they don't appreciate all the effort relatives in the passport country have gone to in preparing for their return. Learning to live with the great mystery of paradox—that life is not always an either/or scenario—is an imperative lesson for TCKs and all in their families and communities. Until any of us learns that seemingly opposite realities can be mutually embraced, we are left with no choice but to deny *either* the joy or the pain. If we deny the joy, we are left with the pain only—and that's not a good place to be. If we deny the pain, it may seem for a while it is only joy, but, in time, refusing to deal with the pain of loss will come out in other ways. It's not easy to live in this paradox while it is happening, but it is vitally important for TCKs and those with whom they are close to remember that mourning a loss doesn't mean the mourner isn't recognizing the good in the present and future.

HIDDEN LOSSES

Everyone's life is filled with the tangible and intangible. What is it that makes a house a home? Surely it is more than the furniture or the color of the rug. Yet the tangibles are part of the intangible. The old fading recliner reminds us of Grandma and when we sat on her lap listening to her read us stories. We see the chair and feel a twinge of nostalgia for days that are no more, but we are comforted by the smells of her cooking and the sound of her bright laughter. In that moment, the tangible and intangible mix and we know we are home.

Though third culture kids have a wealth of tangible and intangible realities that give their lives meaning, many of the worlds they have known are far away. Therefore, what they loved and lost in each transition remains invisible to others and often unnamed by themselves. Such losses create a special challenge. Hidden or unnamed losses most often are unrecognized, and therefore the TCK's grief for them is also unrecognized—and unresolved. It's hard to mourn appropriately without defining the loss.

These hidden losses also are recurring ones. The exact loss may not repeat itself, but the same *types* of loss happen again and again, and the unresolved grief accumulates. These hidden losses vary from large to small.

Loss of their world. With one plane ride the whole world as TCKs have known it can die. Every important place they've been, every tree climbed, pet owned, and virtually every close friend they've made are gone with the closing of the airplane door. The sights and smells of the market, waves of people walking, darting between honking cars as they cross the streets, store signs written in the local language—everything that feels so familiar and "home" are also gone. TCKs don't lose one thing at a time; they lose everything at once. And there's no funeral. In fact, there's no time or space to grieve, because tomorrow they'll be sightseeing in Bangkok as well as four other exciting places before arriving at Grandma's house to see relatives who are eagerly awaiting their return. Or, if they're sad to leave friends and family in their passport country, they'll soon be caught up in the busyness of adjusting to a new land and finding new friends. How can they be sad? Remember, as they move from one world to another, this type of loss occurs over and over.

Loss of status. With that plane ride also comes a loss of status. Whether in their passport or host country, many TCKs have settled in enough to establish a place of significance for themselves. They know where they belong in the current scene and are recognized for who they are and what they can contribute. Then suddenly not only their world but also their place in it is gone. As they travel back and forth between home and host country, this loss is repeated.

Loss of lifestyle. Whether it's biking down rutty paths to the open-air market, taking a ferry to school, buying favorite goodies at the commissary or PX, or having dependable access to electricity and water—all familiar habits can change overnight. Suddenly, traffic is too heavy for bike riding and stuffy buses carry everyone to school. Local stores don't have the items you want, while your electricity and water can go off for three days at a time. All the comfortable patterns of daily living are gone, and with it the sense of security and competency that are so vital to us all. These are major losses, and they happen more than once. Definitely, a sense of cultural balance is lost.

Loss of possessions. This loss doesn't refer to possessions of monetary value, but to the loss of things that connect TCKs to their past and, again, their security. Because of weight limits on airplanes, favorite toys are sold. Tree houses remain nested in the foliage waiting for the next attaché's family. Evacuations during political crises mean all possessions are left behind. And so it goes.

> At one conference, TCKs were asked to name some of their hidden losses. All sorts of answers popped up.
>
> "My country" (meaning the host country).
> "Separation from my siblings because of boarding school."
> "My dog."
> "My history."
> "My tree."
> "My place in the community."
> "Our dishes."
> Dishes? Why that?

> "We'd lived in Venezuela the whole 18 years since I'd
> been born. I felt so sad as I watched my parents sell our
> furniture. But when we got back to England and my mom
> unpacked, I suddenly realized she hadn't even brought our
> dishes. I said, 'Mum, how could you do that? Why didn't you
> bring them?' She replied, 'They were cracked, and it's easier
> to buy new ones here.' She didn't understand those were the
> dishes we'd used whenever my friends came over, for our
> family meals, for everything. They were not replaceable
> because they held our family history."

The lack of opportunity to take most personal possessions from one place to another is one of the differences in international mobility compared with mobility inside a particular country. If someone moves from Amsterdam to Rotterdam, usually a mover comes, loads up the furniture and dishes along with everything else, and drives the truck to the new home. Although the house and city are different, at least familiar pictures can be hung on the wall, the favorite recliner can be placed in the living room, and some sense of connectedness to the past remains.

In international and intercontinental moves, however, shipping the entire household is often impossible. Shipping costs much more than the furniture is worth. Instructions come from the organization (or parents) to keep only those possessions that can fit into a suitcase. Many things are too big or bulky to pack. It becomes simpler and more efficient and economical to start over again with new things at the next place.

Loss of relationships. Not only do many people constantly come and go in the TCKs' world, but among these chronically disrupted relationships are those that are core relationships in life—the ones between parent and child as well as with siblings, grandparents, aunts, uncles, and cousins. Dad or Mom may go to sea for six months. Grandparents and other extended family members aren't merely a town or state away—they're an ocean away. Education choices such as boarding school or staying in the home country for high school can create major patterns of separation for families when the children are still young. Many TCKs who returned to their home countries for secondary school grew up as strangers to their brothers and sisters who remained with their parents in the host country during those same years.

> Until Ruth Van Reken was thirty-nine and started writing
> the journal that turned into *Letters Never Sent* (the story of
> her own TCK journey), she had no idea that the day her par-
> ents and siblings returned to Nigeria for four years and left
> her in the United States was the day her family—as she had
> always known it—died. Never again did all six children live
> with two parents as a family unit for any extended period

of time. As she wrote, Ruth allowed herself to experience for the first time the grief of that moment twenty-six years before—a grief almost as deep as she would have experienced had she gotten a phone call that her family had been killed in a car wreck.

Loss of role models. In the same way we "catch" culture almost instinctively from those around us, we also learn what to expect at upcoming stages of life by observing and interacting with people already in those stages.

In a gathering of older ATCKs, we again asked the question, "What are your hidden losses?" One gentleman answered, "Role models." He had only recently realized that during his 12 years in a boarding school from ages 6 to 18, he had not had a model for a father who was involved in his family's life. Although he was a successful businessman, he had been married and divorced four times and was estranged from his adult children.

From our role models, we decide what and who we want to be like when we become adults. Additionally, peer role models may not be present in the lives of TCKs. The delayed adolescent response often noted in TCKs may be the result of that fact. While living overseas as teenagers they aren't around peers and slightly older adolescents, such as college or the career-beginning age group, from their passport culture, so they are deprived of role models for young adulthood.

Loss of system identity. As mentioned before, many TCKs grow up within the friendly (or unfriendly as a few might say) confines of a strong sponsoring organizational structure, which becomes part of their identity. They have instant recognition as a member of this group. Then at age 21 the commissary card is cut up, the support for education stops, invitations to organizational functions cease, and they are on their own as "adults." TCKs understand this change and probably maintain personal friends within the original system, but their sense of loss of no longer being part of that system is real. In fact, some TCKs have told us that this "graduation to adulthood" felt like their own families disowned them.

Loss of the past that wasn't. Some TCKs feel deep grief over what they see as the irretrievable losses of their childhood. ATCKs from the pre-jet set days remember the graduation ceremony parents couldn't attend because they were a continent away. Other TCKs wish they could have gone to school in their native language. Some regret that they had to return to their passport country with their parents; they wanted to stay in the host country.

> Chris, a Finnish TCK, returned to Helsinki after a childhood in Namibia. While living there, separation from extended family seemed normal. All the other TCKs she knew had done the same. But that hadn't been the experience for her Finnish relatives. One evening, just after Christmas, Chris listened to her cousins reminisce about their childhood in Finland. They talked of family Christmas traditions, summer

vacations at the family cottage on the lake, birthday celebrations and weddings when the family gathered. Suddenly, Chris felt overwhelmed by what she had missed growing up. Later, in a gathering of TCKs from various countries, Chris spoke of how living overseas had robbed her of knowing the closeness of her extended family back home.

Loss of the past that was. While some TCKs grieve for experiences they missed, other TCKs grieve for the past no longer available to them. People who live as adults in the same country where they grew up can usually go back and revisit their old house, school, playground, and church. In spite of inevitable changes, they can still reminisce "on site," but a highly mobile TCK often lacks this opportunity. And for many whose host countries have experienced the devastation of war or great political turmoil, the world they knew will never be accessible again, even if they physically return. This is a great loss.

In any of the hidden losses we've just mentioned, the main issue again is not the grief, per se. The real issue is that in these types of invisible losses, where the tangible and intangible are so inextricably intertwined, no one actually died or was divorced and nothing was physically stolen. Contrary to obvious losses, there are no markers, no rites of passage recognizing them as they occur—no recognized way to mourn. Yet each hidden loss relates to the major human needs we all have of belonging, feeling significant to others, and being understood. The majority of TCKs are adults before they acknowledge and come to terms with the depth of their grief over any or all of these areas of hidden loss.

Hidden losses and fear aren't the only reason for unresolved grief, however. Even when losses are recognized, other factors may prevent a healthy resolution of grief.

LACK OF PERMISSION TO GRIEVE

ATCK Harry wrote to the alumni magazine of his school in response to earlier letters in which various ATCKs had talked about painful issues from their childhood. "Stop fussing," he wrote. "Don't you think any kid in the Harlem ghetto would trade places with you in a second?"

Sometimes TCKs receive a very direct message that lets them know it's not okay to express their fears or grief. Many are asked to be "brave soldiers," perhaps particularly in the military and missionary context. Colonialists' offspring were encouraged to "keep a stiff upper lip." In *Military Brats,* Mary Edwards Wertsch wrote of a girl who came down the stairs one morning and asked her mom, "What would happen if Dad got shot in Vietnam?" The mother's instant reply was "Don't—you—*ever*—say—that!"[6]

Also, when parents are serving noble causes—saving the country from war, representing the government on delicate negotiations, or preaching salvation to a lost world—how can a child admit grief or fear? The child would feel too much shame for being selfish, wrong, or not spiritual or patriotic enough if they acknowledged how much it hurt to leave or be left. In such situations, TCKs may easily learn that negative feelings of almost any kind, including grief, aren't allowed. They begin to wear a mask to cover those feelings and conform to the expectations and socially approved behavior of the community.

TCKs who grow up in a missionary community may face an added burden. Some mission people see an admission of painful feelings as a lack of faith. TCKs who want to keep their faith often feel they can't acknowledge any pain they have experienced. Conversely, other TCKs from such communities take the opposite tack; they believe that in order to deal with their grief, they must deny the faith they've been taught. They, too, have forgotten (or never grasped?) the paradoxical nature of the TCK experience we mentioned earlier.

LACK OF TIME TO PROCESS

Unresolved grief can also be the result of insufficient time to process loss. Any person who experiences loss needs a period of time to face the pain, mourn and accept the loss, come to closure, and move on. In the era when most international travelers went overseas by ship, the trip could take weeks, providing a built-in transition period that allowed time for the grief process. In today's world of jet travel, however, there is no transition time to deal properly with the inevitable grief of losing what has been left behind. A world disappears with the closing of the airplane door and when the door is opened, the receiving community is excited to welcome the returnees. How can TCKs mourn losing the world they've loved when, because there is no visible ceremony such as a funeral, the community surrounding them has no idea of the depth of their loss? In fact, they can become impatient if these TCKs are not ready to move on immediately into the many wonderful plans prepared for them.

LACK OF COMFORT

The presence or lack of comfort is another huge factor in whether grief is resolved. In 1984, Sharon Willmer first identified this as a key issue for TCKs when she wrote Dave Pollock, "If someone were to ask me, 'From your experience as a therapist and friend of [TCKs], what do you see as the [TCKs'] greatest need?' I would reply, beyond the shadow of a doubt. . . that they need to be comforted and helped to understand what it means to be a person."[7] We've already begun looking at the issues relating to personal identity, but to understand why people need comfort and why it's often missing for TCKs, we must first look at what comfort is and isn't and how it differs from encouragement.

Merriam-Webster's Collegiate Dictionary defines *comfort* as "consolation in time of trouble or worry."[8] Comfort doesn't change the situation itself, nor can it take away the pain, but it relays the message that someone cares and understands. Comfort validates grief and gives permission for the grieving process to take place. For example, when a person walks up to a widow standing by her husband's casket and puts an arm around her shoulder, that gesture, with or without words, is comforting. It can't bring the husband back to life or stop the tears or the pain, but it lets the widow know her grief is accepted and understood. She's not alone in her sorrow.

Unfortunately, in their very efforts to help another person "feel better," people often confuse comfort with encouragement and end up giving neither. Encouragement is a person's attempt to change the griever's perspective. It may be a reminder to look at the bright side of a situation instead of the loss or to think about a past success and presume this present situation will turn out just as well.

Obviously there's a time for both comfort and encouragement, but what happens when the two are confused? If the grieving widow is told that it's a good thing at least her husband had a substantial life insurance policy, how does she feel? Neither comforted nor encouraged! When encouragement is given before comfort, the subtle or not so subtle message is "Buck up; you *shouldn't* feel so low." It becomes a shame message rather than an encouragement.

Perhaps because a TCK's losses are far less visible than the widow's, this mix-up between comfort and encouragement can sometimes prevent TCKs from being comforted. There are several ways people may unknowingly try to encourage rather than comfort TCKs and thus accomplish neither.

Discounting grief. As TCKs and their families prepare to board the plane, Mom and Dad admonish them not to cry by saying, "Don't worry. You'll make new friends quickly once we get there." In not acknowledging the pain involved in the good-bye, they communicate the hidden message that their son or daughter *shouldn't* be sad. What's the big deal about saying good-bye to these friends when they can be so easily replaced? Somehow, though, the TCKs still feel sad and end up thinking something must be wrong with *them*. After a while there is nothing to do but bury the pain.

Comparing grief to a higher good. When TCKs express sadness at an approaching move or loss, adults may try to cheer them up with the reminder that the reasons behind this lifestyle—and thus the losses involved—are of such importance (defending or representing the country, saving the world, earning enough money to pay for the child's later educational bills) that the TCKs *shouldn't* complain about a few hardships along the way. Unfortunately, this noble reasoning still is not comforting; in fact, it is shaming. Generally, TCKs already understand—

and often agree with—the reason why their parents have a particular career and lifestyle. Most TCKs aren't asking their parents to change. All they're trying to say is that, in spite of what they *know,* it still hurts to leave friends and a place they love dearly.

Denying grief. It's not only TCKs who may deny their grief; adults around them often do the same. To comfort another person, to say "I understand," is to admit there's a reason for grieving. Adults who busily mask their own sense of loss by denial can't afford to admit they understand the sad TCK. If they did, their own internal protective structures might tumble down and leave them quite unprotected.

One therapist asked us if anyone had ever done a study on how parents react when they know they must send their kids away to school at age six. Bowlby[9] and others have written about how early separations between parents and children affect a child's ability to attach later to those parents or others, but we know of no official study regarding how the parents cope. In asking ATCKs for their thoughts on this, a number have told us how their parents stopped hugging them in their early years so these ATCKs wouldn't "miss it" (the hugs) when they left for school at the age of six. Surely this was a loss for both parent and child.

Once again, the losses TCKs encounter—recognized or unrecognized—and the grief that follows aren't in themselves the biggest problems. These losses are natural, and when that grief can be expressed, the grief is good—a productive way to deal with the pain. The biggest problem is *unresolved* grief. Grief that is not dealt with directly emerges in some way—in forms that are destructive and that can last a lifetime. That's "bad grief," and it needs attention and resolution. Part III offers many concrete suggestions for how to deal with losses as they happen in positive ways so grief does not need to accumulate in the ways it has for so many TCKs in the past.

Lessons from the TCK Petri Dish

When we look at some CCKs, it is easy to think, "Well, the mobility issues that affect TCKs really don't apply. An international adoptee makes one long original trip and then may stay in one home for the rest of his or her childhood. Children of minorities or educational CCKs may have one address from birth to university. How can these issues of mobility apply to them?"

This question is all part of the ongoing discovery process. For us, it is relatively clear how living and growing up among many cultural worlds creates issues of identity and belonging for many types of CCKs. We are not yet as clear on why it is that so often when we discuss issues related to transition, loss, and unresolved grief, so many CCKs who did not grow up in a traditional TCK environment also come to us with tears to say how helpful it was to find new language and understanding for their own story. In some situations, it seems even the aspect of mobility between cultural worlds is hidden: the educational CCK who goes between majority and minority culture each day, the domestic CCK whose family relocated often but never outside the country, the bicultural child who changes cultural worlds with each visit to Grandma and Grandpa.

But for many other types of CCKs (and for non-CCKs as well), it seems the places they relate to are not the physical transitions as much as the emotional experiences we describe. In particular, they tell of their hidden losses and how others do not understand. The international adoptee may wonder what it would have been like to grow up in the land of his birth. The immigrant's child tells of the loss she feels when she visits her cousins in the Philippines and realizes they have close family ties she will never have because of the distance. But, like TCKs, to express such things seems ungrateful for the obvious good and blessings they also have in life. Others try to remind them of their "blessings" before acknowledging the reality of their losses. In days ahead, our awareness of the parallels between all types of CCKs in this area will, we believe, only increase.

We hope that a deeper understanding of the dynamics of issues related to mobility will help all TCKs/ATCKs and other groups of CCKs/ACCKS—including their families and all who work with them—find ways to work through the challenges so they can enjoy the adventures of life even more fully. But we also trust that understanding matters such as the hidden losses of life, the way lack of permission to grieve or discounting of grief can unintentionally happen, will allow people of all backgrounds—TCKs/CCKs or not—to translate these principles back to their own stories and find new language and understanding for their journeys too.

Part II

The TCK Profile

IN PART I WE FOCUSED PRIMARILY on defining third culture kids and explaining their world. Now we will look in depth at the specific benefits and challenges of this experience. Some benefits and challenges are seen most clearly in the shorter term, while others become more obvious with time.

We will examine the character traits this lifestyle fosters along with how it affects interpersonal relationships and developmental patterns. While we most often use the term TCK alone for simplicity's sake, these are characteristics that often become even more visible in adulthood for ATCKs. Because this is a group profile, not every characteristic will fit every person. But the "a-ha!" moment of recognition, which we have seen among countless TCKs and ATCKs, tells us these characteristics are valid as an overall representation of their world.

~~~~~~

CHAPTER 6

Benefits and Challenges

Besides the drawbacks of family separation and the very real adjustment on the permanent return to the [home country], a child growing up abroad has great advantages. He [or she] learns, through no conscious act of learning, that thoughts can be transmitted in many languages, that skin color is unimportant... that certain things are sacred or taboo to some people while to others they're meaningless, that the ordinary word of one area is a swearword in another.

We have lived in Tulsa for five years... I am struck again and again by the fact that so much of the sociology, feeling for history, geography, questions [about] others that our friends' children try to understand through textbooks, my sisters and I acquired just by living.[1]

—Rachel Miller Schaetti

Introduction: The TCK Profile

~~~~~~~~~~~~~~~~~

The often paradoxical benefits and challenges of the TCK Profile are sometimes described as being like opposite sides of the same coin, but in reality they are more like the contrasting colored strands of thread woven together into a tapestry. As each strand crosses with a contrasting or complementary color, a picture begins to emerge, but no one strand alone tells the full story. For example, the high mobility of a TCK's life often results in special relationships with people throughout the world, but it also creates sadness at the chronic loss of these relationships. That very pain, however, provides the opportunity to develop a greater empathy for others. A TCK's expansive worldview, which enriches history classes and gives perspective to the nightly news, also makes the horror of the slaughter of

Sudanese citizens in the refugee camps of Darfur a painful reality. That same awareness can be what motivates a TCK's concern for solving those kinds of tragic problems. And so it goes.

Some of the characteristics—as well as the benefits and challenges—are primarily a result of the cross-cultural nature of the third culture experience. Others are more directly shaped by the high mobility of the lifestyle. Most of the profile, however, is this weaving together of these two dominant realities.

We begin by discussing some of the most common general benefits and challenges we have seen among TCKs and ATCKs, but before we do, let us make it clear once more that when we use the word *challenge,* we purposefully do not infer the word *liability.* A challenge is something people have the choice to face, deal with, and grow from. A liability can only be something that pulls someone down. Some may say we concentrate too much on the challenges, but if that criticism is valid, it is for a reason. We have seen the benefits of this experience enrich countless TCKs' lives, whether or not they stop to consciously define or use them. Many have also found unconscious ways to deal with the challenges and make them a productive aspect of their lives in one way or another. We have also seen, however, that for some TCKs (and those around them) the unrecognized challenges have caused years of frustration as they struggle to deal with matters that have no name, no definition. In the process, they have lost sight of the benefits they have also received. It is our hope that in naming both the benefits and challenges, and then offering suggestions in Part III on how to build intentionally on the strengths and deal productively with the challenges, many more TCKs will be able to maximize the great gifts that can come from their lives and live out with joy the richness of their heritage. We begin.

Expanded Worldview versus Confused Loyalties

BENEFIT: EXPANDED WORLDVIEW

An obvious benefit of the TCK experience is that while growing up in a multiplicity of countries and cultures, TCKs not only observe firsthand the many geographical differences around the world, but they also learn how people view life from different philosophical and political perspectives. Some people think of Osama bin Laden as a hero; others believe he's a villain. Western culture is time and task oriented; in Eastern culture, interpersonal relationships are of greater importance. The TCK's awareness that there can be more than one way to look at the same thing starts early in life. We listened to these rather remarkable stories during a meeting in Malaysia with TCKs ages five to twelve who were all growing up in Asia.

"You know, last year we had to hide on the floor for four days because of typhoons."

"We couldn't go out of our house in Sri Lanka for a week when everybody in town started fighting."

"On our vacation last month we got to ride on the backs of elephants and go look for tigers."

"Well, so did we!" countered another seven-year-old from across the room. "We saw six tigers. How many did you see?"

And so it went.

Eventually New Year's Day came up as part of a story. We asked what we thought was a simple question. "When is New Year's Day?" Instead of the simple "January 1" that we expected, many different dates were given—each young TCK trying to defend how and when it was celebrated in his or her host country. We knew that if we had asked most traditional groups of five- to twelve-year-olds in the United States about New Year's Day, this discussion wouldn't be occurring. Most of them probably would have no idea that New Year's Day could be dates other than January 1.

This may seem like a small detail, but already these children are learning how big and interesting the world they live in is and how much there will be to discover about it all through life. Many readers may not know that Henry Robinson Luce was an ATCK born and raised in China until he first set foot in the United States at age 15. He founded *Time* magazine in 1923 and *Life* magazine in 1936. He couldn't find enough international news in local publications, so he decided to fix the problem by starting these publications.[2]

Interestingly, many of today's commentators in print and on cable news channels are also TCKs or other versions of CCKs with global childhoods. Fareed Zakaria, born in India, spent time as a foreign student in, and ultimately immigrated to, the United States. He has become an award-winning author and commentator on international relationships and policies. In a column he wrote for *Newsweek*, Zakaria states:

> I've spent my life acquiring formal expertise on foreign policy. I've got fancy degrees, have run research projects, taught in colleges and graduate schools... I couldn't do my job without the expertise... [but] my biography [of living in countries outside his own during his formative years] has helped me put my book learning in context, made for a richer interaction with foreigners and helped me see the world from many angles.[3]

Zakaria goes on to talk about the need to develop deeper understandings of other countries than our own and concludes, "There are many ways to attain this, but certainly being able to feel it in your bones is one powerful way."[4]

CHALLENGE: CONFUSED LOYALTIES

Although their expanded worldview is a great benefit, it can also leave TCKs with a sense of confusion about such complex things as politics, patriotism, and values. Should they support the policies of their home country when those policies are detrimental to their host country? Or should they support the host country even if it means opposing policies of their own government?

Joe, the American ATCK raised in Argentina and educated in a British school who was introduced in chapter 4, writes about divided loyalties:

> When I came to the U.S., there was the matter of pledging allegiance to the American flag. I had saluted the Union Jack, the Argentine flag, and now I was supposed to swear loyalty to a country which, in 1955, didn't even have decent pizza or coffee. Worse, Americans, many of them, were still McCarthyites at heart, and feared anything tainted with foreignisms.
>
> The unfortunate side effects of a multicultural upbringing are substantial, of course. Whose side are you on? I had a dickens of a time with my loyalties during the Islas Malvinas war (no, make that the Falkland Islands war). After all, as an eleven-year-old I had sworn undying fealty to Juan Domingo Peron and his promise that he would free the Malvinas from British enslavement. After the army booted him out of Argentina, I figured I was off the hook. But could I really be sure? On the other hand, I whistled "Rule Britannia" at least three times a week and really felt proud to know that a massive British force was headed to the Falklands and that British sovereignty would be asserted, unequivocally. I was dismayed by the profound indifference to this war exhibited by Americans.[5]

Confused loyalties can make TCKs seem unpatriotic and arrogant to their fellow citizens. If Joe is a good American, how could he ever pledge allegiance to Argentina and Britain—or be angry with his own country for not getting involved in someone else's war? If British TCKs who grew up in India try to explain negative remnants of the colonial era to fellow classmates in England, they can seem like traitors. Australian children in Indianapolis schools have been rebuked for refusing to pledge allegiance to the American flag each morning, even though they have stood respectfully during that daily ritual.

In *Homesick: My Own Story,* Jean Fritz writes of her experiences as an American TCK in China during the 1920s. She attended a British school in China but defiantly refused to sing "God Save the King" because it wasn't *her* national anthem. She was an American, although she had never spent a day in the United States in her life. Throughout the growing turmoil that led to the revolution in 1927, Jean dreamed of her grandmother's farm and garden in Pennsylvania, fantasizing over and over about what it would be like to live and go to school in America. Finally, after what seemed like an endless boat ride and many struggles, Jean arrived at that long-awaited first day in an American school. Here's what happened.

> "The class will come to order," she [Miss Crofts, the teacher] said. "I will call the roll." When she came to my name, Miss Crofts looked up from her book. "Jean Guttery is new to our school," she said. "She has come all the way from China where she lived beside the Yangs-Ta-Zee River. Isn't that right, Jean?"
>
> "It's pronounced *Yang-see,*" I corrected. "There are just two syllables."
>
> Miss Crofts looked at me coldly. "In America," she said, "we say *Yangs-Ta-Zee.*"
>
> I was working myself up, madder by the minute, when I heard Andrew Carr, the boy behind me, shifting his feet on the floor. I guess he must have hunched across his desk, because all at once I heard him whisper over my shoulder:
>
> "Chink, Chink, Chinaman
> Sitting on a fence,
> Trying to make a dollar
> Out of fifteen cents."
>
> I forgot all about where I was. I jumped to my feet, whirled around, and spoke out loud as if there were no Miss Crofts, as if I'd never been in a classroom before, as if I knew nothing about classroom behavior. "You don't call them Chinamen or Chinks," I cried. "You call them *Chinese.* Even in America you call them *Chinese.*"
>
> "Well, you don't need to get exercised, Jean," she [Miss Crofts] said. "We all know that you are American."
>
> "But that's not the *point!*" Before I could explain that it was an insult to call Chinese people *Chinamen,* Miss Crofts had tapped her desk with a ruler.
>
> "That will be enough," she said. "All eyes front."[6]

Which country had Jean's greatest loyalty and devotion—the United States or China? Did she know? All her life she had thought of herself as American, yet now here she was defending the Chinese. Certainly Miss Crofts and Jean's classmates couldn't understand why she would want to defend a people and a country halfway around the world from them—particularly at the expense of getting along with people from her own country. Because Jean physically looked like her classmates, those around her had no idea that Jean had spent her life studying about the Chinese culture and people and that throughout her life people from that world had been her playmates and friends.

More difficult than the questions of political or patriotic loyalties, however, are the value dissonances that occur in the cross-cultural experience. As we said earlier, TCKs often live among cultures with strongly conflicting value systems. One culture says female circumcision is wrong. Another one says female circumcision is the most significant moment in a girl's life; it is when she knows she has become an accepted member of her tribe. One culture says abortion is wrong; another says it is all right for specific reasons up to certain points in the pregnancy. Still other cultures practice abortion based on the gender of the baby: males are wanted; females are not.

In each situation, which value is right? Which is wrong? Is there a right and wrong? If so, who or what defines them? Conflicting values cannot be operational at the same time in the same place. How do TCKs decide from all they see around them what their own values will and won't be? Deciding on what are the core personal beliefs and values we will hold on to no matter where we are compared to understanding what are simply cultural differences is an important task for everyone in the process of developing a sense of personal identity. For TCKs, however, it can be a special challenge.

This expanded worldview and its resulting confusion of loyalties and values can be a greater problem for those who return to cultures that remain relatively homogenous. In a study of Turkish TCKs, Steve Eisinger discovered that "the statistics regarding public opinion . . . indicate that this expanded worldview may not be necessarily viewed as a positive characteristic."[7] In appendix B, Japanese researcher Momo Kano Podolsky describes how Japanese TCKs, or kikoku-shijo, were originally looked down on in the early days of their returning to Japan. While that opinion has now been reversed in Japan, the new ideas that the TCKs bring back, and their refusal to follow unthinkingly the cultural patterns of preceding generations, can sometimes make them unwelcome citizens in their own countries—whatever that country and culture might be.

Three-Dimensional View of the World versus Painful View of Reality

BENEFIT: THREE-DIMENSIONAL VIEW OF THE WORLD

As TCKs live in various cultures, they not only learn about cultural differences, but they also experience the world in a tangible way that is impossible to do by reading books, seeing movies, or watching nightly newscasts alone. Because they have lived in so many places, smelled so many smells, heard so many strange sounds, and been in so many strange situations, throughout their lives when they read a story in the newspaper or watch it on TV, the flat, odorless images there transform into an internal 3-D panoramic picture show. It's almost as if they were there in person smelling the smells, tasting the tastes, perspiring with the heat. They may not be present at the event, but they have a clear awareness of what is going on and what it is like for those who are there.

> Each summer Dave Pollock led transition seminars for TCKs. During one of these, he asked the attendees, "What comes to your mind if I say the word *riot*?" The answers came back, "Paris," "Korea," "Iran" "Ecuador."
> Next question. "Any details?"
> More answers: "Broken windows." "Water cannons." "Burned buses." "Tear gas, mobs." "Burning tires."
> Burning tires. Who would think about burning tires except somebody who had smelled that stench?
> "Tacks."

Anyone might think of guns in a riot, but why tacks? Because this TCK had seen tacks spread on the streets of Ecuador to flatten tires, so people couldn't travel during a riot. It makes sense, but probably only someone who had seen it would name it.

Having a 3-D view of the world is a useful skill not only for reading stories but for writing them. For TCKs who like to write, their culturally rich and highly mobile childhoods give them a true breadth of hands-on experiences in many places to add life to their work. Pearl S. Buck and John Hersey were among the first ATCKs who recorded in words the world they had known as children growing up in China. In a feature article for *Time* called "The Empire Writes Back," Pico Iyer gives an account of an entirely new genre of award-winning authors, all of whom have cross-cultural backgrounds.

> Authors from Britain's former colonies have begun to cap-
> ture the very heart of English literature, transforming the
> canon with bright colors and strange cadences and foreign
> eyes. They are revolutionizing the language from within.
> Hot spices are entering English, and tropical birds... magi-
> cal creations from the makers of a new World Fiction.[8]

Iyer goes on to describe the great diversity of each writer's background and then states,

> But the new transcultural writers are something different.
> For one, they are the products not so much of colonial divi-
> sion as of the *international culture* that has grown up since
> the war, and they are addressing an audience as mixed up
> and eclectic and uprooted as themselves.[9]

Without ever using, or perhaps even knowing, the term *third culture kids*, Iyer has conveyed vividly the richness of their experience. In the last few years, the ranks of TCK authors have swelled. Beside Pico Iyer and his book *The Global Soul*, the list now includes such names as Khaled Hosseini (*The Kite Runner* and *A Thousand Splendid Suns*), William Paul Young (*The Shack*), and the many books of Isabel Allende, including *My Invented Country*.

CHALLENGE: PAINFUL AWARENESS OF REALITY

With this three-dimensional view of the world, however, comes the painful reality that behind the stories in the news are real flesh-and-blood people—not merely flat faces on a TV screen. When an airplane crashes in India or a tsunami rips the coasts of Thailand, TCKs find it appalling that their local evening newscasters seem to focus mainly on how many citizens of their particular country died— almost as if the other lives lost didn't matter. As they watch an empty-eyed woman and desperate man search vainly for their child amid the rubble of an earthquake in China, ATCKs know that loss is as painful as their own would be if they were in that situation. Many of them know that when bombs drop on Baghdad or Beirut, people scream with fear and horror there just as they did on September 11, 2001, when airplanes hit the twin towers of the World Trade Center in New York.

Many TCKs have seen war or faced the pain of evacuation and its disrup-
tion. For some it has happened in their host cultures. In others, it has happened in their passport culture. Either way, with this global lifestyle, they are often an ocean apart from their families at times of great political and social upheaval or even natural disasters. A special hardship is that others around them may have no idea why a war or an earthquake drifting by on the scrolling news line on CNN makes such a difference to this TCK or ATCK.

As a child, Samar grew up as a Lebanese citizen living in Liberia and attended a U.S.-based international school. Her father had a thriving business until the civil war in Liberia began. After her family fled back to Lebanon, more civil unrest hit that land and they then immigrated to France. In time, Samar and her family returned to Lebanon and lived amid the continuing tensions there. Eventually, Samar married her Lebanese sweetheart, Khaled, and they moved to the United States while Khaled finished a medical residency program. Samar made friends with local citizens and pushed her new baby's stroller while walking with other young moms in the park. Within these social interactions, they all appeared to be living similar lifestyles.

Then the unrest in Lebanon flared up once more. While the other moms continued talking about the color of their kitchen curtains and making playdates for their children, Samar suddenly lost interest in such discussions. Her life became centered on CNN and MSNBC, trying to figure out from the onscreen images how close the fighting was to her parents' home. Every thunderstorm made her want to hide, because it reminded her of the sounds of war in both Liberia and Lebanon. She found herself resenting her newfound friends for their seeming lack of interest not only in her family, but in all those others who suffered because governments had chosen to wage their wars where real people like her and her family lived.

Cross-Cultural Enrichment versus Ignorance of the Home Culture

BENEFIT: CROSS-CULTURAL ENRICHMENT

TCKs and ATCKs usually have a sense of ownership and interest in cultures other than just that of their passport country. They set their Internet homepages to receive news from the places they've lived. They enjoy aspects of the host culture others might not appreciate. While the smell of the Southeast Asian fruit *durian* would precipitate a gag reflex in most of us, TCKs who grew up in Malaysia inhale the scent with glee, for it is the smell of home. Those who grew up in India use *chapatis* to pick up the hottest curry sauce. Still other TCKs and ATCKs sit cross-legged on the floor whenever they have a choice between that and a lounge chair. They consider these aspects of their lifestyle part of the wealth of their heritage.

Perhaps more important than what they have learned to enjoy from the more surface layers of other cultures, however, is the fact that most TCKs have gained valuable lessons from the deeper levels as well. They have lived in other places long enough to learn to appreciate the reasons and understanding behind some of the behavioral differences rather than simply being frustrated by them as visitors tend to be. For example, while a tourist might feel irritated that the stores close for two hours in the middle of the day just when he or she wants to go shopping, most TCKs can understand that this custom not only helps people survive better if the climate is extremely hot, but it's a time when parents greet the children as they return from school and spend time together as a family. Many TCKs learn to value relationships above convenience as they live in such places, and it is a gift they carry with them wherever they may later go.

CHALLENGE: IGNORANCE OF HOME CULTURE

The irony of collecting cross-cultural practices and skills, however, is that TCKs may know all sorts of fascinating things about other countries but little about their own.

> Tamara attended school in England for the first time when she was ten. Until then she had attended a small American-oriented school in Africa. In early November, she asked her mother, "Mom, who is this Guy Fawkes everybody's talking about?"
>
> Tamara's mom, Elizabeth, a born and bred English-woman, tried to hide her shock at her daughter's ignorance. Tamara seemed so knowledgeable about countless global matters—how could she not know a simple fact about a major figure in British history? And particularly one whose wicked deed of trying to blow up the Parliament was decried each year as people throughout the country burned him in effigy? Elizabeth hadn't realized that while Tamara had seen the world, she had missed learning about this common tradition in her own country.

TCKs are often sadly ignorant of national, local, and even family history. How many rides to various relatives' homes are filled with parents coaching TCKs about who is related to whom? Many kids simply haven't been around the normal chatter that keeps family members connected.

One major advantage TCKs have in today's world of the Internet, Skype, blogging, Facebook, and YouTube compared to previous generations of TCKs is a better means of keeping up with pop culture, including current movie stars, politicians, musicians, and other public figures, as well as fads and trends. Many older ATCKs remember all too well when reentering their passport culture after being away for years the reactions from their peers to an innocent question such as, "Who's Elvis?" Such questions could lock them forever into the "Camp of Inner Shame." These TCKs, along with their friends, wondered how they could be so stupid—not realizing that ignorance is not the same as stupidity. They were definitely not in cultural balance.

There is, however, an important point to make here. In recent years, personnel directors, parents, and even some educators from international schools have stated that with all the new technological changes, TCKs no longer have any cultural adjustment "problems." In fact, some have seemed almost dismissive. One principal from an international school in the United States said emphatically that his students had none of these TCK challenges because they went online every morning to read the newspapers from their passport countries. What he and others forget, however, is that while media is one place of cultural learning, knowledge of facts alone isn't enough to put someone in cultural balance. Cultural cues and nuances are picked up unknowingly from our environment.

Take humor, for example. When people switch cultures, humor is another unknown. Jokes often are based on a surprise, an indirect reference to something current, or a play on words that have a double meaning specific to that culture or language. Few things make people, including TCKs, feel more left out than seeing everyone else laughing at something they can't understand as funny. Or, conversely, they try to tell a joke that was hilarious in their boarding school, but nobody laughs in this new environment.

Probably most TCKs have some story about getting caught in an embarrassing situation because they didn't know some everyday rule of their passport culture that is different from their host culture. One TCK couldn't pay her bill because she had forgotten to mentally add the tax to the amount listed on the menu. Another was shamed by his visiting relatives because he came into the room and sat down before making sure that all the oldest guests had found their places. Not knowing cultural rules can also be dangerous.

> In the village in Mali where Sophie had grown up, passing anyone—male or female—on the street and not saying hello created instant social disfavor. In London the rules were different, as she learned in a police seminar on rape prevention during her first semester at university. "Never look a stranger in the eye," the policeman said. "After attacking someone, a man often accuses the woman of having invited him with her look." And Sophie had been smiling at strange men all over the city!

Lessons from the TCK Petri Dish

All these benefits and challenges are a mere beginning of the TCK Profile, but they are characteristics many other CCKs tell us are familiar to them as well. Which "home country" does the child of a binational couple support in the World Cup series? How does an immigrant child exlpain to grandparents in the country of origin that she never had to bargain in market before when they ac-ccuse her of paying an exorbitant price for vegetables at market? What happens when an educational CCK wants to further explore new ideas learned at school and parents fear he will forget his roots? For these and other reasons, different goups of CCKs can all resonate with these descriptions. We continue our dicussion by looking at common personal strengths and struggles many TCKs and other CCKs often seem to share.

CHAPTER 7

Personal Characteristics

The benefits of this upbringing need to be underscored: In an era when global vision is an imperative, when skills in intercultural communication, linguistic ability, mediation, diplomacy, and the management of diversity are critical, global nomads are better equipped in these areas by the age of eighteen than are many adults.... These intercultural and linguistic skills are the markings of the cultural chameleon—the young participant-observer who takes note of verbal and nonverbal cues and readjusts accordingly, taking on enough of the coloration of the social surroundings to gain acceptance while maintaining some vestige of identity as a different animal, an "other."[1]

—Norma M. McCaig
Founder, Global Nomads International

NORMA M. MCCAIG, one of the true pioneers in raising global awareness of the issues facing TCKs, was a business ATCK herself and worked extensively with international companies preparing employees and their families for overseas assignments before her death in 2008. In this chapter and the next we will discuss many of the characteristics and skills (their benefits and their corresponding challenges) of the TCKs that she mentions.

Cultural Chameleon: Adaptability versus Lack of True Cultural Balance

BENEFIT: ADAPTABILITY

TCKs usually develop some degree of cultural adaptability as a primary tool for surviving the frequent change of cultures. Over and over TCKs use the term *chameleon* to describe how, after spending a little time observing what is going on, they can easily switch language, style of relating, appearance, and cultural practices to take on the characteristics needed to blend better into the current scene. Often their behavior becomes almost indistinguishable from longtime members of this group and they feel protected from the scorn or rejection of others (and their own ensuing sense of shame) that often comes with being different from others. A quote from the *Financial Times* after the inauguration of President Barack Obama talks of how he "benefited from his chameleon power to make a lot of different people feel he represents them…"

Cultural adaptability may begin as a survival tool, but it also has immensely practical benefits. TCKs usually learn to adjust with relative calm to life where meetings may start the exact minute for which they have been scheduled or two hours later, depending on which country they're in. Partly because of the frequency with which they travel and move, TCKs can often "roll with the punches" even in unusual circumstances.

> Nona and her ATCK friend, Joy, waited in vain for a bus to carry them from Arusha to Nairobi. They finally found a taxi driver who would take them to the Tanzanian/Kenyan border and promised to find them a ride the rest of the way. At the border, however, the driver disappeared. Night was approaching, when travel would no longer be safe.
>
> As Nona watched in amazement, Joy walked across the border to find another taxi. She soon returned to the Tanzanian side, got Nona and the bags, and returned to a waiting driver who took them to Nairobi. Later, Nona complimented Joy, "If it was me by myself, I'd still be sitting at the border, waiting for that first driver to come back."
>
> Joy replied, "Well, there are times when all I can think is, 'This is going to make a great story in three months, but right now it's the pits.' But I always know there's a way out if I can just think of all the options. I've been in these kinds of situations too many times to just wait."

CHALLENGE: LACK OF TRUE CULTURAL BALANCE

Becoming a cultural chameleon, however, brings special challenges as well. For one thing, although in the short term the ability to "change colors" helps them fit in with their peers day-by-day, TCK chameleons may never develop true cultural balance anywhere. While appearing to be one of the crowd, inside they may still be the cautious observer, the *wallflower* described in chapter 4—always a bit withdrawn and checking to see how they are doing. In addition, those around them may notice how the TCK's behavior changes in various circumstances and begin to wonder if they can trust anything the TCK does or says. It looks to them as if he or she has no real convictions about much of anything.

Some TCKs who flip-flop back and forth between various behavioral patterns have trouble figuring out their own value system from the multicultural mix they have been exposed to. It can be very difficult for them to decide if there are, after all, some absolutes in life they can hold onto and live by no matter which culture they are in. In the end, TCKs may adopt so many personas as cultural chameleons that they themselves don't know who they really are. Even when they try to be "themselves," they are often simply exchanging being chameleons in one group rather than another.

> Ginny returned to Minnesota for university after many years in New Zealand and Thailand. She looked with disdain on the majority of her fellow students who seemed to be clones of one another and decided she didn't want to be anything like them. She struck up an acquaintance with another student, Jessica, who was a member of the prevailing counterculture. Whatever Jessica did, Ginny did. Both wore clothing that was outlandish enough to be an obvious statement that they weren't going to be swayed by any current fads.
>
> Only years later did Ginny realize that she too had been a chameleon—copying Jessica—and had no idea of what she herself liked or wanted to be. She had rejected one group to make a statement about her "unique" identity, but she had never realized that among their styles of dress or behavior might be some things she did, in fact, like. Since she had totally aligned herself with Jessica, Ginny never stopped to think that some of Jessica's choices might not work for her. Was it all right for her to like jazz when Jessica didn't? What types of clothes did she, Ginny, really want to wear? It was some time before she was able to sort out and identify what her own gifts, talents, and preferences were in contrast to those she had borrowed from Jessica.

Hidden Immigrants: Blending In versus Defining the Differences

While virtually all TCKs make cultural adaptations to survive wherever they live, traditionally most TCKs—such as the children of early colonialists in the United States—were physically distinct from members of the host culture and easily recognizable as *foreigners* when living there. Even today, the child of the Norwegian ambassador in China would likely not be mistaken for a citizen of the host culture. As mentioned earlier in our discussion on identity, when TCKs are obvious foreigners, they are often excused—both by others and by themselves—if their behavior doesn't exactly match the local cultural norms or practices. No one expects them to be the same based on their appearance alone. Only when these TCKs, who are clearly foreigners in their host culture, reenter their home culture do they face the prospect of being the hidden immigrants we discussed in chapter 4.

As we also mentioned there, a frequently overlooked, but important, factor is that in our increasingly internationalizing world, many TCKs are becoming hidden immigrants in the host culture as well. Asian American children may look like the majority of others when they are in Kunming, China; a Ugandan diplomat's child may be mistaken for an African American in his classroom in Washington, D.C. So why is this hidden diversity an important issue?

For one thing, being a hidden immigrant gives those TCKs who desire it the choice to be total chameleons in their host culture in a way other non-look alike TCKs can't do. Once they adapt culturally, people around them have no idea they are actually foreigners, and the TCK may like this type of relative anonymity. A second reason to be aware of the potential for a hidden immigrant experience in the host culture is to recognize that some TCKS who prefer *not* to adapt to the surrounding scene will often find a way to proclaim that they are different from those around them, as other TCKs do upon reentry to their passport culture. This can result in some interesting behavior! Here are three different responses from TCKs who were hidden immigrants in their host culture.

BENEFIT: BLENDING IN

The first is Paul, an international business TCK who was born in Alaska and then lived in California and Illinois until he was nine. At that time, his family moved to Australia, where his father worked for an oil company. Paul tells us his story.

> My first year of school in Australia was horrible. I learned that Americans weren't very popular because of a nuclear base they'd set up near Sydney. People protested against the "ugly Americans" all the time. I felt other students assigned me guilt by association just because I was a U.S. citizen.

> Looking back, I realize the only kids who were good to me
> didn't fit in either.
>
> By the end of the first year, I'd developed an Austra-
> lian accent and learned to dress and act like my Australian
> counterparts. Then I changed schools so I could start over
> and no one knew I was American. I was a chameleon.

As a hidden immigrant in his host culture, Paul made a choice an obviously foreign TCK could never make. Until he chose to reveal his true identity, no one had to know that he was not Australian. Theoretically, some might argue that he made a poor choice, but from Paul's perspective as a child, blending in to this degree gave him the opportunity not only to be accepted by others, but also to more fully participate in school and social events while he remained in Australia. On the other hand, TCKs who choose this route also say they live with a fear of others discovering who they really are and sometimes feel as if they are living a double life.

CHALLENGE: DEFINING THE DIFFERENCES

While Paul chose to hide his identity by becoming a chameleon, Nicola and Krista are TCKs who reacted in an opposite way. They became the screamers we mentioned before. Because they looked like those around them, they felt they would lose their true identity if they didn't find some way to shout, "But I'm *not* like you." This is how each of them coped.

> Nicola, a British TCK, was born in Malaysia while her father
> served with the Royal Air Force. He retired from the service
> when Nicola was four years old. The family moved to Scot-
> land, where Nicola's father took a job flying airplanes off the
> coast of Scotland for a major oil company.
>
> At first, Nicola tried to hide her English roots, even
> adopting a thick Scottish brogue. In spite of that, by second-
> ary school she realized something inside her would never fit
> in with these classmates who had never left this small town.
> She looked like them, but when she didn't act like them they
> teased her unmercifully for every small transgression. It
> seemed the more she tried to be like them, the more she was
> having to deny who she really was inside.
>
> Finally, Nicola decided to openly—rather defiantly, in
> fact—espouse her English identity. She changed her accent
> to a proper British one and talked of England as home. She
> informed her classmates that she couldn't wait to leave Scot-
> land to attend university in England. When Nicola arrived

in Southampton on her way to the university, she literally
kissed the ground when she alighted from the train.

Krista is an American business TCK raised in England
from age six to sixteen. She attended a British school for six
months before attending the local American school. We were
surprised to hear her tell of how fiercely anti-British she
and her fellow classmates in the American school became.
In spite of the prevailing culture, they steadfastly refused
to speak "British." They decried Britain for not having
American-style shopping malls and bought all their clothes
at American stores like The Gap and Old Navy during their
summer leave in the United States. And why did everyone
insist on queuing so carefully anyway? It looked so prim
and silly. She couldn't wait to return to the U.S. permanently where everything would be "normal."

The difficulty for Nicola and Krista, however, was that in trying to proclaim
what they consider their true identity, they ultimately formed an "anti" identity—be that in clothes, speech, or behavior. Unfortunately, when TCKs make
this choice, they also cut themselves off from many benefits they could experience in friendships and cultural exchange with those around them from the local
community. In addition, as TCKs scream to others, "I'm not like you," people
around soon avoid them and they are left with a deep loneliness—although it
might take them a long time to admit such a thing.

Prejudice: Less versus More

BENEFIT: LESS PREJUDICE

The opportunity to know people from diverse backgrounds as friends—not
merely as acquaintances—and within the context of their own cultural milieu
is another gift TCKs receive. They have been members of groups that include a
striking collection of culturally and ethnically diverse people, and most have the
ability to truly enjoy such diversity and to believe that people of all backgrounds
can be full and equal participants in any given situation. Sometimes their unconscious, underlying assumptions that people of all backgrounds are still just
that—people—can surprise others, and the TCKs in turn are surprised that this
isn't necessarily "normal" for everyone else.

One white ATCK living in the suburban United States had an
African American repairman arrive to fix a leaky faucet. As

> the repairman prepared to leave, he said, "I can tell you've
> been around black people a lot, haven't you?" Since the
> ATCK had grown up in Africa, she had to agree, but asked,
> "Why do you say that?" He replied, "Because you're com-
> fortable with me being here. A lot of white people aren't."
> And she was surprised because she hadn't been thinking
> about racial relationships at all. To her, they had simply
> been talking about fixing faucets and paying the bill.

TCKs who use their cross-cultural experiences well learn there is always a reason behind anyone's behavior—no matter how mystifying it appears—and may be more patient than others might be in a particular situation to try to understand what is going on.

> When ATCK Anne-Marie returned to Mali as a United Na-
> tions worker, she heard other expatriates complaining that
> the Malians who worked in the local government hospital
> never planned ahead. The medicine, oxygen, or other vital
> commodities were always completely gone before anyone re-
> ported that it was time to reorder. This had caused endless
> frustration for the UN workers.
>
> While listening to the usual grumbling during morning
> tea one day soon after she arrived, Anne-Marie interrupted
> the flow of complaints. "I understand your annoyance," she
> said, "but did it ever occur to you what it's like to be so
> poor you can only worry about each particular day's needs?
> If you haven't got enough money for today, you certainly
> aren't worrying about storing up for tomorrow."

Of all the gifts we hear TCKs say they have received from their backgrounds, the richness and breadth of diversity among those they truly count as friends is one they consistently mention among the greatest.

CHALLENGE: MORE PREJUDICE

Unfortunately, however, there are a few TCKs who appear to become *more* prejudiced rather than less. There may be several reasons for this. Perhaps it is because historically many TCKs' parents were part of what others considered a special, elite group (such as diplomats or high-ranking military personnel) in the host country. The parent's position often brought special deference, and the children had little contact with the local population outside of servants in the home or the drivers who took them to school or shopping. In such situations, a sense of entitlement and superiority over the host nationals can easily grow.

The movie *Empire of the Sun* gives a clear picture of what this privileged lifestyle has been for some TCKs. The story opens with the scene of a young British lad being driven home from school in the back seat of a chauffeured limousine while he stares uncaringly out the windows at starving Chinese children on the streets. As he enters his home, the young man begins to order the Chinese servants around as if they were his slaves.

One day all is changed. When the British boy tries to tell the maid what to do, she runs up and slaps him. The revolution has come, and years of suppressed bitterness at his treatment of her erupt. It takes World War II and several years of incarceration in a concentration camp before this TCK finally understands that the world is not completely under his control.

While this may seem like an exaggeration in today's world, when adults from any expatriate community constantly speak poorly of the host culture residents in their presence, TCKs can pick up the same disdain and thereby waste one of the richest parts of their heritage.

Decisiveness: The Importance of Now versus the Delusion of Choice

BENEFIT: THE IMPORTANCE OF NOW

Because their lifestyle is transitory, many TCKs have a sense of urgency that life is to be lived *now*. They may not stop to deliberate long on any particular decision because the chance to climb Mt. Kilimanjaro will be gone if new orders to move come through. Do it now. Seize the day! Sushi is on the menu at the shop around the corner today. Better try it while you can. Some may fault them for impulsiveness, but they do get a lot of living done while others are still deciding what they do or don't want to do.

CHALLENGE: THE DELUSION OF CHOICE

For the same reason that some TCKs seize every opportunity, other TCKs seem, ironically, to have difficulty in making or feeling excited about plans at all. So often in the past their desires and intentions to do such things as act in a school play, run for class office, or be captain of the soccer team were denied when Dad or Mom came home one day and said, "Well, I just received orders today; we are shipping out to Portsmouth in two weeks." No matter how much the TCKs thought they could choose what they wanted to do at school or in the neighborhood, it turned out that they had no choice at all. They weren't going to be there for the next school year or soccer season after all. Off they went, their dreams vanishing. In Portsmouth, or wherever their next post was, the TCKs asked themselves, "Why even make plans for what I want to do? I'll just have to leave again."

These preempted plans can lead to what some mental health professionals call a "delusion of choice." In other words, a choice to act is offered ("Would you like to run for class president next year?"), but circumstances or the intervention of others arbitrarily eliminates that choice ("Pack your bags; we're leaving tomorrow."). Reality for many TCKs is feeling choiceless. The achievement of a goal, the development of a relationship, or the completion of a project can be cut short by an unexpected event or the decision of a personnel director.

For some TCKs, decision making has an almost superstitious dimension. "If I allow myself to make a decision and start taking the necessary steps to see it through, something will happen to stop what I want." For others, this delusion of choice is wrapped in a theological dimension. "If God finds out what I really want, he'll take it away from me." Rather than be disappointed, they refuse to acknowledge to themselves, let alone to others or to God, what they would like to do.

Other TCKs and ATCKs have difficulty in making a choice that involves a significant time commitment because they know a new and more desirable possibility may always appear. Signing a contract to teach in Middleville might be a wise economic move, but what if a job opportunity opens in Surabaya next week? It's hard to choose one thing before knowing all the choices. Experience has taught them that life not only offers multiple options, but these options can appear suddenly and must be acted on quickly or they will be gone. Yet the very fact that one choice might preclude another keeps them from making any choice at all.

Chronically waiting until the last minute to plan rather than risking disappointment or having to change plans can be particularly frustrating for spouses or children waiting for decisions to be made that will affect the entire family. Adult TCKs also may miss significant school, job, or career opportunities. It becomes such a habit to wait that they never follow through on leads or fill out necessary forms by the deadline.

One of the most disabling outcomes of this delusion of choice is that it can lead some TCKs and ATCKs to take on a *victim mentality*. They may fuss or complain bitterly about their circumstances, but seem unable to make the choices necessary to extricate themselves from the situation or change things even when they could. No matter what others may suggest to ameliorate the circumstances, the ATCKs always have a reason that person's suggestion won't work. Perhaps this is another way of avoiding one more disappointment in life. "If you don't hope, then you can't be disappointed." It may also be that with choice comes responsibility, with the internal message "If you don't try, you can't fail." It's simply safer not to try than to risk disappointment or failure. For whatever reason, this place of being seemingly unable to make even the simplest choice to begin to change unwanted circumstances is a sad reality for some ATCKs we have met.

Relation to Authority: Appreciative versus Mistrustful

BENEFIT: APPRECIATIVE OF AUTHORITY

For some TCKs, living within the friendly confines of a strong organizational system is a positive experience in their lives. Relationships with adults in their community are basically constructive and nurturing. There may be almost a cocoon atmosphere on their military base, or embassy, business, or mission compound. The sense of structure under such strong leadership gives a feeling of great security. This world is safe. The struggles of others in the world can be shut out at least for some time and perks such as generators, special stores, and paid vacations are all part of a wonderful package deal. As adults, they look back on their TCK childhood and those who supervised their lives with nothing but great fondness.

CHALLENGE: MISTRUSTFUL OF AUTHORITY

Other ATCKs and TCKs feel quite differently. For all the reasons (and maybe more) mentioned under "The Delusion of Choice," they begin to mistrust the authority figures in their lives, easily blaming virtually all of their problems in life on parents or organizational administrators who made autocratic decisions about where and when they would move with little regard for their needs or the needs of their family. One of them told us,

> My parents finally got divorced when Mom said she wouldn't make one more move. The company had moved my dad to a new position every two years. Each time we went to a different place, even different countries—sometimes in the middle of the school year, sometimes not. My mom could see how it was affecting us children as well as herself. We would finally start to find our own places within the new group when it was time to move again. Mom asked Dad to talk to the managers of his company and request they leave us in one place while we went through high school at least. They

said they couldn't do it as they were amalgamating their headquarters and the office in our town was being phased out. Dad didn't want to find a new job, and Mom wouldn't move, so they got divorced. I've always been angry about both my Dad's decision and the company's.

In the end, some TCKs who have had their life unhappily affected because of decisions made by others tell us they will starve before risking the possibility that the direction of their lives will be so profoundly affected once more by the decision of someone in authority over them.

Arrogance: Real versus Perceived

At times, the very richness of their background creates a new problem for TCKs. Once, after a seminar, a woman came up to Dave Pollock and said, "There's one issue you failed to talk about tonight and it's the very thing that almost ruined my life. It was my arrogance."

Unfortunately, *arrogance* isn't an uncommon word when people describe TCKs or ATCKs. It seems the very awareness that helps TCKs view a situation from multiple perspectives can also make TCKs impatient or arrogant with others who only see things from their own perspective—particularly people from their home culture. This may happen for several reasons.

1. *A cross-cultural lifestyle is so normal to them that TCKs themselves don't always understand how much it has shaped their view of the world.* They easily forget it's their life experiences that have been different from others', not their brain cells, and do consider themselves much more cosmopolitan and just plain smarter, or at least more globally aware, than others.
2. *This impatience or judgmentalism can sometimes serve as a point of identity with other TCKs.* It becomes one of the markers of "us" versus "them." It's often easy for a get-together of TCKs to quickly degenerate into bashing the stupidity of non-TCKs. The irony is that the TCKs are then doing unto others what they don't like having done unto themselves—equating ignorance with stupidity.

Sometimes TCKs and ATCKs appear arrogant because they have chosen a permanent identity as being "different" from others.

Todd, an ATCK, was angry. His parents could do no right. His sponsoring organization had stupid policies, and his American peers ranked among the dumbest souls who had ever been born. Todd castigated everyone and everything. Mark, his good friend, finally got tired of the tirades and pointed out the pride and arrogance coming out in his words.

"You know, Todd," Mark said, "it's your experiences that have been different—not your humanity. I think if you try, you might discover you are not as different from the rest of the world as you seem to feel. You know, you're a normal person."

At that, Todd fairly jumped out of his chair. "The last thing I want to be is 'normal.' That idea is nauseating to me."

This "I'm different from you" type of identity is often a defense mechanism to protect against unconscious feelings of insecurity or inferiority. It is another expression of the "screamer" we have discussed. But a "different from" identity has a certain arrogance attached to it. TCKs often use it to put other people down as a way to set themselves apart or boost their sense of self-worth. "I don't care if you don't accept me, because you could never understand me anyway." TCKs chalk up any rejection they feel or interpersonal problems they have to being different, rather than taking a look to see if they themselves might have added to this particular problem.

At other times, however, what is labeled as arrogance in TCKs is simply an attempt to share their normal life experiences. People who don't understand their background may feel the TCKs are bragging or name dropping when they speak of places they have been or people they have met. Non-TCK friends don't realize TCKs have no other stories to tell.

And sometimes there may be a mix of both real and perceived arrogance. The conviction or passion with which TCKs speak because of what they have seen and/or experienced makes them seem dogmatic and overly sure of their opinions. Is that arrogance? It's hard to know.

Lessons from the TCK Petri Dish

CCKs of all backgrounds tell us how they have learned to play the appropriate role for whichever cultural community they are in, often changing roles as needed. They also know what it means for others to make false assumptions about who they are when they are defined by their appearance or traditional models of "diversity," which miss the hidden diversity created by their life experiences. We look next at the benefits that McCaig also referred to that can develop into true life skills.

CHAPTER 8

Practical Skills

> One day I poured out my bitter complaints to a senior mis-
> sionary. I could not understand why the mission imported
> thirty Canadian and U.S. young people to do famine work,
> when not one of the more than fifteen resident MKs [mis-
> sionary kids]—experienced in language and culture—had
> been asked to help. He told me to quit complaining and sign
> on. I did.[1]
>
> —Andrew Atkins

THE FEELINGS ANDREW EXPRESSES REFLECT the fact that growing up as a TCK not only increases an inner awareness of our cultur- ally diverse world, but the experience also helps in the development of useful personal skills for interacting with and in it. Some of these characteristics are acquired so naturally they aren't recognized, acknowledged, or effectively used—either by ATCKs or others—as the special gifts they are. At the same time, some of the skills also have a flip side, where a skill becomes a liability, as we will see in the discussion of social and linguistic skills in this chapter.

Cross-Cultural Skills

As TCKS have the opportunity not only to observe a great variety of cultural practices but also to learn what some of the underlying assumptions are behind them, they often develop strong cross-cultural skills. More significant than the ease with which they can change from chopsticks to forks for eating, or from bowing to shaking hands while greeting, is their ability to be sensitive to the more hidden aspects or deeper levels of culture and to work successfully in these areas. For ATCKs who go into international or intercultural careers, this ability to be a bridge between different groups of people can be useful in helping their company or organization speak with a more human voice in the local community and be more sensitive to the dynamics of potentially stressful situations in the international work environment.

> Nancy Ackley Ruth, an ATCK who is a highly sought cross-cultural trainer, conducts seminars called "The Added Value of TCKs in the Workplace." In these seminars, she tells of a situation where a corporation wanted to branch out and begin doing business internationally. The CEO in the United States set up a conference call with potential new partners in the Middle East. When the potential partners did not join the call at the appointed time, he became frustrated. Next, his impatience could barely be contained when they at last joined the call but began what he termed "chitchat"—each one asking about the other's family, the weather, and so on. Finally, the CEO could take it no longer and interrupted the conversation to remind them that there was only a half hour left to do their business.
>
> The voices on the other end of the call became strangely quiet as the CEO tried to proceed. A junior partner, Tom, sitting beside the CEO passed him a note that read, "You may not realize it but you *were* doing business. In that part of the world, relationships must be established before business deals can be done."
>
> In the end, the CEO almost lost the contract. It was only when Tom, who was an ATCK, urged the CEO to visit these potential business partners in person and to take him along as cultural interpreter that the business deal got back on track.[2]

Perhaps it's obvious from this story why an ATCK's experience in very different cultures and places around the world can be helpful in the global workforce. ATCKs also often find themselves particularly qualified not only for the corporate world, but for jobs or situations such as teaching or mentoring. In these days when developing "global awareness" among education majors is a major emphasis in universities, ATCKs who go into this field are already well equipped in this area.

> When a magazine for teachers asked ATCK Fran to write on global awareness in the classroom, she happily wrote about all the TCKs and other CCKs the teachers needed to consider as a hidden diversity among their students. After all, she had been doing many seminars on how teachers needed to realize those around the globe had come to them, particu-

larly in the form of CCKs. Fran worked hard and sent it in
to the magazine.

The editor didn't reply for a few days. When she did
e-mail back, she said, "I'm sorry, but we didn't want you
to write about the students; we wanted you to write about
global awareness in the classroom."

Fran, of course, thought she had! In the end, she had
to enlist the help of her copy-editor friend, Sally, who was
born and bred in the U.S., to help her understand what it
was the magazine wanted. When Sally explained that they
wanted to emphasize how it was good for teachers to travel
so they could begin to understand that others had different outlooks, or to see the sights they were going to teach
about, Fran had to laugh at herself. Talk about a cultural
misunderstanding! She and the editor used the same words
with totally different understandings of what they meant.
If worldview is the lens through which we see and interpret the world, then it was apparent they had two different lenses. Fran realized what they were asking for was
so basic to her as part of her life experience that it hadn't
occurred to her it was something teachers would have to
learn!

Why is it that this innate global awareness can be such an asset to ATCKs
in a profession such as teaching? First, it helps them understand the students
better. The fact that most TCKs have attended schools with a wide variety of
cultural learning and teaching styles gives them firsthand insight into their students' struggles with language, spelling, and conceptual differences, whether
those students are from a local ethnic subculture or have lived in another country. ATCKs, of all people, should be willing to allow for differences in thinking,
writing, learning, and language styles.

Second, ATCKs can well use their 3-D view of the world. They have firsthand
stories to augment the facts presented in geography or social studies textbooks.
They may be able to bring life to the textbook's chapter on how the Netherlands
reclaimed its land from the sea because they have walked on those dikes. Maybe
they have seen the prison cells in the Philippines where American and Filipino
POWs were held during World War II. From whatever countries where they have
lived or traveled, ATCKs can bring their students fresh and personalized ways of
looking at the world.

Most ATCKs have gone to school in places where there were a large variety
of races and cultures in their classrooms. As teachers, ATCKs can bring a vital
understanding in helping their students see how they share common feelings and
humanity with their peers from various backgrounds, even when circumstances
may differ.

> Nilly Venezia, an ATCK who is founder and director of
> Venezia Institute for Differences and Multiculturalism,
> works with both Jewish and Palestinian children in the Gaza
> Strip. She has designed storybooks for children to help her
> students focus on their shared humanity rather than the
> political issues in their environment. The stories may be set
> in different cultural or geographical places reflecting where
> the students come from, but the focus will be one that all
> students can relate to, such as the fear of a bully, visiting
> Grandma's home, or sharing jokes with friends. Nilly be-
> lieves that "emotions are the universal language" and that if
> we can help children connect in areas where they are alike,
> we can go a long way to establishing positive connections
> between very different groups.[3]

Because of their own experiences, TCKs and ATCKs can be effective mentors for new students coming to their school or community from different countries or cultures or even other parts of their own country. They know what it is
like to be the new kid on the block and how painful it can be if no one reaches
out to a newcomer and, conversely, how wonderful it is when someone does. In
so many areas, they can effectively help others settle in more quickly—and less
traumatically—than might happen otherwise.

Sometimes TCKs can be connectors or mediators between groups that are
stereotypically prejudiced against one another.

> Francisco is a black Panamanian TCK. At age six, he moved
> to the United States while his stepfather pursued a military
> career. Initially, Francisco lived in the predominantly white
> culture in the community surrounding the army base. Here
> he learned firsthand the shock of being the target of racist
> slurs and attacks. Later his parents moved and he went to
> a more racially diverse high school where he became a cha-
> meleon who apparently fit perfectly into the African Ameri-
> can community. Eventually most of his friends saw him as
> Francisco and forgot, if they ever knew, that his roots were
> not the same as theirs.
>
> One day, however, a heated discussion erupted among
> his black friends about why "foreigners" shouldn't be al-
> lowed into the country. Finally, Francisco spoke up and said,
> "You know, guys, what you're saying about them, you're
> saying about me. I'm not a citizen either. But foreigners
> have flesh and blood like me—and like you." Then Francisco
> pointed out how this kind of group stereotyping was why
> he and they as black people had known prejudice. Francisco
> reminded them that he—their personal friend, a foreigner—

was living proof that people of all backgrounds, races, colors, and nationalities were just that—people, not statistics or embodiments of other people's stereotypes.

Observational Skills

TCKs may well develop certain skills because of the basic human instinct for survival. Sometimes through rather painful means, they have learned that particularly in cross-cultural situations it pays to be a careful observer of what's going on around them and then try to understand the reasons for what they are seeing.

> One TCK received the "nerd for life" award when, on his first day of school "at home," he carried his books in a brand new attaché case—just like the one his dad took to work. The attaché served a most utilitarian purpose—keeping books together in an easily transportable manner. But in this new school, a backpack slung over one shoulder (and one shoulder only) served the same purpose in a far more socially acceptable manner.

Through such experiences, TCKs learn firsthand that in any culture these unwritten rules govern everyone's acceptance or rejection in a new setting. In addition, they have seen how behavior unnoticed in one place may cause deep offense in another. Something as seemingly insignificant as raising a middle finger or pointing at another person with your chin can have vastly different meanings depending on the culture. Mistakes in conscious and unconscious social rules—whether eating style, greetings, or methods of carrying schoolbooks—often send an unwanted message to people in the new culture. Observing carefully and learning to ask "How does life work here?" before barging ahead are other skills TCKs can use to help themselves or others relate more effectively in different cultures.

> Mariella, a German ATCK who had grown up in India, took a job working for an NGO hospital in Ghana. It wasn't long before she heard complaints from the expatriate staff that the patients often threw their prescriptions away immediately after exiting the doctor's office. That seemed odd to her as well, so Mariella began investigating.
>
> She soon noticed that when the new doctor from Germany dispensed these prescriptions, he always sat sideways at the desk. The patients were on the doctor's left side as he wrote notes on their charts using his right hand. Whenever the doctor finished writing the prescription, he would pick it up with his free left hand and give it to the patient.

This process probably would not have caused a second thought in Germany, but Mariella knew from her childhood in India that there the left hand is considered unclean because it is the one used for dirty tasks. Giving someone anything with that hand is both an insult and a statement that the object being offered is worthless. She wondered if that might be the case in Ghana as well and asked her new Ghanaian friends about this. When their replies confirmed her suspicion that using the left hand in Ghana had the same connotation as she remembered from her childhood in India, Mariella understood why the patients didn't fill the prescriptions! She suggested the doctor turn his desk around so all the patients sat at his right and that way he would naturally give out the prescriptions in a culturally appropriate manner. He followed her advice and the problem disappeared.

Social Skills

In certain ways, learning to live with the repetitive change that often characterizes their lifestyle gives many TCKs and ATCKs a great sense of inner confidence and strong feelings of self-reliance. While not always liking change—and sometimes even hating it—TCKs do expect to cope with new situations. Many have moved in and among various cultural worlds so often that, while they may not know every detail of the local culture, they can see beyond that to the humanity of the people in front of them.

When commentators marveled at the ease with which President Obama connected with various racial and social groups throughout his 2008 presidential campaign, it seemed they had no comprehension how his TCK/CCK childhood had shaped him to enable him to move with ease across these traditional boundary lines. His story transcends not only typical racial boundaries but also economic, social, and cultural boundaries. Growing up as the son of a single mom who needed food stamps at one point, moving to Indonesia with his mother and stepfather where he attended the local schools with Indonesian children, going with his mother to the local American Embassy on weekends to eat hamburgers with other Americans, and returning to the mixed cultural milieu of Hawaii and his white grandparents all formed in him this comfortableness of moving into various communities with

ease. It allowed him to ascend to the heights of the social
ladder during his time as a law student at Harvard but then
return to the inner city of Chicago to be a community organizer. This type of fluidity to move and function with quiet
confidence in various cultural worlds is common for many
TCKs—even those not running for president!

It seems many TCKs and ATCKs can also generally approach various changes
in their life circumstances with some degree of confidence because past experience has taught them that given enough time, they will make friends and learn
the new culture's ways. This sense that they'll be able to manage new situations—
even when they can't always count on others to be physically present to help in a
crisis—often gives them the security to go take risks others might not take.

This type of confidence comes out in various ways. It may involve believing
you are able to work with others to solve the world's problems or it may manifest
in simpler ways. Helga, a Belgian ATCK, planned to go alone on a five-week trip
to Australia and New Zealand. Some friends were shocked.

"Do you know anyone there?" they asked.
"Not yet," she replied.
"Well, how can you just go? Aren't you scared to stay
with people you don't know? How will you find them at the
airport? What kind of food will you eat?"
Actually, she hadn't thought of it. She'd just presumed
one way or another it would all work out. As a teenager
and university student, she'd often traveled halfway around
the world alone to see her parents during school vacations.
Customs and language barriers were no longer intimidating.
Lost luggage could be dealt with. She had a great time.

But there is a flip side to this type of confidence as well. While TCKs develop
feelings of confidence in many areas of life, there are other times or situations in
which they may be so fearful of making mistakes they are almost paralyzed. Paul,
the American TCK who grew up in Australia whom we mentioned earlier, moved
once more as a teenager—a critical age when peer approval is essential. Here's
what he said about that move.

I changed worlds once more at age fourteen when my dad's
company moved him from Australia to Indonesia. But the
consequence of switching worlds at that age is you can't
participate in the social scene. Everyone else seems to know
the rules except you. You stand at the edge, and you shut
up and listen, mostly to learn, but you can't participate. You
only sort of participate—not as an initiator, but as a weak
supporter in whatever goes on—hoping that whatever you

do is right and flies okay. You're always double-checking and making sure.

Just as true chameleons move slowly while constantly checking which color they should be to blend into each new environment, so TCKs can appear to be socially slow while trying to figure out the operative rules in their new situations. To avoid looking foolish or stupid, they retreat from these situations in such ways as overemphasizing academics or withdrawing in extreme shyness. Even those who have been extremely social in one setting may refuse to join group activities in the next place because they have no idea how to do what everyone else already can. Maybe they have returned home to Sweden from a tropical climate and have never learned to ice skate, toboggan, or ski. They would rather not participate at all than let anyone know of their incompetence.

Insecurity in a new environment can make TCKs withdraw even in areas where they have knowledge or talent. It's one thing to join the choir in a relatively small international school overseas, but quite another to volunteer when you are suddenly in a school of 3,000 students. Who knows what might be expected? Who knows how many others are better than you? And so the TCK holds back to wait and watch, even when it might be possible to be involved.

While these TCKs are trying to figure out the new rules and if or where they might jump in, people around them wonder why they are holding back. If the TCKs do jump into the fray, it's easy for them to make "dumb" mistakes and be quickly labeled as social misfits. This can lead to another problem. Because TCKs often don't feel a sense of belonging, they can, as did both Paul as mentioned in this chapter and Ginny in chapter 7, quickly identify with others who don't fit in. Unfortunately, this is often the group that is in trouble with the school administration or one in which scholastic achievement is disdained. Later, if the TCKs want to change and make friends with those more interested in academic success, it may be difficult because they have already been labeled as part of the other group.

Linguistic Skills

Acquiring fluency in more than one language is potentially one of the most useful life skills a cross-cultural upbringing can give TCKs. Children who learn two or more languages early in life, and use these languages on a day-to-day basis, develop a facility and ease with language unlike those who learn a second language for the first time as teenagers or adults.

Bilingualism and multilingualism have advantages besides the obvious one of communicating with various groups of people. For instance, Jeannine Heny, an English professor, believes learning different languages early in life can sharpen thinking skills in general and actually help children achieve academically above their grade level.[4] Learning the grammar of one language can strengthen grammatical understanding in the next one.

Strong linguistic skills also have practical advantages as the TCK becomes an adult. Some careers are only available to people fluent in two or more languages. One American ATCK works for a large international company as a Japanese/English translator. She learned Japanese while growing up and attending local schools in a small town in Japan. Another American ATCK works as an international broadcaster using the Hausa language he learned as a child in Nigeria.

Even if a career isn't directly involved with language, opportunities to take jobs in certain countries may require language acquisition. There's no doubt that a job applicant who already speaks the country's language will see his or her resume land a lot closer to the top of the pile than those who will have to spend a year in language school. Even when the language required isn't one the ATCK already knows, the fact that he or she is obviously adept at learning more than one language improves job opportunities as well.

Along with the many advantages, though, there are some precautions to take in a multiple language environment. Speaking another language, and knowing it well enough to think in it, are not the same, and that difference can be critical. During a seminar in Asia where many of the expatriates were in cross-cultural marriages, this issue of multiple languages in the home came up. Teachers from an international school told the following tale.

> A few years ago, we had three children from the same family arrive at our school. To be honest, we thought they were all developmentally delayed. They spoke adequate English but something didn't seem quite right. We eventually discovered that their parents were from two different cultures and neither of them spoke one another's mother tongue, so the family used English at home. Unfortunately, the parents' English wasn't very good, and therefore their children had never experienced any language deeply enough to think in. Once the children were in an environment where they could learn language for concepts as well as facts, they did well in school.

The teachers who told this story commended the parents on teaching their children several languages and agreed that most children could learn them simultaneously. Their one caution, however, was to remind the parents that children need to learn in at least one language deeply enough and richly enough to think in it.

Children who learn one language well can often go on to learn others at a very deep level. However, when learning a new language as an adult, the thinking process of our mother language often superimposes itself on the second language, which makes learning the new language more difficult. It also inhibits us from fully understanding the thinking patterns of those who use that language. When children learn languages, they instinctively pick up the nuances of how people in that culture think and relate to one another. Adults often translate word for word and never gain an understanding of how the same word may have a different implication in another language. Ironically, however, learning the nuances for certain words in their adopted language can sometimes keep TCKs from fully understanding the nuances of the translation of that same word in their mother tongue. This happened to JoAnna.

> For years, American friends of ATCK JoAnna told her that she was the most guilt-ridden person they'd ever met. No matter what happened—if a glass fell out of someone's hand, a friend lost her notebook, or someone bit his lip—JoAnna always said "Sorry."
>
> The instantaneous answer always came back. "What are you sorry for? You didn't do anything."
>
> JoAnna's equally instantaneous reply was also always the same. "I know I didn't do anything. I'm just sorry."
>
> For years this exchange was a point of significant frustration for both JoAnna and her friends. She couldn't get out of the habit of saying sorry and her friends couldn't get over being irritated by it. None of them understood the impasse.
>
> When she was in her forties, JoAnna went to live in Kenya for a year. During a hike in the woods with Pamela, another American, Pamela said, "I'll be glad when I get back to the States where everyone doesn't say 'sorry' all the time."
>
> JoAnna asked why that was a problem.
>
> "It drives me crazy," Pamela said. "No matter what happens, everyone rushes around and says, *Pole, pole sana* (which means 'Sorry, very sorry'). But most of the time there's nothing to apologize for."
>
> For the first time, JoAnna understood her lifelong problem with the word "sorry." For Pamela, a U.S. citizen, "sorry" was primarily an apology. She had never realized in this African context that people were expressing sympathy and empathy rather than apologizing when they used that word. For JoAnna, in the African language she had learned as a child, and in the two she had learned as an adult, "sorry" was used as both an apology and as an expression of sympathy. It had never occurred to her that "sorry" was only an apology word to most listeners using American English. No wonder she and her American friends had misunderstood each other. They weren't speaking the same language!

Although the linguistic gifts for TCKs are primarily positive ones, there are a few pitfalls to be aware of. These include being limited in any one language, becoming a "creative speller," and losing fluency and depth in the child's native language. As we saw in chapter 4 with Ilpö, no matter how bright the child is, the specialized terminology needed for studying medicine (or fixing cars, discussing computers, studying science, etc.) may be missing if someone is working in many languages. Ultimately, he or she may never have time to learn the more specialized meanings and usage of each. JoAnna's story demonstrates how idiomatic expressions or non-literal meanings of common words can also cause confusion in such situations.

Interestingly enough, it's not simply those who work or study in entirely different languages who may find themselves linguistically challenged. Perhaps for the very reason it seems so minor, TCKs who speak and write English find it very difficult to keep American and English spelling straight. Is it *color* or *colour? Behavior* or *behaviour? Pediatrician* or *paediatrician?* Even worse, how do you remember if it's *criticise* or *criticize* when *criticism* is spelled the same everywhere? While this may seem a minor irritation, it can become a major problem when, for example, a British student transfers to a school in the United States (or an American-based school in another country), where teachers may not be sensitive to this issue.

These differences in spelling provide a special challenge to schools everywhere that have a mix of nationalities among their students. Many solve the problem by keeping both an English and American dictionary available to check on the variations that come in on assigned papers. With a sense of humor, an understanding teacher, or a spell checker appropriate for the current country, most TCKs weather this particular challenge successfully.

The most serious problem related to learning multiple languages at an early age, however, is that some people never become proficient in their supposed mother tongue—the language of their family roots and personal history. Among TCKs, this occurs most often among those who come from non-English speaking countries but attend international schools overseas where classes are predominantly taught in English. Fortunately, schools like the International School of the Hague have begun developing some very strong programs to help students maintain fluency in their mother tongue, but many schools do not yet offer such programs. When that is a boarding school with little home (and thus language) contact for months at a time, language can become a major issue when the TCK returns to his or her parents, with the supposed mother tongue becoming almost a foreign language. Families whose members lack fluency in a common language by which they can express emotions and profound ideas lose one critical tool for developing close, intimate relationships.

> Kwabena is a Ghanaian TCK who faced the problem of
> never gaining fluency in his parents' languages. His father
> was from the Ga tribe, his mother from the Anum tribe.
> Kwabena was born in predominantly English-speaking

Liberia, where his father worked for several years. Eventually, the family moved to Mali, where French was the official language. The family could only make occasional visits back to the parents' villages in Ghana, where his grandparents spoke only the local languages. By the time Kwabena reached his teens, he sadly realized he could never talk to his grandparents and ask for the family stories all children love to hear because he couldn't speak enough of their language and they couldn't speak the English, French, or Malian languages he knew.

Most TCKs we know, however, count the benefits of having facility in two or more languages as another of their greatest practical blessings. What is more, it's just plain fun to watch a group of ATCKs at an international school reunion suddenly break into the greetings or farewells of the language they all learned in some far away land during their youth. At that moment, language becomes one more marker of all they have shared in the world that now may seem invisible to them. It reminds them of the depth of experience and life they do, in fact, share with others of their "tribe."

Lessons from the TCK Petri Dish

The more we have heard from other groups of CCKs, the more we realize how frequently the practical skills learned in their interactions with many cultures during childhood have been overlooked. Often the majority culture is oblivious to the cross-cultural skills the child of a minority is using each day simply to succeed in school. Surely children in refugee camps learn great observation skills related to determining when it is safe to venture forth or not. Looking at the specifics of the TCK experience helps us to recognize similar abilities that other CCKs develop so naturally from their life experiences that they, and others, often don't realize the assets they have. Now we move on to two challenges TCKs and other CCKs often face: rootlessness and restlessness.

CHAPTER 9

Rootlessness and Restlessness

Being a TCK has given me a view of the world as my home and a confidence in facing new situations and people, particularly of other countries and cultures. However, it has its negative side [because] Americans and foreigners have a problem relating to me, for I am not a typical American! The hardest question still to answer is where I am from. What is my place of origin?[1]

—Response to an ATCK survey

WHILE THIS WRITER OBVIOUSLY ENJOYED THE TYPE OF confidence a TCK childhood can foster, he or she also brings up two very common characteristics TCKs often share—a deep sense of rootlessness and restlessness. These are such key aspects of the TCK Profile that they deserve a chapter of their own.

Rootlessness

There are several questions many TCKs have learned to dread. Among them are these two: "Where are you from?" and "Where is home?"

WHERE ARE YOU FROM?

Why should anyone dread such a seemingly simple question? Consider Erika again.

Like most other TCKs, when Erika hears that question, her internal computer starts the search mode. *What does this person mean by "from"? Is he asking my nationality? Or maybe it's "Where were you born?" Does he mean "Where are you living now?" or "Where did you come from today?" Or does he mean "Where do your parents live now?" or "Where did you grow up?" Actually, does he even understand what a complicated question he asked me or care? Is he simply asking a polite, "Let's make conversation about something while we stand here with shrimp on our plates" question, or is he really interested?*

Erika decides what to answer by how she perceives the interest of the person who asked or what she does or doesn't feel like talking about. If the new acquaintance seems more polite than interested, or if Erika doesn't want a lengthy conversation, she gives the "safe" answer. During college she simply said, "Wisconsin." Now she replies, "Dayton." It's the "where I'm living now" answer.

If Erika does want to extend the conversation slightly or test out the questioner's true interest, she throws out the next higher level answer: "New York"—still a fairly safe answer. It's where she visited during each home leave and where her family's roots are.

If the person responds with more than a polite, "Oh," and asks another question such as, "Then when did you move to Dayton?" Erika might elevate her reply to a still higher level, "Well, I'm not really from New York, but my parents are." Now the gauntlet is thrown down. If the potential new friend picks up on this and asks, "Well, where are you from then?" the conversation begins and Erika's fascinating life history starts to unfold. Of course, if the newcomer doesn't follow up on that clue and lets the comment go, Erika knows for sure she or he wasn't really interested anyway and moves the conversation on to other topics—or simply drops it altogether.

On days when Erika feels like talking more or wants to make herself stand out from among the crowd, however, she answers the question "Where are you from?" quite differently. "What time in my life are you referring to?" she asks. At this point the other person has virtually no choice but to ask Erika where she has lived during her life and then hear all the very interesting details Erika has to tell!

WHERE IS HOME?

While this question at first seems to be the same as "Where are you from?" it is not. In some cases, TCKs have a great sense of "at-homeness" in their host culture. As long as Erika's parents remained in Singapore, "Where's your home?" was an easier question to answer than "Where are you from?" She simply said, "Singapore." Both her emotional and physical sense of home were the same.

Other TCKs who have lived in one city or house during each leave or furlough may have a strong sense of that place being home. In January 1987, the U.S. ambassador to Ecuador spoke at a conference about TCKs in Quito and said, "I think every expatriate family should buy a home before going abroad so their children will have the same base for every home assignment. My kids feel very strongly that Virginia is home even though they've lived outside the States over half their lives." This is undoubtedly an excellent idea, and one to be seriously considered when at all possible.

When, for various reasons, buying a house in the home country isn't a viable option, some TCKs still develop a strong sense of "home" in other ways. Often TCKs whose parents move every two years rarely consider geography as the determining factor in what they consider home. Instead, home is defined by relationships.

> When Dave Pollock asked Ben, a TCK from the diplomatic community, "Where's your home?" Ben replied, "Egypt."
> Dave was somewhat surprised as he'd not previously heard Ben talk about Egypt, so Dave asked how long he had lived there.
> "Well," Ben replied, "actually, I haven't been to Egypt yet, but that's where my parents are posted now. They moved there from Brazil right after I left for university, so when I go home for Christmas vacation, that's where I'll go."

For some TCKS, however, "Where is home?" is the hardest question of all. *Home* connotes an emotional place—somewhere you truly belong. There simply is no real answer to that question for many TCKs. They may have moved so many times, lived in so many different residences, and attended so many different schools that they never had time to become attached to any. Their parents may be divorced and living in two different countries. Denis tells his story.

> When someone asks me, "Where is your home?" I tell them I don't know and that I don't really have a home. The reason is my parents got divorced when I was one year old and I was a TCK with my mother. My mother is originally from

Taiwan but she now lives in London. "Home" should be where my mom is, but she moved to a new country after I stopped living with her. London isn't home. My father has lived in Switzerland for about thirty years now; I could call that home but I can't because I've lived with him for about one year total. My conclusion is that home is where I currently am. So now my home is Luzern, Switzerland, even though I don't speak a word of German and I've only been here for eight months.

Some TCKs have spent years in boarding schools and no longer feel a close attachment to their parents. In fact, they may feel more emotionally at home at boarding school than when thinking of their parents' home. Paul Seaman writes,

> "Home" might refer to the school dormitory or to the house where we stayed during the summer, to our family's home where our parents worked, or, more broadly, to the country of our citizenship. And while we might have some sense of belonging to all of these places, we felt fully at home in none of them. Boarding life seemed to have the most consistency, but there we were separated from our siblings and shared one "parent" with other kids. As it grew colder, we could look forward to going home for the holidays. We were always eager to be reunited with our families, but after three months of separation from our friends, we were just as eager to go back. Every time we got on the train, we experienced both abandonment and communion.[2]

No matter how home is defined in terms of a physical place, the day comes for many TCKs when they realize it is irretrievably gone. For whatever reasons, they, like Erika, can never "go home." Now when someone asks Erika where her home is, she simply says, "Everywhere and nowhere." She has no other answer.

Restlessness—The Migratory Instinct

In the end, many TCKs develop a *migratory instinct* that controls their lives. Along with their chronic rootlessness is a feeling of restlessness: "Here, where I am today, is temporary. But as soon as I finish my schooling, get a job, or purchase a home, I'll settle down." Somehow the settling down never quite happens. The present is never enough—something always seems lacking. An unrealistic attachment to the past, or a persistent expectation that the next place will finally be home, can lead to this inner restlessness that keeps the TCK always moving.

Inika had waited for what seemed like forever to return to her host country, Guatemala. She finally found a job that offered her the prospect of staying there for many years, possibly even until she retired. Two weeks after arriving, however, Inika felt a wave of panic. For the first time in her life, there was no defined end point. Now she had to be involved with the good and bad of whatever happened in this community. She wondered why she felt like this so soon after reaching her goal. Then she realized that throughout her life, no matter where she had lived, any time things got messy (relationships with a neighbor, zoning fights in the town, conflicts at church), internally she had leapfrogged over them. There was always an end point ahead when she knew she would be gone—the end of school, the end of home leave, or something. Suddenly, that safety net had disappeared. For the first time in her life Inika either had to engage completely in the world around her or start forming another plan to leave.

Obviously, it is good to be ready to move when a career choice mandates it, but to move simply from restlessness alone can have disastrous effects on an ATCK's academic life, career, and family.

Without question, there are legitimate reasons to change colleges or universities. Sometimes TCKs who live a continent away must enroll in a university without having the opportunity to visit beforehand. After arriving, they discover that this school doesn't offer the particular courses or majors they want. Perhaps they change their interest in what career they want to pursue and this school doesn't offer concentrated studies in that field. In such situations, there is no choice but to change. Some TCKs, however, switch schools just because of their inner migratory instinct. Their roommates aren't quite right; the professors are boring; the weather in this place is too hot or too cold. They keep moving on, chronically hoping to find the ideal experience. Unfortunately, frequent transfers can limit what TCKs learn and inhibit the development of their social relationships.

Once through with school (or after dropping out), a TCK who has moved often and regularly may feel it's time to move even when it's not. Some ATCKs can't stay at one job long enough to build any sort of career. Just as they are anticipating a position of new responsibility and growth, that old rolling stone instinct kicks in. They submit their letter of resignation and off they go—again always thinking the next place will be "it."

Sylvia raced through life. In the ten years following her graduation from university, she acquired two master's degrees, had seven career changes, and lived in four countries. One day it struck her that while she had a vast

amount of broad knowledge and experience, her career was
going nowhere. And she wasn't sure she still wanted, or
knew how, to settle down.

Some feel almost an obligation to be far from their parents, siblings, or even
their own children. When it is possible to live closer, these adult TCKs choose not
to. They have spent so much time separated from family that they don't know
how to live in physical proximity—or don't want to. Others, like Bernie, have
learned to deal with interpersonal conflict, including family conflict, by separating from the situation. He said, "I loved growing up with high mobility. Every
time there was a problem, all I had to do was wait and either the people causing
the problem left or I left. I have handled all of my life's conflicts the same way."
Camilla is another example of how this restlessness works.

Camilla, a foreign service ATCK, attended twelve schools in
sixteen years all around the globe. Now, every two years,
an internal clock goes off that says, "This assignment is up.
Time to move." She has changed jobs, houses, cities, and—
twice—husbands in response to that message.

Unfortunately, her migratory instinct has affected Camilla's children. Although she has noticed their insecurities
developing as she perpetually uproots them, Camilla appears powerless to settle down. The overt reason for change
always seems clear. "I don't like the neighborhood we're in,"
or "My boss simply doesn't understand me," or "I have a
nasty landlord." It never occurs to her that she is replaying
a very old tape that says, "No place can ever become permanent; don't get too attached," or "If you have a problem, just
leave." Nor does she realize it might be possible to replace
the old tape with a new one that plays a message that could
serve her better in some of these situations—that she can
also make a choice to stay.

Some TCKs have an opposite response to their highly mobile background.
They have moved so many times, in so many ways, and to so many places, they
swear they will find a place to call their own, put up the white picket fence, and
never, ever, move again. Lakisha, a non-TCK married to an ATCK, told us:

When I met Antwayne, I think I fell in love with his passport as much as I did with him. I was intrigued with all the
places he had been and everything he had seen. I envisioned
a life of worldwide travel and living in all sorts of exotic
places. Unfortunately, I assumed wrong. When my father
surprised us with a lovely bungalow for our wedding present, Antwayne was thrilled. That was the first time he

shared with me how he had always dreamed of finding a place to call his own and settle down. This was it. So I'm still reading my travel magazines and dreaming.

Lessons from the TCK Petri Dish

A few years ago, one ATCK's father came to Ruth and said, "My daughter isn't rootless and restless because she's a TCK. She's rootless and restless because she's part of the Gen X generation." Is that true? If we stop to consider what creates these two characteristics in TCKs, it's not hard to see how it could be happening for countless others in today's world. When a child is biracial, bicultural, and an immigrant and educational CCK all at the same time, where do his roots lie? If another child has moved time and again as a domestic CCK, she can easily develop the same patterns of restlessness for all the same reasons a traditional TCK does. This seems to be another area where lessons learned from the TCK experience can be more fully explored and applied to the broader range of fellow CCKs. Next we take a further look at how the TCK experience, including this rootlessness and restlessness shapes the patterns of TCK relationships.

~~~~~~~~~~~~~~~~~~~~~~~~~~~~~~~~~

CHAPTER 10

Relational Patterns

> Multiple separations tended to cause me to develop deeper
> relationships more quickly. Also, when I was with family or
> friends, we tended to talk about things that matter spiritu-
> ally, emotionally, and so on. I still become impatient with
> [what I see as] superficiality.[1]
>
> —Response to an ATCK survey

R ELATIONSHIPS ARE ANOTHER AREA AFFECTED BY THE
paradoxical nature of the TCK experience. The wealth of friends from so
many places and backgrounds is often beyond measure, yet the chronic
cycles of leaving add so much loss as well.

As we've seen, TCKs often define their sense of rootedness in terms of relationships rather than geography. Because of that, many TCKs will go to greater
lengths than some people might consider normal to nurture relational ties with
others—be they family members, friends with whom the TCKs have shared
boarding school years, or other important members of their third culture community. Unfortunately, the same mobility that creates such bonding can result
in relationships being a source of great conflict and pain as well. The cycle of frequent good-byes inherent in a highly mobile lifestyle can lead TCKs and ATCKs
to develop patterns of self-protection against the further pain of separations that
may affect relationships throughout their lives.

Large Numbers of Relationships

TCKs usually develop a wide range of relationships as they or people around them habitually come and go. New friends enter their lives while old friends become another entry in their burgeoning address books.

"I could travel to almost any country in the world and stay with a friend," Tom bragged after one transition seminar. This may sound like an exaggeration, but for many adult TCKs it's the truth. With friends from their childhood now in countless places, TCKs build a rich international network that is useful for all sorts of things—from finding cheap room and board while traveling to setting up business connections later in life.

The problem with having this many relationships, however, is that eventually they simply can't all be maintained—even on Facebook. Renee learned this the hard way.

> ATCK Renee's list of friends on Facebook grew to over 800 names. Each time she posted her information, many friends replied. She tried to answer each one personally with a short note, but in the end, no matter how hard she tried to keep up, her messages to answer always exceeded the time available to do so. She fell farther and farther behind on individual answers, but presumed her friends would understand she was thinking of them through her general postings.
>
> Then she attended a wedding and met an African friend from her five years in Malawi. When Renee rushed to greet him warmly, his response was exceedingly cool.
>
> "Seems like you've forgotten us," he said.
>
> Renee was dumbfounded. "How can you say that?"
>
> "Well, you haven't called for months, and you don't write us personally anymore. My wife and I have been wondering what we've done to offend you."
>
> Of course, Renee felt terrible that she had hurt her friends, but finally had to accept the sad reality that she wasn't going to be able to keep up with every wonderful person she had ever met—even in today's high-tech age.

Deep and Valued Relationships

Throughout the world, relationships move through various levels of communication as people get to know each other. While there are undoubtedly different ways this happens in various cultures, here is a common pattern for how relationships are established.

1. *Superficial level: This involves conversation generally referred to as "small talk."* How are you? Where are you from? The weather or today's headlines.
2. *"Still safe" level: This is an exchange of no-risk facts.* Where did you go on vacation last year? What sights did you see?
3. *Judgmental level: Here, we begin to risk a few statements about our opinions on politics, religion, or other matters about which our new friend might disagree with us.*
4. *Emotional level: We begin sharing how we feel about life, ourselves, and others* (e.g., that we're sad, glad, worried, or depressed).
5. *Disclosure level: We reveal our most private thoughts and feelings to another person, confessing secret dreams as well as painful failures.* This stage involves an honesty and vulnerability that lead to true intimacy. Most of us only have a few people in our lives with whom we share at this level. Some people have no one to share such a place.

One common complaint from at least Canadian and U.S. American TCKs is that they feel people in their home cultures are "shallow." Conversations with peers seem boring, and the TCKs long for the good old days with their international friends. Why is this such a common complaint?

It has to do with these levels of relationships. People in different cultures not only enter but move through the various levels at different paces. Some cultures jump past the small talk quickly and treat strangers like long-lost cousins, inviting them to stay the night, eat what they want, and come as often as they wish. In other cultures nobody bothers to go next door to say hello to the family that just moved in from who knows where.

For various reasons, TCKs seem prone to passing quickly through levels 1 and 2 and getting immediately into topics that fall into level 3. In other words, while others are still at the "polite" stages, TCKs are offering opinions on and asking what others think about such topics as how the president's term is going, what the government should do on its immigration policy, or whether the United Nations should intervene in some new world crisis. When others either don't seem to care about such things or don't want to express their opinions, TCKs deem them shallow—and who knows what those others think of the TCKs?

Why do TCKs often jump into these at least supposedly deeper levels of communication faster than others? There are a number of reasons. One of these is cultural habit. On an Internet chat group for TCKs, this matter of relational levels became a hot topic of discussion. An interesting response came from a Dutch ATCK, Ard A. Louis, who grew up in Gabon and now lives in New York. He wrote:

> At least among educated Europeans, it's very common to discuss politics or other potentially divisive topics upon a first encounter. In fact, sometimes we look for something to argue about on purpose. Part of being "educated" is being

able to talk about art, philosophy, politics, etc.... and argue
your points if need be.

This is very different with Americans, who seem always
to look for points of common interest. For example, how often when you meet someone do they ask where you're from
and then try to find some point of commonality like "I've
been there" or "Do you know so and so?"

Another very common topic of discussion is pop culture,
especially movies/TV shows most people have seen. (Pop culture is the great unifying factor in the U.S.—and being well
versed in its history helps tremendously in fitting in.) Thus,
a very common first impression of Europeans arriving in
the U.S. is that Americans are superficial because they seem
to have no opinions about even their own political situation,
let alone what's happening in the rest of the world.[2]

Ard's point is that the methods and styles of relating to one another differ
from culture to culture according to cultural habit. When we discuss entering
relationships at a "deeper level," perhaps this is only in comparison to particular
cultures, as Ard discusses in his impression of U.S. culture. In reality, discussing
politics in some cultures may be no closer to true intimacy than talking about
the weather in other cultures. This, of course, calls into question the universality
of how the levels themselves are defined.

Another ATCK recounted how this mix-up of culturally appropriate relationship styles caught him unaware.

I'd never met this Israeli businessman before that evening,
but during supper I asked him how the political situation
in Israel was doing. Another U.S. American, Lisa, who was
also eating with us almost spit out her food and instantly
changed the subject of conversation. When we finished that
new topic and I went back to my original question, Lisa had
the same reaction. Afterwards she told me how horribly
rude I'd been to ask such a question of someone I barely
knew. Frankly, I was stunned. Here was a guy with lots
of information about key world issues and Lisa thought I
shouldn't talk about it. So I asked her why. She told me in
her family you were never allowed to talk about religion or
politics because that always caused trouble and I wondered:
What else would you talk about? Until I heard about these
different levels of communication and personal relationships, I couldn't understand why I shouldn't start with political questions.[3]

There are three other reasons TCKs may jump more quickly than others into what we are calling deeper levels of relationship:

1. *Practice: Many TCKs know how to get into relationships fairly quickly when they want to simply because they have had to start so many.* They have learned to observe the dynamics of a situation, ask questions that can help open a door, hopefully be sensitive to cultural cues of what is or is not appropriate for this group, and respond appropriately when others approach them.
2. *Content: The store of knowledge from the various experiences they have had feeds into many different topics, so they often at least think they have something relevant to say.* Because of their parents' careers, TCKs often grow up in homes where discussions on a current political crisis, starving children, religious views, or solutions to the economic woes of the country are standard fare. To express opinions on these topics is normal and people around them seem interested because the TCK's firsthand insights may help others understand the complexity of issues in the newspaper or on television that are happening an ocean away.
3. *Sense of urgency: TCKs may also jump into deeper levels of communication quickly because there is little time to develop a particular relationship.* They understand that if something doesn't happen now, perhaps it never will. TCKs routinely meet people of incredible diversity who can teach them so much about their part of the world. Why waste time in small talk? In one sense, almost everyone can be an instant friend. Because they have connected at a relatively deep level, many of these quick relationships do become long-term friendships—or at least part of that bulging address book for occasional telephone calls, Facebook list, and yearly letters.

In *Military Brats*, Mary Edwards Wertsch discusses the "forced extroversion" the military lifestyle fosters because time is too short to wait to make friends. She says one technique she used to break into new groups was the "confessional impulse." In quickly spilling family secrets (a level 4 or 5 disclosure), she sent a message that she wanted to invest in a new friendship. Often her confession was met by a mutual confession from the new friend. Wertsch also says that military kids might be more willing to be open than their civilian counterparts because they probably won't be around to deal with any negative consequences from these confessions.[4]

Non-TCKs who are used to staying at the first or second level of relationships for relatively long periods may misread TCKs who jump in at a deeper level. This type of confusion happened at a camp where Dave Pollock served as a seminar leader.

> Several days after camp started, a group of tearful, non-TCK young women sought Dave out. They felt completely

confused by actions of the TCK males. A young man would
engage one of these young women in, to them, deep and
meaningful conversation, and she would think he was interested in her. But the next day he would do the same with
someone else. After three days the young women were confused, angry with each other, and angry at the young men.

When Dave spoke to the guys, they were shocked that
these girls thought they had even considered anything more
than a friendship for this week at camp. The TCK young
men said they had no romantic presuppositions whatsoever.
They just wanted to get to know these young women, find
out what they thought about life, the world, their faith, and
other assorted interesting topics. It seemed like a perfect
chance to understand more about non-TCK Americans. But
the seriousness of the conversation communicated a level of
warmth and relationship that meant something quite different to the young women.

TCKs usually place a high value on their relationships—especially those
from their TCK world. Often the style and intensity of friendship within the international third culture is quite different from the types of friendship they have
in their home country. Most expatriate families live far from relatives and tend
to reach out to one another as surrogate families in times of need. When there is
a coup, it's the friends in this international community who are together in the
fear, the packing, the wondering, and the leaving. Without doubt, a great deal of
bonding that lasts a lifetime takes place at such times.

Relationships—both with friends and family at home as well as with friends
from their third culture world—are also valued because they give the TCKs a
sense of connectedness. These relationships are the one place TCKs can say, "Do
you remember when . . . ?" and someone actually does!

A TCK's wedding is usually quite a sight. When Robin married Kevin, her high school sweetheart from boarding school,
you would have thought you were in Africa rather than in
New York. Papier mâché palm trees framing a painted mural
of a tropical beach decorated the reception hall. Kevin and
his groomsmen all wore flowing robes from Sierra Leone.
Robin's dad wore a country-cloth chief's robe as he walked
her down the aisle. Friends came from far and near, filling the pews with equally colorful attire. The wedding had
turned into a mini-reunion. Watching these TCKs chatter
unceasingly throughout the reception was like watching long-
lost family members reunite. There was no question about
how they viewed their relationships from the past.

Effects of Cycles of Multiple Losses on Relationships

While many TCKs jump into relationships with both feet, others approach any new relationship with caution. In a 1986 survey of 300 ATCKs, 40 percent of the respondents said they struggled with a fear of intimacy because of the fear of loss.[5] Too many close friends have moved away. Frequent, painful good-byes make some TCKs unwilling to risk emotional involvement again.

Often these TCKs are labeled as quiet or shy. They never take available opportunities to be deeply engaged in their schools or communities. Even TCKs who are regarded as gregarious, open, and friendly because of their skill at jumping into the second and third levels of communication often refuse to move on to the fourth and fifth levels of true intimacy. They manage to erect walls, usually without realizing it, to keep out anyone trying to come closer.

> When Fiona became engaged to Jack, she couldn't believe that someone would actually be with her for the rest of her life, so she prepared for what seemed the inevitable loss by presuming Jack would have a fatal car wreck before their marriage. When that didn't happen, she feared it would happen on their honeymoon. After safely returning from their honeymoon, Fiona worried whenever Jack was a few minutes late coming home from work. On their first anniversary, he was over two hours late due to an electrical failure in the mass transportation system. By the time he got home, she had started crying with an "I knew it would happen" despair, had begun to plan his funeral, and wondered how long you had to be married before you didn't need to return the wedding gifts.
>
> Although Jack is living to this day, for a long time after the wedding Fiona couldn't understand why she always seemed to fuss over insignificant details—like whose turn it was to take out the garbage—just when she and Jack felt especially close. She finally realized that deep inside such closeness terrified her because she still feared losing it. Fussing was her way to keep up a wall of safety. Fiona had been losing people she loved dearly since first separating from her parents at age six when she left for boarding school, and it took a long time for her to let her guard down and dare to believe Jack would be staying.

As we saw in our discussion on the stages of transition, people try to protect themselves from the pain of losing a precious, or at least valued, relationship in various ways. TCKs are no different. Here are three common ways it happens.

1. *Refusing to care.* Some try to limit their vulnerability to impending grief by refusing to acknowledge they care for anyone or anything. In the end, however, they know a pain of loneliness far greater than the one from which they are running. The independence they have been so proud of turns into a profound isolation that keeps them prisoner until the day they become willing to once more feel the pain of loss in order to know the joy of closeness.

2. *Quick release.* A second common response for people trying to avoid the pain of losing a relationship is called the "quick release." This is a form of the "leaning away" we discussed in chapter 5 as part of the leaving stage of transition. When friends are about to leave, or when TCKs think they themselves might be leaving, their response is frequently to let go too soon. Friends stop calling each other and don't visit, play together, or go out for lunch. Each wonders what he or she did to upset the other one. A "quick release" also happens at points when some kind of temporary separation is about to occur. Many ATCKs talk of how easily they have an argument with a spouse the night before one of them is leaving for a short business trip the next day—an unconscious attempt to protect against loss based on past patterns rather than the reality of the moment.

   Some ATCKs who themselves have commonly used anger as part of their quick release (or had it used by those they were separating from) may see any type of anger as a precursor to separation and emotionally detach at the first sign of it.

   > Garth and his new bride had their first argument. He told us later, "I knew right then she was going to leave me." Inside, he went stone cold toward her. *Let her leave. I don't care. I don't know why I married her anyway,* he thought. When he finally realized his wife had no intention of leaving, he began to think through his reaction and what had happened. He remembered frequent arguments with his parents just before he left for boarding school, probably each of them unconsciously trying to make the leaving easier. Garth began to realize that because of that previous pattern, he made automatic assumptions that any conflict meant the impending loss of a relationship.

3. *Emotional flattening.* Refusing to feel the pain is another common response of TCKs to the multiple losses due to the high mobility of their lives. Even when TCKs feel intensely about leaving a friend or relative, some refuse to acknowledge the hurt to others or themselves. It's almost as if they will themselves to be emotionally flat—feeling neither great joy nor great pain. They say they don't like messy good-byes and, in fact, refuse to say them. Becky and Mary Ann were two ATCKs caught in this pattern.

Becky and Mary Ann met at a Global Nomads International
conference. For both of them, this was the first time they
had consciously reflected on how their pasts as TCKs had
affected them. Each had basked in the joy of discovering another person who understood her deep, inner, secret places.
They had laughed together, cried together, and talked inces-
santly. Suddenly the conference was over, and that inevitable moment of saying good-bye had come.

Becky and Mary Ann stood by the elevator as Mary
Ann prepared to leave for the airport. Chances were great
they would never see each other again; they lived an ocean
apart. As they looked at one another, each knew she had let
the other into a space usually kept off limits. What did they
do now?

After a brief, uncomfortable stare, both broke into wry
smiles of understanding.

"So what do we say?" Becky asked first.

"I guess there's not much to say but the usual," and
Mary Ann paused, bent her right arm up so the palm of
her hand faced Becky. Like a windshield wiper making one
sweep across the windscreen, Mary Ann moved her forearm
from left to right while saying *"Byyee."*

"I guess you're right, Mary Ann. So *byyee*," and Becky
mirrored the perfunctory farewell wave Mary Ann had just
made.

Then they laughed. For some, this might have seemed
an incredibly cold way to say good-bye after they had
shared their lives so intensely. For them, however, it was
a moment of recognition, of understanding how each had
learned to avoid painful farewells. They simply didn't acknowledge them! But, in another way, it also represented
the sum of all they had shared that needed no verbal explanation.

Unfortunately, however, not all who exercise the protective mechanism of
emotional flattening realize it as poignantly as Mary Ann and Becky did at their
moment of parting. Even more unfortunately, this flat emotional response can
be transferred from avoiding the pain of farewells to all areas of life. Sometimes
what is praised as confidence and independence among TCKs may actually be a
form of detachment. In his book *Your Inner Child of the Past*, psychiatrist Hugh
Missildine cites the work of John Bowlby and says that whenever there is a prolonged loss of relationship between parent and child, for *whatever* reason, children go through grief, despair, and, finally, *detachment* as they try to cope with

that loss.[6] Historically, many TCKs have known profound separation from their parents at an early age when they went to boarding schools around the age of six. While this practice has changed markedly and relatively few TCKs leave home this early anymore, attachment can still be a huge issue for the ATCKs who did leave home at a young age. In addition to going away for schooling, however, the chronicity of separating so repeatedly from friends and other relatives can lead to a habit of detachment for many TCKs, whether they went to boarding school or not. They simply refuse to let themselves care about or need anyone again. The sad thing is, when pain is shut down, so is the capacity to feel or express joy.

This detachment response can be devastating in a marriage. The ATCK's partner feels rejected because there are too few external demonstrations of love from the ATCK. Conversely, no matter how many romantic gestures are offered to the ATCK, nothing seems to spark a warm response.

It can be equally painful for the child of such an ATCK. Some ATCK parents seem genuinely unable to delight openly in the pure joy of having a child, of watching that child grow, of playing games together, or of reading stories at bedtime. Not only do the children miss the warmth and approval they long for, but the ATCK parent also loses out on one of the richest relationships possible in life.

On the other hand, however, we have seen how TCKs who learn to deal in healthy ways with the cycle of relationships they face become richer for it. They do, in fact, have a wealth of experiences to share and rich diversity among those they have met, and they have every possibility for making truly deep friendships that last across the years and miles. As TCKs become skilled at going through the process of transition in the healthy ways we discuss in later chapters, they can learn to enjoy each relationship they have, whether it be a long- or short-term friendship. Because all people lose relationships at one time or another, they can share the transitional skills they've learned for themselves to help others cope during their life transitions as well.

Lessons from the TCK Petri Dish

Again, many of these patterns appear in the TCK experience not primarily because they are TCKs, but because they are human beings who are all in the process of negotiating relationships and connections with others—and trying to protect themselves from being hurt. For other CCKs and people of all backgrounds, taking a look inside this petri dish will hopefully open the discussion for how the multiple layering of cross-cultural relationships and the growing complexity of our world in general affect our relationships in these and other ways.

CHAPTER 11

Developmental Issues

Sometimes I think the cement of my being was taken from one cultural mould before it was cured and forced into other moulds one after the other, retaining bits of the form of each but producing a finished sculpture that fit into none. At other times I think of myself like the fish we caught [while we were] snorkelling off Wewak. My basic shape camouflages itself in the colours of whatever surroundings I find myself in. I am adept at playing the appropriate roles. But do I have a colour of my own apart from those I appropriate? If I cease to play any role would I be transparent? To mix metaphors, if I peeled away the layers of the roles I adopt would I find nothing at the centre? Am I after all an onion—nothing but the sum of my layers?[1]

—*Sophia Morton*

IN HER POWERFUL ESSAY "LET US POSSESS ONE WORLD," Sophia reflects on the basic questions that TCKs (and all others) must ultimately answer: Who am I? What does it mean to be human, and what does it mean to be this *particular* human—me?

Developing Personal Identity

In 1984, Sharon Willmer, an ATCK and therapist for TCKs, spoke at a conference about TCK issues and said that one of the greatest challenges she found among her TCK clients was that few of them had any idea what it meant to be a person. During her talk, Sharon explained how every person—regardless of race, nationality, background, economic status, educational experience or lack thereof—is a relational, emotional, intellectual, creative, physical, volitional, and spiritual being. At birth, before a moment of cultural influence, these are the baselines of what it means to be human. Figure 11-1 illustrates this concept using the iceberg analogy introduced earlier.

Because of this, every person has specific, legitimate needs.[2] These include the need for strong relationships: a sense of belonging, of being nurtured and cared for, of internal unity, of significance, of being able to make meaningful choices, and a feeling of knowing ourselves and being known by others. Every human also has the need to express in some way these emotional, creative, intellectual, volitional, and spiritual aspects of his or her being. These needs are what define us as human, and to deny any of them is to deny something precious and important about ourselves. Part of cultural training is teaching us socially acceptable ways to have these needs met. Furthermore, it is the specific mix and manner in which we meet or express these universal needs that lead to our sense of unique, personal identity.

So why is finding that sense of identity such a particular problem for TCKs? Obviously, this is an important issue for non-TCKs as well. At first glance, it may seem that finding a sense of identity is difficult for TCKs simply because of all the cultural or national confusion we've talked about: "Am I an Austrian or a Brazilian?" "Do I fit better in a village setting or a mansion?" But having a strong sense of who we are is more than just knowing our nationality or culture, though that is part of it. It's a matter of answering these questions: Who am I as *this* person? What are my gifts? Strengths? Weaknesses? Where do I fit or belong? We seek answers to these questions in any culture.

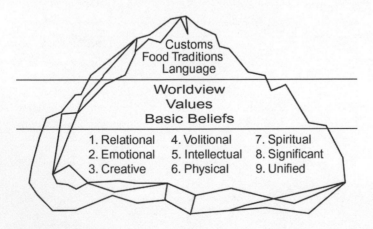

Figure 11-1 The Expanded Iceberg
(© 2006 Ruth E. Van Reken)

But challenges to personal identity also come from another unlikely source for TCKs. As we said in chapter 6, in matters related to a global awareness or interacting with adults, TCKs often seem far older than their years. In relationships with peers in their passport cultures, they often seem quite immature. People often tell them, "I can't believe you're only 14 [or whatever age]. You seem much older." Equally often (and probably behind their backs), these same people marvel at the TCKs' lack of sophistication or social skills. TCKs feel this discrepancy too and soon begin to wonder which person they really are: the competent, capable, mature self or the bungling, insecure, immature self? That's part of the problem in trying to figure out who they are; in many ways they're both. We call this *uneven maturity*. Why is this such a common issue for many TCKs?

Uneven Maturity

Before we can understand why TCKs seem to face such an uneven task to moving into true maturity, let's stop and remind ourselves of some fundamental developmental tasks we all face on our path from infancy to adulthood. Figure 11-2 gives us some clue of how and why it develops.

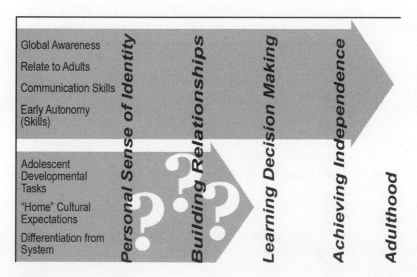

Figure 11-2 Uneven Maturity for TCKs
(© 2008 Barbara H. Knuckles)

When we look at this model, we see five emotional and psychological developmental tasks every child must go through to move in a relatively smooth manner from dependent infant to a mature, responsible adult. As we can also see from this grid, there are some aspects of the TCK lifestyle that may accelerate the normal process and other places where the same experience can slow it down a bit. We'll look at the normal stages first and then at some of the factors for the early maturity, as well as the delayed adolescence that is often characteristic of many TCKs.

Developmental Tasks

From birth, children of every race, color, creed, or background begin to perform various developmental tasks. They move from rolling over to sitting, crawling, standing, walking, and, finally, running. Each task is sequential. If a broken leg keeps a child from learning to stand, he or she must still learn that task when the leg heals before walking, let alone running. Although we all use and build on these foundational accomplishments throughout life, when they happen as expected, we take them for granted. This is what life "should" be. However, if a child isn't walking by two, something is out of sync. Pediatricians call it *delayed development* and begin to investigate the reasons for this delay. But how does this relate to the TCK experience?

While learning to run and talk are two early physical developmental tasks, there are other important steps in every child's growth from infancy to becoming a mature adult. The following are some of these critical emotional and psychological developmental tasks we all face.

1. *Establishing a personal sense of identity.* This begins early on as children begin to differentiate their sense of self from their parents (think "terrible twos"!). It's also a process of discovery: Who am I? What makes me *me*? Where do I fit in my family and group?
2. *Establishing and maintaining strong relationships.* Young children initially bond to their immediate families, but the teenage years are when relationships with the larger world of peers become critical if we are to move on into adulthood.
3. *Developing competence in decision making.* Competent decision making is based on the assumption that the world is predictable and that we have some measure of control. In ideal situations, children and adolescents learn to make decisions under the protection of the family and then move on to making their own choices.
4. *Achieving independence.* When we have the stability of knowing what the rules of the family and culture are and have learned to make competent decisions, we can begin moving toward the independence of adulthood.

5. *Adulthood.* With the first four stages complete, we are ready to move on into adulthood. We have established a sense of "otherness" from our parents and families of origin. We are confident, ready and able to take responsibility for our decisions and actions.

Traditionally, most people moved through the various stages of each of these developmental tasks while living in one physical place or among one primary culture group. In that context, the world stayed constant. That meant there was a solid place against which rules could be tested and where decisions made could have a relatively predictable outcome. The process for moving through these developmental tasks happened as normally as learning to walk and talk does for most children. No one thought much about it. But this traditional world is not the one in which TCKs grow up. As a result, these developmental tasks are often being interrupted, or expedited, and it is from that process we see both early maturity and delayed adolescence. Here are some reasons for both among TCKs.

EARLY MATURITY

It's not only others who see TCKs as "more mature." They often feel more comfortable with older students rather than fellow classmates when they begin college back in their passport countries. Others are amazed at their confidence to travel the world alone or how well they communicate with adults. There are several reasons for these places where they seem "ahead of the game."

1. *Broad base of knowledge and awareness.* TCKs often have an "advanced for their years" knowledge of geography, global events, and politics in other countries and are interested in topics not usually discussed by younger people in their home cultures. Many TCKs have learned unusual practical skills at a very young age as well—such as how to set up solar energy panels to keep computers running for translation work in the Amazon jungle.
2. *Relationship to adults.* TCKs generally feel quite comfortable with adults because they have had lots of experience with them. Generations usually mix much more in third culture communities than in the home country. Why? Because, at least traditionally, many expatriate communities live within relatively defined parameters: kids attend the same school; most of the parents appear at the same international or organizational functions; families may go to the only international church in town; and they bump into one another frequently in the one or two grocery stores that carry foods imported from their particular homeland. Since the children may already be friends through school, families visit as families rather than as adults only. In certain situations—such as homeschooling—some TCKs spend more time with adults than children, which makes them come across almost as "mini-adults."

3. *Communication skills.* Children who speak two or more languages fluently also seem like mini-adults. How could they have learned to speak like this so soon in life? Multilingual TCKs generally feel at ease using their languages to communicate with quite diverse groups. In fact, TCKs often serve as translators for their parents—again, a task usually reserved for adults. All this continues to increase their exposure to, participation in, and comfort with a world of culturally diverse adults as well as other children and gives them an unusual air of maturity.

4. *Early autonomy.* In many ways, many TCKs have an earlier sense of autonomy than peers at home. By their early teenage years, TCKs literally know how to get around in the world and enjoy functioning in quite diverse ways and places. This may be the result of traveling alone to boarding school or having the opportunity as young children to explore their surroundings freely by trikes, bikes, and hikes. A reliable, safe public transportation system in some countries adds to that sense of autonomy. Many TCKs in Japan take the train to school for two hours each way, every day, in early elementary grades. When one TCK lived in Australia, he took a ferry and bus by himself to school every day at age eleven, while his friends back in the United States waited at the corner of their street for the school bus to pick them up.

DELAYED ADOLESCENCE

Ironically, while in many ways TCKs seem advanced for their years, there are also many ways they seem to lag far behind. In a survey of nearly 700 ATCKs, Ruth Hill Useem and Ann Baker Cottrell observed that it wasn't unusual for TCKs to go through a delayed adolescence, often between the ages of 22 and 24, and sometimes even later.[3] TCKs who have never heard the expression "delayed adolescence" have still sensed that they are definitely out of sync with their peers but can't figure out why.

What exactly does *delayed adolescence* mean? And why is it a characteristic of many TCKs? Let's first define adolescence itself. Here's one definition:

> Adolescence essentially begins when physiologically normal puberty starts. *It ends when the person develops an adult identity and behavior* [italics added]. This period of development corresponds roughly to the period between the ages of 10 and 19 years.[4]

Basically, then, delayed adolescence simply means that it is taking TCKs longer than what has traditionally been considered "normal" to complete the emotional and psychological developmental tasks that move us from infancy to adulthood. The tasks we listed earlier—developing a sense of personal identity, building strong relationships, developing competence in decision making, and achieving independence—are all part of that process. Delayed adolescence doesn't mean TCKs can't complete these tasks. It simply means it may take a bit more time. Don't forget: a child who breaks a leg before learning to walk will, in fact, walk in the end, but not as soon as others.

But the question remains: Why is delayed adolescence so common for many TCKs? Figure 11-3 helps us understand some of the reasons.

1. *Cross-cultural mobility in developmental years.* This reason relates to why cross-cultural transitions and high mobility *during developmental years* are so significant. As we've said before, part of completing these developmental tasks involves a testing of the rules, values, and beliefs learned in childhood during these adolescent years. One common way teens test is through direct challenges, something parents of teenagers around the world know only too well: "Why do I have to be in by midnight?" "Who says I can't wear my hair like this?" After the testing is a period of integrating the cultural practices and values we decide (often unconsciously) to keep. We then use these to make decisions about how we will live as autonomous adults rather than continuing to live as children guided by external, parental rules alone. When the cultural rules are always changing, however, what happens to this process? This is, again, why the issues of cultural balance and mobility—and the age or ages when they occur—become very important. Often at the very time TCKs should be testing and internalizing the customs and values of whatever culture they've grown up in, that whole world, its familiar culture, and their relationships to it can change overnight with one plane ride. While peers in their new (and old) community are internalizing the rules of culture and beginning to move out with budding confidence, TCKs are still trying to figure out what the rules are. They aren't free to explore their personal gifts and talents because they're still preoccupied with what is or isn't appropriate behavior. Children who have to learn to juggle many sets of cultural rules at the same time have a different developmental experience from children growing up in one basically permanent, dominant culture that they regard as their own.

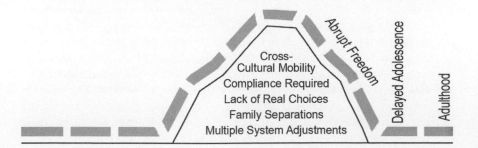

Figure 11-3 Delayed Adolescence for TCKs
(© 2008 Barbara H. Knuckles)

2. *Extended compliance required.* Some TCKs experience delayed development because of an extended compliance to cultural rules. In certain situations, TCKs are not as free as peers at home might be to test those rules during their teenage years. For instance, some TCKs need to comply with the status quo in a given situation for their own safety and acceptance. Instead of freedom to hang out with friends in shopping malls or on the street corners, many TCKs find themselves restricted, perhaps for safety reasons, to the military base or diplomatic compound. If they don't want to be kidnapped or robbed, they must obey regulations that might not be necessary in the home country. Also, some TCKs belong to organizations with fairly rigid rules of what its members (and their families) may and may not do. An embassy kid doing drugs or a missionary daughter who gets pregnant can result in a quick re-patriation for the family. In such cases, not only might the parents lose their jobs, but the TCKs might well lose what they consider to be home. This adds pressure to follow community standards longer than they might otherwise.

3. *Lack of opportunities for meaningful choices.* In the situations just mentioned, when TCKs aren't as free as their friends in the home country might be to make some of the decisions about where they will go and what they will do, they don't have the same opportunity to test parental and societal rules until a later period in life than usual.

4. *In addition, as we saw in the discussion of the delusion of choice in chapter 7, the fact that life is often unpredictable makes it hard for many TCKs to make decisions.* It's difficult to make a competent decision if the basis used to de-cide something is always changing. As mentioned before, a TCK's lifestyle in many third culture communities is frequently dictated by the sponsor-ing agency. If the U.S. Navy assigns a parent for a six-month deployment, it doesn't matter what the TCK does or doesn't decide about it—that parent will be going. For these reasons and probably more, some TCKs don't learn to take responsibility for the direction of their lives. They are more prone to just "letting it happen."

5. *Family separations.* TCKs who are separated from their parents during ado-lescence may not have the normal opportunity of challenging and testing parental values and choices as others do. Some who were separated in early years find themselves wanting to cling to parental nurture and make up for early losses. They don't want to move into adulthood yet. Still others who have spent years away from home may idealize their parents in almost fan-tasy form. To challenge anything about their parents would call that dream into question. In situations such as these, we've seen many TCKs delay the normal adolescent process of differentiating their identity from that of their parents until their late twenties or even into their thirties.

6. *Operating between different systems.* Incompatible educational and social factors also contribute to at least the appearance of delayed adolescence. The Danish TCK who graduates from an American-based international school

may return to Denmark and discover that she must do two more years at the secondary level before going to university. Suddenly she is grouped with those younger than herself and treated as their peer. This is especially traumatic if she's become accustomed to being seen as older than her years.

7. *The social slowness discussed earlier can contribute to delayed adolescence by severely impeding the normal developmental task of establishing and maintaining strong relationships—particularly with peers and members of the opposite sex.* Judith Gjoen, a Dutch ATCK who grew up in Indonesia and is now a clinical counselor in Norway, wrote about the difficulties Europeans face on their return home after attending a predominantly international school.

> Dating is very American. Scandinavian ways of interrelating between the sexes are much more informal. There is much more flexibility in the sex roles. All boys learn to knit; all girls learn carpentry. Furthermore, a young person's identity is not so strongly connected to "dating status." From a Scandinavian perspective, the American way can be slightly overdone and hysterical. You are not prepared for the European way of being together [males and females] when you have been socialized into an American system.[5]

The development of other social skills may also be delayed by not knowing the unwritten rules in the TCK's age group back home or in the new culture. How loud do you play music? How long do you talk on the phone? When do you engage in chitchat and when in deeper conversations? How do you behave with a friend of the opposite sex? When the rules around them have changed, TCKs sometimes retreat into isolation from others rather than try to cope.

Sometimes the very maturity noted earlier coupled with the sometimes more hidden delayed adolescence may lead to unforeseen problems. The initial attraction of a young TCK to older, more mature people may result in the choosing of an older marriage partner. Unfortunately, while the "early maturity" of the TCK may make such a match seem like a good idea, the deeper delay in development may scuttle the relationship later on. Sometimes the TCK isn't as ready for the responsibility or partnership of marriage as he or she appeared to be because the issues of personal identity, good decision making, and ability to build strong relationships haven't been resolved. Other times, as in any marriage, when the younger partner goes on to develop a deeper, truer maturity, the older spouse doesn't always continue to grow at the same rate. This can leave the younger partner disappointed, disillusioned, or dissatisfied.

Uneven maturity offers almost paradoxical benefits and challenges, as do all other TCK characteristics. The very reasons for some of the delays in adolescence are rooted in the greatest benefits of the third culture experience. Once they are aware of and understand the process, however, TCKs and/or their parents can be alert to and guard against a certain smugness or sense of elitism they sometimes exhibit about how "mature" they are, while at the same time not panicking about areas where they still need to catch up. Given time, the maturity process will sort itself out into a more even flow as they, like others, move on through adolescence—delayed or not—into adulthood. In the end, through this very process of having to figure out some of these matters with conscious thought rather than an unconscious process, many TCKs and ATCKs find themselves with a very clear and strong sense of personal identity. Perhaps some of their process is only defined as "uneven" because it is judged by models that may not be as standardized as once thought in these days of changing cultural patterns around our world.

Delayed Adolescent Rebellion

A delayed adolescence is painful enough for the TCK who keeps wondering why he or she can't be like others, but even more painful—not only for TCKs, but for their families as well—is a delayed adolescent rebellion: when the normal testing of rules either starts unexpectedly late or becomes exaggerated in an all-out, open defiance of nearly every possible convention the family and/or community hold dear and extends far beyond the adolescent years. Obviously, this type of rebellion also occurs in families that don't live abroad, but we want to look at a few specific reasons for a delayed rebellion in some TCKs and then at why it often continues later than the normal teenage years.

1. *Extension of delayed adolescence.* In any journey to adulthood, there are always those who in the process of testing the rules of their upbringing decide they will avoid adults' expectations, no matter what. For whatever reasons, they assume an "anti-identity." This process of rebellion is often an offshoot of normal adolescent testing of cultural norms. When that normal process is delayed for all the reasons mentioned earlier, the rebellion that often comes during that time will be delayed.
2. *End of the need for compliance.* Sometimes it seems that young people who have been forced to comply with a fairly rigorous system throughout their teenage years decide to try everything they couldn't do before, once they are finally free from those external constraints. Rather than the usual process of testing rules a few at a time while still under a parent's watchful eye, they go off to university and seemingly "go off the deep end."

   This form of rebellion may actually be a positive—though slightly misguided—move toward independence. In these situations, parents and others may need to understand the reason for the behavior and be patient in the process, while also pointing out (when possible) that some of this behavior may be counterproductive to the goal of the independence they seek.

3. *Loneliness*. Sometimes the rebellion is a plea for help. We have met many TCKs who have tried to express to their parents that they need a home base; that they feel desperately lonely when vacation time comes and everyone else goes home and they stay in the dorm because their parents are still overseas and relatives in the home country seem like strangers; or that they are struggling in school and want to quit. But the parents never seem to hear. Instead, they send e-mail messages with platitudes like "Cheer up," "It will get better," or "Trust God," or they explain once more why they need to stay in the job they're in.

Eventually, some TCKs finally scream through their behavior the message they have not been able to communicate verbally: "I need you to come *here*—to be near me." When they get arrested for drugs, or get pregnant, or try to commit suicide, they know their parents will come—at least for a short period. Unfortunately, the parents who didn't hear the earlier verbal or nonverbal messages often don't understand, even at this point of major rebellion, the deep loneliness and longing their child is experiencing. They judge the rebellion without understanding the reason and a deeper wedge than ever is driven between parent and child.

At that point, the TCK's behavior may become more extreme than before, and whatever form the rebellion takes—drugs, alcohol, workaholism, some esoteric cause—becomes a way in itself to numb the pain of longing for some type of security and home base. The sad thing is that until the loneliness and longing are addressed, the TCK will stay walled off, often in very destructive behavior, fulfilling the worst prophecies made about him or her.

4. *Anger*. One of the common manifestations of unresolved grief, anger, may erupt in this time of rebellion and intensify it. The anger may be directed at parents, the system they've grown up in, their home country, God, or other targets. Unfortunately, once again people don't always stop to find out what's behind the explosion. The judgment and rejection of the TCK's experience increases the pain and fuels further anger and rebellion.

There is another situation that may be the cause of anger. TCKs who have spent many years physically apart from their parents by being away at a boarding school or back in the passport country, or perhaps even when one parent is away on deployment or frequent short-term assignments, may, as we said, unrealistically idealize them. As young adults, these TCKs begin to discover their own imperfections, realize their parents aren't perfect either, and not only become angry at the loss of their fantasy but also begin to blame their parents for the lack of perfection in *themselves*. "If I'd just lived a normal life or had better parents, I wouldn't be struggling the way I am now." While anger against parents for imperfections in ourselves is probably a normal part of the developmental process for everyone, TCK or not, when parents remain overseas, working through it can be difficult for all concerned.

The bottom line is that no matter what the reason for the anger, it's often turned against the parents and may be expressed in an almost punitive rebellion—the TCKs want to hurt those who they feel hurt them.

A major problem with delayed adolescent rebellion, however, is that rebellion in the mid-to-late twenties may have a destructive effect far beyond that of teenage rebellion.

> Pierre was a diplomat's son from Switzerland who grew up in four different South American countries. During his early twenties, when friends asked how he had liked his nomadic lifestyle, he always replied, "Oh, I loved it! It never bothered me to pack up and move. We always knew there was something very exciting ahead. I've lived in nine different countries."
>
> After marriage and three children, however, the story changed. Certain job situations didn't work out. He became tired of trying to find ways to support his wife and children. In the end, he became totally disenchanted with family life and the attendant responsibilities and simply walked away from everything he'd apparently valued before. "I've spent my life," he replied to those who questioned him, "doing what everyone else wanted me to do and I'm tired of it. Now I'm finally going to do whatever I want to do."

We stress that this type of rebellion is neither desirable nor necessary. The TCK as well as parents, family, and friends are all wounded in this process. Being aware of some of the reasons delayed rebellion occurs may sometimes prevent it, or it may help the family deal with delayed adolescence in its early stages, so they and their TCKs aren't held prisoners to destructive behavior. Perhaps the best preventive measure parents and other adults can take against this type of rebellion is to make sure, even in situations where their TCKs are raised in a strong organizational (or family) system, that there are opportunities for the children to make real choices in matters that don't compromise their safety or the agency's effectiveness. This says to the child, "I am listening to you. Your needs are heard. You don't have to scream to get my attention." Most importantly, TCKs and ATCKs who read these lines and recognize themselves need to know they have the choice to take responsibility for their own actions and find help for their behavior rather than continuing to blame others for how awful their lives have been or become. (See chapter 19 for further help in this area.)

Identity in a "System"

TCKs who grow up in the subculture of the parents' sponsoring organization have a few extra factors to deal with in this process of establishing a sense of identity. Although in reality these issues are extensions of what we have already discussed, it's important to understand how growing up in what is often a fairly structured community can be one more factor in a TCK's developmental process.

There can be many benefits to living in a carefully defined system. In many situations, the whole system of the sponsoring organization serves to some extent as both family and community. It provides materially as a good parent might, with air travel paid for, housing provided, and perhaps special stores made available. In many cases, as mentioned earlier, it also provides specific guidance or regulations for behavior.

An organizational system is one of the places where the need for belonging can truly be fulfilled because there are clear demarcations of who does and doesn't belong. Some TCKs have a deeper sense of belonging to that community than they will ever have with any other group and feel secure within the well-ordered structure of their particular system.

Other TCKs, however, feel stifled by the organizational system in which they grew up. They may be straining at the bit to get out of what they see as the rigid policies of the system. They realize that they have had almost no choice in countless matters that have deeply affected their lives—such as when and where their parents moved, where they could go to school, how to behave in certain common circumstances, or how they could express their inner passions. They see their organization as an uncaring nemesis and feel intense rage at a system that requires conformity to rules and regulations regardless of individual preferences. Some blame the system for ruining their lives.

Certainly anyone who grows up in a clearly defined system is very much aware of how the group expects its members to behave. Failure to conform brings great shame on the TCK or the whole family. In many cases, the rules of these systems are a higher priority than the rules of the family, superseding decisions parents would normally make for their own children—such as when and where the children go to school.

What might make the difference in how or why an organizational system seems so positive for one person and restrictive for another? At the risk of oversimplifying, and recognizing that there are many differences in how each agency may be run, Figure 11-4 outlines the basic ways Barb Knuckles has identified of how TCKs relate to the system in which they grew up—from the perspective of their own personal makeup, gifts, and personality. Understanding this perspective can help us answer the preceding question.

1. *A TCK who fits the system.* Feeling comfortable is relatively easy for those whose personality and interests pretty well fit within the structure or rules

	Child's Identity	Adult's Identity Choices
child, adult fits	**intuitively conforms** system based identity protects system to protect self	intuitively conforms identity depends on system other options threaten identity
		intuitively conforms identity transcends system(s) secure self, confident
child, adult does not fit	**strives to conform** system based identity may protect, resent system	striving for outward conformity shame based identity lacking knowledge of real self
		conforms (thoughtfully and selectively) Identity transcends system(s) may stay or move on, without shame
	neither resists nor conforms inner directed (naïve) identity chooses alternatives	inner directed (alternative) choices identity transcends system(s) remains and conforms selectively
		inner directed (alternative) choices identity transcends system(s) moves into more compatible system
	resists system, rebels system based anti-identity fights system to preserve self	sheds anti-identity in favor of freedom begins to develop real self moves between and in systems at will
		reactionary anti-identity rebellion counterfeits real freedom work of establishing real identity is postponed

Figure 11-4 BarbekModel: Identity Related to Systems
(Barbek System and Identity Model © 2008 Barbara H. Knuckles)

of the system under which they have grown up. It might be an easygoing military kid who never seems to question authority, a pragmatic missionary kid who doesn't see the point of the fancy accessories in a Lexus, or a diplomat's kid who is an extrovert and thrives on meeting new people. They can go along with how life works in this system and it doesn't conflict with how they think, what they like to do, what they want to be, or, most important, who they are by their very nature. There is room in this system to express who they are at this core. It's a pretty good match.

2. *A TCK who doesn't fit the system but attempts to conform.* Other children don't match the system as well. Secretly, they prefer rap music while others around them are denouncing it as junk. They long for color and beautiful decor but live in a plain, brown, adobe-type home within a system that feels it isn't spiritual to focus on worldly beauty. They find crowds of new people frightening, but they paste on a smile and act cordial to the dignitaries at the

never-ending receptions. They have learned not to reveal their feelings or desires, because they learned early on that it was wrong to feel or think that way. Instead of being able to explore the mystery of their own personality and set of gifts, they feel ashamed of this secret longing and try harder and harder to be what they perceive the system says they should be.

The major problem for members of this second group is that their sense of identity comes almost totally from an external system rather than from the unique mix and validity of who they are deep within. If this type of conformity doesn't change at some point, people in this group may become more and more rigid over the years in adhering to the system that now defines them. They fear that if they let any part of it go, they will lose themselves because they don't know who they are without this structure to hold them together.

3. *A person who doesn't completely fit the system but doesn't realize (or at least seem to mind) it.* People in this group go ahead and listen to rap—not to be rebellious, but because they like it. It doesn't occur to them—or worry them—that others might disapprove. If told that others might disapprove, they would likely respond, "That's okay. If they do, I'll use my earphones." They stay in their rooms and read—not because they're rejecting the social scene, but because they love to read. They make decisions that don't quite match those of everyone else—not for the sake of being different but simply because they prefer they way they've chosen. They don't feel compelled to be exactly like everyone else but are happy to join with others when they do share an interest. Perhaps they have the inner security to be independent because many of their foundational needs of relationship and belonging have been well met in early years within their family. Maybe it just happens to be one of the attributes of their personality. Either way, they are discovering and operating from who they are inside rather than letting their environment define them.

4. *A person who doesn't fit the system, knows it, and spends years of his or her life proving it.* People in this group like to think of themselves as members of the group just discussed, but they're not. For whatever reasons, they learned early on that at least parts of them didn't fit the system. Perhaps they cried their first night at boarding school and were told to be brave—but they couldn't stop crying. Maybe they honestly wanted to know why things should be done one way rather than another but were given the unsatisfactory reply, "Because I said so." Still, the burning question inside wouldn't go away. Unfortunately, as they keep bumping into something that doesn't fit them inside, some TCKs finally decide—consciously or unconsciously—to throw out everything the system stands for. They'll be anything *but* that system.

The irony is that these outwardly rebellious TCKs actually get their identity from the very system they're rejecting. People who are determined to prove who they are not rarely go on to discover who they are.

It's important to remember that it's not wrong to be part of a strong organizational system. An organization is an efficient and necessary way of forming a community into functional groups, usually for the purpose of accomplishing a common goal. We can relate to it, be part of it, and even have some of our core needs of belonging met by it. But it's not, by itself, who we are. Once that's understood, Barb's model shows what can happen when TCKs and ATCKs can take a better look at their group and determine which parts of the system do or don't fit with who they are, keeping in mind that they don't have to reject or retain an entire system.

By the time we sort through these many challenges, it's easy to wonder once again if any TCK can survive. Dirk, a German TCK who grew up in Taiwan and went to university in the United States, has learned to live with the challenge of many cultures and places by living fully in whichever one he is currently in while not denying the others are also part of his life. He uses a computer metaphor to describe this phenomenon.

> I just build windows. I know that all my windows are open, but I have to operate in the one that's on the screen. When I'm in America, I activate the American window. When I'm in Germany, I activate the German window and the American window goes on the back burner—and so do the people in it.

In summary, when thinking about TCKs' identity and development issues, don't forget the interweaving of challenges with great benefits. TCKs find in their experience numerous opportunities for fulfilling their basic human needs in the most profound ways of all, and they often emerge with a very secure self-identity. We have seen that TCKs who dare to wrestle through the hard questions of life can develop a deep and solid sense of purpose and values that go deeper than those who are not forced to sort through such questions to the same degree. In addition, the exposure to philosophical, political, and social matters that are almost part and parcel of the TCK experience means there is every potential for substantive intellectual development. By its diversity alone, a TCK's world creates questions to ponder. This is one aspect of personhood that has every potential to be filled to overflowing for TCKs. Of all the TCKs we have met or worked with, very few would ever exchange the richness of their lives to avoid the inevitable challenges they have faced along the way.

Lessons from the TCK Petri Dish

Recently we heard that some that some sociologist has declared that the "normal" ending of adolescence for the population of at least the U.S. is now age 25 or later, rather than 18 as in the past. Articles in magazines frequently talk about the "boomerang kids." In earlier generations, kids went off to university and never came home again. What is going on? Why is it taking so long for children to "grow up" in today's world?

Perhaps this is one of the key places where the TCK Petri dish can begin to raise the question of what is the difference developmentally for children who grow on up among many cultural complexities, as CCKs of all backgrounds do, compared to those who grew up in the traditional monocultural experience of yesteryear. If developmental patterns are judged by old standards, formed when most people grew up in one basic cultural environment, then how can we take into account the "new normal" of what it means to grow up in a constantly changing world—a world where role models don't exist because the jobs that many of today's youth will get haven't been created yet? No one has walked this way before. Perhaps a closer look at the TCK developmental experience might shed light for not only other CCKs, but for all those growing up in a world where the stability of former years seems like only a dream.

And now we examine one of the greatest TCK challenges of all—unresolved grief.

CHAPTER 12

Unresolved Grief

There was no funeral.
No flowers.
No ceremony.
No one had died.
No weeping or wailing.
Just in my heart.
I can't...
But I did anyway,
and nobody knew I couldn't.
I don't want to...
But nobody else said they didn't.
So I put down my panic
and picked up my luggage
and got on the plane.
There was no funeral.[1]

—"Mock Funeral" by Alex Graham James

IN CHAPTER 5 WE DISCUSSED SOME OF THE REASONS FOR unresolved grief. Initially, some TCKs and ATCKs feel a bit skeptical when they first hear us say that is one of the two major challenges of the TCK experience. After all, they aren't walking around feeling sad every day. When they think about the past, they remember happy times. The whole idea of grief seems not only nebulous, but also perhaps a tad ridiculous. They wonder exactly what we're talking about—or if we're being a bit extreme.

First, we remind you this is a profile. Surely there are TCKs and ATCKs (and we hope increasingly more of them) who have had their share of mobility and losses but managed to deal with them in basically positive ways throughout life. They don't exhibit many of the behaviors we are about to describe. They have maintained solid, close relationships in each place and stage of life, and things are going well. We are delighted each time we meet someone with that story.

Second, we want to point out that there seems to be some age-related issues to how and when people may notice or begin to deal with some of these things. When Ruth first published *Letters Never Sent*, in which, at age 39, she first named some of her own losses, several people sent her surveys of high school– and university-aged TCKs to prove this was her unique experience. Most respondents to these surveys indicated they were "just fine." At first, Ruth was willing to accept their judgments, but then she realized in her high school and university years, she had been "just fine" as well. Only in living longer did she begin to see patterns of behavior that followed her no matter where she went or what environment she was in. And in rereading these surveys, she realized that the seeds for unresolved grief were there. One statement in particular stood out: "I miss being home, but I know it's right for me to be at boarding school because if I were home, my parents wouldn't be able to do their work." That may sound noble for a 10-year-old child, but by age 35 or 40 the lens on that experience might be quite different.

At any rate, the purpose of this discussion is not to make everyone think they aren't true TCKs or ATCKs if this doesn't relate to them. But we have seen what we write here often enough to know that some readers will recognize themselves, their children, their students, or their friends in the following descriptions.

Expressions of Unresolved Grief

Unresolved grief will always express itself somehow. Often it will be in ways that appear completely unrelated to feelings of grief and apparently focused on very different events. As we said in chapter 5, the typical reactions of unresolved grief include denial, anger, bargaining, depression, and acceptance, but not always in a linear or even obvious fashion.[2] Many have asked us how these stages might be expressed in the third culture experience. Here are some examples of common reactions we see as TCKs try to deal with or reduce the pain of their losses.

DENIAL

Some TCKs and ATCKs refuse to admit to themselves the amount of sadness they have felt. "It didn't bother me to leave my parents for boarding school when I was six. I was so excited to go that once I got on the train, I didn't even think about them anymore." While this may be their conscious recollection of events, they forget that if a six-year-old *doesn't* miss Mommy and Daddy when he or she leaves for months at a time, something must be fundamentally wrong with that relationship—or they have already disconnected. Grief is normal when separating from those we love.

Others admit these separations were painful but claim to have gotten over them. Yet, as we've already seen, they continue to live lives that wall out close relationships to others—including spouses and children.

ANGER

The most common responses triggered by unresolved grief are defensiveness and a quick, flashing anger totally out of proportion to what are seemingly small circumstances in anyone else's mind. These types of responses can have devastating consequences in every context: marriage, work, social relationships, and parenting. For some, the anger is sublimated and eventually finds expression when TCKs take up a "righteous cause." They can defend the need for justice, environmental matters, civil rights, political reform, or religious practices with adamancy and vigor because no one can argue with their sense of outrage on such matters. Those who try will, of course, be seen as fools. This is not to say TCKs and others shouldn't be involved with such issues, but there is often a level of intensity that seems to go beyond the cause itself.

In any of these situations, people complain about how difficult the angry TCK is to live, work, or deal with, but few try to understand the pain behind the anger. Somewhere along the way the TCK decided the pain was simply too much to bear and replaced grief with anger as anesthesia for the pain. Unfortunately, anger ultimately increases the pain as the TCK's world becomes more isolated and lonely; no one wants to be near such an angry person.

BARGAINING

Once it becomes clear that a loss is inevitable, we begin to try to figure out ways to deal with it that might ameliorate the intensity of what is ahead. We are beginning to accept the reality of what we can't change, but can't yet accept the finality of all this loss may entail. For TCKs, they may begin planning how "one day" they will return to the land they are leaving. Friends set up Facebook accounts. Sometimes it takes the form of planning for how to take parts of the present into the future place. Pam Davis, a counselor for TCKs, says that for all the stages, "Bargaining is okay. It's a part of the process." It's a beginning step for how to deal with the losses productively.

SADNESS/DEPRESSION

Kübler-Ross called this stage depression; others prefer to call it sadness to differentiate this normal occurrence from a more chronic depressive condition. Either way, a feeling of sadness and lack of interest or energy is another manifestation of grief. This may be the time when TCKs listen to sad songs on the radio, don't have much energy to complete school or work assignments, and may not even want to contact old friends, let alone make new ones. This stage is when the reality of the loss hits. We can no longer deny what is occurring, the anger wasn't enough to stop it, the bargaining made us realize we can't outsmart or outrun it, and it seems we are left powerless. No wonder we are sad. But in that powerlessness, the anger against the circumstances turns back against ourselves and it can, in fact, turn into a true depression if the grief gets bottled up for too long. We have met far too many ATCKs who have struggled for years with major depression because they never found a way through this stage. Just remember: sadness and depression (as well as denial, anger, and withdrawal) are normal in any grief process and must be respected as such. The problem, however, is when TCKs, ATCKs, or anyone gets stuck here because they have never been able to name the grief and mourn the loss in healthy ways.

WITHDRAWAL

Withdrawal is another way that TCKs express anger and/or sadness as they attempt to avoid feeling the pain of their losses. For some, physical and emotional withdrawal can be part of grief turned into a true clinical depression. If withdrawal becomes severe, with the TCK isolating from everyone and virtually everything, professional help needs to be sought with someone who understands the TCK experience. Sadly, we know of TCKs who have ended their lives or finally lashed out at others following such despair.

But other times, withdrawal is simply another way to avoid their own pain. Some TCKs refuse to make contact with anyone from the past. They write infrequent e-mails home from university. Phone calls are rare, and text messages are brief. On the other hand, we have also seen TCKs use this as a conscious or unconscious way to strike out at parents and hurt them for "dragging me away from the place I love"—be it home or host country.

Emotional withdrawal as a protective mechanism can continue in some situations for many years. We've heard story after story from parents of ATCKs whose adult children were in the midst of a life crisis but told their parents, "Don't come. You can't do anything." Parents are often confused, not knowing what to do. They fail to recognize that their children may have emotionally withdrawn and denied their need for support rather than risk being disappointed that, once again, no one will be physically or emotionally present in their times of crisis.

REBELLION

If the normal anger felt in any grief situation isn't dealt with, it can easily take the form of extreme rebellion. Whatever they know the parents dislike, they will do. These are the screamers to the extreme, in behavior, language, dress, and values. For some, rebellion takes an inward, silent form; for others, it's blatant and loud. Either way, rebellion becomes the nearly impenetrable shield behind which the pain is deeply hidden. Each time a new circumstance comes that threatens to break through the fragile protection and expose the pain, it's like something inside the TCK metaphorically grabs a trowel and slaps on more plaster to reinforce the shield. Until he or she is willing to let the protection be gently removed so the wound can be exposed to light and air, however, healing cannot begin. Too often, it winds up in the forms of delayed adolescent rebellion we mentioned earlier. One sad fact: We have yet to meet an outwardly defiant, rebellious TCK or ATCK who, when talked to long enough, doesn't have a place of deep wounding or profound loss within. Unfortunately, that TCK's protective behavior has too often been punished before anyone stopped to see what the wound or loss might be.

VICARIOUS GRIEF

Transferring the focus from personal grief to that of others is another way to express unresolved grief. A TCK might sit at an airport weeping as he or she watches total strangers say good-bye. Some TCKs go into professions where this vicarious grief finds a more active, long-term expression.

> As a child, ATCK Joan spent twelve years in boarding schools. On a conscious level, she remembered the fun of game nights, the senior banquet, and the lifelong friends she had made. She denied any particular sadness from these years of family separation, outside of the initial tears of farewell in first and second grades.
>
> After college, however, Joan found herself working in a daycare center. She explained her choice of career by saying, "I just want to help kids whose parents must work not to feel lonely. I like to sit and hug them all day so they know they're wanted and loved. Kids need to be nurtured."
>
> Joan realized after several years that she was excessively involved with every child under her care, trying to protect each one from emotional pain. Her anger sparked against parents who forgot to bring their child's favorite teddy bear. She fought with other workers if they sharply reprimanded a child.
>
> Finally, Joan began to recognize that her deep involvement with these children reflected more than a normal

concern for them. It stemmed from the extreme loneliness she had felt when separated from her own parents during her years at boarding school, which began when she was six. Instead of directly dealing with the loss of day-by-day parenting she had experienced, Joan had unconsciously tried to deal with her own grief by making sure no child under her care would feel that same pain.

Even ATCKs who don't express their grief through a profession often become the "rescuers" of the community. For whatever reasons, they are the unofficial dorm counselors, the ones who befriend the lonely people around, who may take in the homeless. All of these can, in fact, be noble and positive gestures, but if their activities are really a substitute for working out their own grief, their behavior eventually will become counterproductive. They may be so involved in rescuing others that they may never rescue themselves.

DELAYED GRIEF

TCKs may go through life without showing or consciously feeling any particular sadness and then suddenly find to their great surprise that a seemingly small incident triggers a huge reaction.

For ATCK Dan, it was the first day his son, Tommy, went off to kindergarten. Dan should have been happy that Tommy was starting this new phase of life. School was only one block away so Dan walked Tommy right to the door, said good-bye, turned around to walk away—and found himself unable to see the sidewalk for the tears that filled his eyes. Once back home, his body sagged against the door as he sobbed uncontrollably. His wife couldn't imagine what had happened. "Is everything all right? Is Tommy okay?" Dan could only shake his head as his body continued to shudder with pain.

Dan was experiencing delayed grief. As he left his son at school, he suddenly had a flashback of his own departure for first grade. But the picture was different from how his son was beginning school. For Dan, the new picture put him inside a small, one-engine plane with four other school kids as it took off from a grassy airstrip. He could still see his parents standing on the edge of the forest waving to him. The memory of what he had felt while returning their farewell wave hit like an engulfing tide as he turned away from Tommy that morning.

Often the people most surprised by the delayed grief are those feeling it. What amazes so many ATCKs is that the grief from losses they have never consciously defined seems to hit them hardest between the ages of 25 and 40. The first glimmerings of their unrecognized grief frequently begin when they have their own children. Sometimes that's when they first ask themselves, "If my parents loved me as much as I love this baby, how could they have ever let me go away?" Or they must face the fact they aren't the perfect parents they were expecting to be.

Even without children, many ATCKs begin to realize that there's a good chance that the rootlessness, withdrawal from close relationships, or whatever they're experiencing isn't going to change no matter how much they change their circumstances. At that point, it's easy for ATCKs to think that if they had lived a "normal" life, they wouldn't have problems. They begin to blame others. Family and friends are shocked that this ATCK who "never had any problems" seems suddenly to be conjuring up all sorts of fantastic painful experiences. Finally, most ATCKs begin to face the fact that some answers for their reactions to life reside inside themselves rather than in outside events and situations. At this time, many finally examine some of this unresolved grief, work through it, and move on in productive, adult ways, using what they have learned from having gone through the grieving process. Chapter 19 suggests specific ways ATCKs can help themselves and be helped in this process.

Lessons from the TCK Petri Dish

Because everyone in this world has suffered loss, everyone also has experienced grief, and the types of behaviors seen in TCKs and ATCKs come out in different details, perhaps, than others of different backgrounds. CCKs, however, may find even the specifics of the losses they feel or the ways they cope have much in common with traditional TCKs. Immigrant children may withdraw from any connection to their parents' mother tongue or passport country, both in their attempt to be "the same as" their peers and because it is too hard to keep connecting with and losing the past. International adoptees often seem to be "doing just fine" throughout their school years, but in young adulthood and mid-thirties they want to discover more of their past and find themselves grieving for parents and a culture they may never know—even while being happy and contented in their current scene.

And now, the good news: grief doesn't need to stay unresolved. It doesn't even need to accumulate. It's time to move on and see what positive, productive, practical steps all involved with children who grow up cross-culturally can do to help them build their lives with strength in what we continue to call the "new normal" for our globalizing days.

Part III

Maximizing the Benefits

NOW THAT WE HAVE LOOKED IN DETAIL at the TCK experience itself, we will move on to specific, constructive ways we all—TCKs, ATCKs, parents, relatives, friends, and sponsors alike—can be involved in maximizing the great potential benefits of this third culture life, and how to deal with the challenges in healthy ways so that the drawbacks, too, become part of the TCK's strength and gifts.

While the early chapters in this part focus more on how parents can help, chapter 17 speaks directly to what the sponsoring organizations or corporations can do to help the families of their employees, and then chapter 19 wraps up our book with specific suggestions for what ATCKs, their families, friends, and/or therapists can do to help put life into perspective, especially when they may have had no help or language while going through this journey.

CHAPTER 13

Building a Strong Foundation

Parents raising global nomads, with the unique challenges, numerous transitions, and extraordinary opportunities presented by travel, must be mindful that their job carries an added layer of responsibility from day one.

As the Dalai Lama says in his famous guide for living, *The Art of Happiness*, "A tree with strong roots can withstand the most violent storm, but the tree can't grow roots just as the storm appears on the horizon." It's a wise lesson for expat parents to keep in mind throughout the process of raising their children abroad.[1]

—Robin Pascoe, from *Raising Global Nomads*

S O FAR, WE'VE LOOKED AT THE WORLD OF TCKS, their common characteristics, and the great gifts and some significant challenges they often face. Now it's finally time to consider the following questions: How *do* third culture families make the most of their experiences in other cultures and places? How can we proactively help TCKs deal with the challenges so that, in learning to work through them, they become part of their strengths as well?

How Parents Can Help

Wise cross-cultural parenting doesn't just happen. Moving to a new culture far from familiar support systems causes new stress for everyone, and parents need to ask some important questions before committing their family to such a major move.

1. *What are family needs that require attention regardless of location?* For example, does any child have a learning or physical disability or a chronic medical condition that requires special care? If so, parents must make sure that those needs can be met in the new location. Will home schooling or tutoring be sufficient if special education programs aren't available in the regular school? Will medical facilities by adequate? In addition, a child's age and level in school are important factors to consider. For instance, the last two years of secondary school aren't usually a good time to uproot teenagers. Not only will they miss graduating with their friends, but it also makes planning for the future harder. It's more difficult to visit potential colleges or universities when they're an ocean away rather than an interstate ride away. Of course, with websites and e-mail these are now not such huge obstacles, but these questions should be considered.

2. *What are the policies of the sending agency or corporation?* Does it look carefully at family and educational needs when moving personnel? In addition to reading the stated policies, parents should also talk with peers in the organization who have already made such a move.

3. *How will existing family patterns and relationships be affected by the move?* In the home culture, parents generally have a support system of extended family, friends, and people from school and church to help raise their kids. A cross-cultural move radically disrupts that support system.

> A Nigerian man told of the surprise he'd felt when he and his wife first moved to the United States so he could pursue a graduate program. In Nigeria, their family had lived in close proximity to grandparents, aunts, and uncles who often functioned as surrogate parents for their children. Finding a babysitter in Nigeria was never a problem. In the U.S., however, they were on their own. No one offered to take their children when they needed to go to class or the store. The special nurturing that comes from living in an extended family had disappeared, and the couple had to develop completely new patterns of parenting.

4. *Do both parents favor the move?* This is a key question. If both parents aren't fully committed to a cross-cultural move, the experience often ends in disaster. Any reluctance easily turns to resentment and hostility under the pressure of adjusting to the assignment. An unwilling parent may use extremely damaging passive-aggressive methods (e.g., emotional withdrawal, drug or alcohol addiction, generalized hostility, or destructive levels of personal criticism) to sabotage the experience for the entire family.

5. *How does the family—and the individuals in it—handle stress?* Parents must realize that not only they but also their children will experience stress in a cross-cultural move. Obviously, stress is part of everyone's life, but some-

times specific individuals or families have a particularly hard time dealing with it. If someone in the family, or the family as a whole, becomes seriously depressed or reacts in an extreme way to stress in general, parents would be wise to seek outside counsel before planning a cross-cultural move. One family whose son had a learning disability decided not to move again until their son finished high school because they realized he could not adjust to new classroom situations and new language environments without going into major withdrawal and depression.

6. *If the family does decide to move, how will it take advantage of the cross-cultural opportunities ahead?* It's a sad waste for families to live in another country and culture and not be enriched by the experience. Without some planning, it's easy for life in the new place overseas to become as routine as it was in suburbia back home. Sadly, the vast resources for learning—whether it be about the history of this new country or the geographical and cultural differences they see around them—are often unthinkingly ignored. One ATCK environmentalist chided her mother, "Mom, we lived in the middle of a tropical rain forest, and you never taught me a thing about it." The truth was that her mother had never *thought* a thing about the trees and plants in their host country any more than those in their home country. To her, they were simply the environment they lived in, not a rain forest to be studied.

7. *What educational options are available in the new setting?* This is a crucial matter to consider before accepting any particular assignment. In the early years of global mobility, schooling options were limited and most TCKs attended boarding school. This has largely changed, but it means parents need to think through even more options. In chapter 15 we look at the pros and cons of various educational choices, but this is a discussion that should happen in the decision-making process as parents consider an overseas assignment.

8. *How will the family prepare to leave?* Once parents decide to make the move, they must consider how to help their children through the transition process (see chapter 14 for a detailed discussion). Closure is as important to a child as it is to an adult. Leaving well has as profound an impact on the ability of children to enter well and adjust successfully as it does on adults.

Cross-cultural living can be a wonderful experience in countless ways, but it is far better when it begins with clear thinking and good planning rather than with naïve visions of a romantic adventure.

Foundation Blocks for Healthy TCKs

Once parents decide to move their family into a cross-cultural situation, it means that they have also decided to raise TCKs. Fortunately, this isn't a malady they inflict on their children; in fact, in most situations it's a great gift. And every parent we have met wants to know how they can help ensure that their children not only survive, but also thrive, in the upcoming adventure.

While there's no perfect formula for "How to Raise TCKs 100 Percent Successfully," the most basic principle is what we said earlier: *never forget a TCK is still a kid and needs consistent, loving parenting like any other child*. The following foundation blocks are reminders of other principles that will help parents build a foundation strong enough to support their children as they explore the new opportunities and challenges they will encounter while living and moving among many cultural worlds. While these guidelines are important for all children, for TCKs, whose world is in continual flux, they are critical.

PARENT-TO-PARENT RELATIONSHIP

We realize not all TCKs live with two biological parents. Some families are blended through marriage or adoption; other TCKs are raised in single-parent families. Regardless, the relationship between parents is of vital importance. There are three critical areas parents must examine.

1. *Commitment to each other. Commitment* may be an unfashionable word to some these days, but it remains an important one. Commitment gets a couple through the days when they wonder if it's worth sticking around. Commitment forces parents who may no longer live together to work out their differences in a way that considers the good of their child. Commitment is what keeps us going rather than throwing in the towel. It's how we grow. Parents considering a change as major as a cross-cultural move need to make sure they are sufficiently committed to one another, their relationship, and their family to make the necessary personal sacrifices to achieve their common goals.
2. *Respect and support for one another.* These go hand in hand with commitment. When kids know their parents' relationship is solid, they feel secure, particularly in the midst of the chaos of a move. They also need to see that their parents *like* each other. Small signs of affection—pecks on the cheek while passing or holding hands while watching TV—may not seem very important, but for children, these types of actions assure them that all is well with Mom and Dad. That's one area they don't have to worry about. If parents are no longer together, showing respect and not demeaning the other parent to any child is also important.
3. *Willingness to nurture the relationship.* A new cultural environment can change a couple's traditional ways of nurturing their relationship. Elegant restaurants aren't available for a lovely anniversary meal. Visitors pop in unannounced any time of the day or night, restricting the opportunities for quiet, private conversations. Couples in cross-cultural settings often have to

find creative ways to keep their relationship vibrant, realizing this is vital to their family as well as themselves.

PARENT-TO-CHILD RELATIONSHIP

Parents are the most important caregivers in any child's life. Indeed, researchers say that this relationship is the single most significant factor in determining how TCKs (or any kids) ultimately fare.[2] This is where children form their first inklings of personal identity. They begin to discover where they belong, that they have value, and that someone believes in them. This profoundly important relationship must be nurtured intentionally, especially in the midst of cross-cultural stress or the chaos of moving.

Children need to be valued. Knowing that what we think and feel makes a difference to those around us is part of feeling significant as a human being. That means someone must know us well enough to be sensitive to what we think and feel. That's what parents do for children. Parents of TCKs communicate that they value their children in all the usual ways parents normally do: by listening when children talk, by asking good questions, by seeking clarification when a child speaks or acts in a way parents don't quite understand, by giving a quiet hug. A special challenge for parents of TCKs, however, is that their children are often growing up in a different world from the one they knew as children. Because the parents are seeing this new world through adult eyes, they may not realize how stressful some cross-cultural situations can at least initially be to their children. Some ATCKs have told us of the extreme fear they felt when they first did such a normal thing as going to a local market—they were targets of constant attention and rude remarks simply because they were foreigners. When their parents said, "Don't be silly; no one is going to hurt you," as they continued walking through the crowd, the fear—and shame for being afraid—only increased. Others have known tremendous stress because of the political climate in the new country. Parents need to listen carefully and not brush off their child's concern or behavior as silly until they understand the reason for it.

> International businessman Byron and his family survived a coup, seemingly unscathed in spite of machine gun fire in their front yard one night. Shortly after the coup, however, one daughter became panicked when the family car developed a flat tire and they stopped by the side of the road to fix it. After a second flat tire the very next day, this daughter refused to take any more car trips with the family.
>
> Why did a simple flat tire cause her so much panic? When questioned, she said something about the "soldiers"; when questioned further, however, the cause of her panic finally became apparent: the first tire went flat near an army

barracks, where soldiers walked around with guns promi-
nently displayed. Their daughter had panicked, afraid that
if the soldiers came after them or started to shoot, there
would be no way for the family to escape because of the flat
tire. With soldiers present throughout the city, she didn't
want to risk being caught in such a situation again.

Another way to let children know they are valued is to include them in the
discussion of decisions that will affect them, such as the possibility of a global
move. Sometimes parents try to protect their children and keep them from worrying by not telling them about an impending move until just before it happens.
Despite the good intentions, such a delay prevents children from having the time
to process the changes that are ahead. Of course, kids don't have the final say in
their parents' career choices, but when included early in discussions and preparations, they hear the all-important message that their needs are respected. They'll
know they are valued members of the family.

The following list of questions from cross-cultural educator Shirley Torstrick
helps parents assess how well they have been listening to their child.[3]

What makes your child really angry?
Who is your child's best friend?
What color would your child like his or her room to be?
Who is your child's hero?
What embarrasses your child most?
What is your child's biggest fear?
What is your child's favorite subject in school?
What is the subject your child dislikes most?
What is your child's favorite book?
What gift from you does your child cherish most?
What person outside your family has most influenced your child?
What is your child's favorite music?
What is your child's biggest complaint about the family?
Of what accomplishment is your child proudest?
Does your child feel too big or too small for his or her age?
*If you could buy your child anything in the world, what would be his or her first
choice?*
What has been the biggest disappointment in your child's life?
What does your child most like to do as a family?
When does your child prefer to do her or his homework?
What makes your child sad?
What does your child want to be as an adult?

It's likely the more of these that parents can answer, the more their kids feel
valued.

Children need to be special. A parent's greatest gift to any child is letting them know beyond any doubt that there is somewhere in this world where they are unconditionally loved and accepted and that no one else could ever replace them. That place is in the family.

For many TCKs, however, the need to feel special is an area of particular vulnerability. Many have parents who are involved in important, high-energy, people-oriented jobs. Sometimes TCKs feel their needs are less important than those with whom their parents work, but this may not be expressed until years after the fact, and parents are surprised. Words like "I felt abandoned" or "I felt like an orphan" shock parents who never knew their kids wanted them to be more emotionally or physically present. Parents of TCKs need to make sure, as they are out dealing with the world, that there are spaces reserved for family time—no matter what other apparently urgent matters arise.

Children need to be protected. Everyone needs a sense of safety before they can move ahead in life. Children especially need to know this—and their main hope for safety is trusting that Mom and Dad will protect them in every way possible. Parents certainly agree; they want to protect their children as well.

For parents, however, protecting their children can be more complicated than they expect when they move to a place with different rules not only for what is acceptable, but also for what is safe. Walking alone to the store might be safe in one environment and risky in another. Parents used to the safety of public transportation in Japan never thought twice about putting their children in a taxi in another country during their vacation. Unfortunately, the taxi driver robbed the children and left them off in a totally different place from where the parents expected them to go.

We stress the importance of protection because of the deep expressions of pain we have heard from TCKs who have felt unprotected by parents or other caregivers. Sometimes they felt pushed out on their own too soon into a new school or community, especially when they didn't know the new language yet. They felt it during leave when it seemed, to the TCKs, that they were put on display against their will for church congregations or relatives.

The worst stories, however, are from those who were left with a caregiver— whether a dorm parent in a boarding school, a domestic worker, a fellow expat in the host country, or a friend or relative in the home country—and were emotionally, physically, or sexually abused by the person parents trusted to take care of them. The trauma is intensified, of course, if the parents refused to believe what had happened, sometimes sending their child back to that same situation. Although no parent would knowingly send a child to an abuser, the fact that often TCKs have been abused by the very people parents trusted can make it seem at some deep level that the parents themselves sanctioned the abuse. This is one reason it often takes years before the child (now an adult) will tell the parents what really happened.

Parents can help children not only feel, but *be*, protected. Children who will attend a school in a new language need to learn at least some words before they begin. TCKs who express resistance at being "little missionaries" or "little ambassadors" shouldn't be forced into that role. Children are persons in their own right, *not merely extensions of their parents*. They need to be respected as such.

With fewer young children away at boarding schools, and with e-mail, instant messaging, Skype, and cell phones, it's much easier to make sure there is a way for children to have direct contact with parents when they are away. Contact must be a priority when children are at school in more remote areas where some of this technology may not be as available. As for all children, it is important to teach TCKs concepts of personal safety and private body zones. Children need to be reminded that their parents will always believe them and protect them—no matter what anyone else might say. And then, if the child *does* report some potential or actual infringement, parents must be prepared to intervene on that child's behalf—even if doing so may put their career at risk. Since the first edition of this book, the number of stories we have heard of child abuse has increased. We believe one reason may be that parents trust others in their expatriate or local communities they know and forget to take precautions they might in other situations.

Children need to be comforted. We talked about the importance of comfort in chapter 5. Being comforted communicates that parents care and understand, even if the situation can't be changed. Parents should remember, particularly in any transition experience, that the quietest, most compliant child may be grieving and need comforting the most.

TCKS' PERCEPTION OF PARENTS' WORK

Nietzsche once said, "I can endure any *how* if I have a *why*." TCKs who understand and value what their parents do are more willing to work through the challenges than those who don't.

Many TCKs feel pride to have parents involved in careers that can make a difference in the world. They feel part-owners (and thus significant) in the process because their family traveled together so Mom or Dad could do the job. Any challenges are small compared to what is being accomplished.

Other TCKs, however, express great bitterness toward parents involved in international careers. What makes the difference? Certainly the parents' attitude toward the job, the host country and culture, and the sincerity of the political or religious beliefs that motivated them to go abroad in the first place are critical factors. Parents who feel and act positively toward their situation and the host country people with whom they are working communicate that attitude to their children. On the other hand, the parent who shows disrespect for the people or culture of the host country can make the young TCK observer wonder why the family is there at all. When the going gets tough, the question can quickly change from "Why are we here?" to "Why don't we go home?" Once that question is raised, the TCKs often begin acting out in ways that may be disruptive to the parent's career: international business kids end up breaking local laws; foreign service kids start covering the embassy walls with graffiti; missionary kids blatantly smoke, drink, use drugs, or get pregnant; military kids may join an antiwar demonstration.

A particular irony can happen, however, when parents feel it's time to repatriate. Some TCKs who have valued what their parents are doing question how these parents could be "giving up." For them, leaving casts a retrospective doubt on their whole experience. Once more, communication is important: parents should let children know of the upcoming move and the true reasons for it—even if the children have difficulty listening.

POSITIVE SPIRITUAL CORE

This foundation block is the child's awareness that there is a stable spiritual core in their parents' lives and in the life of the family as a whole. Barbara Schaetti talks about this as a final step in a TCK's identity development.

> Certainly it is valuable to be able to understand different truths as represented in different cultures, to withhold judgment and interpretation. This is part of the global nomad birthright. At the same time, however, it is important for the adult global nomad to plant his or her feet in personal truth, one not dependent on circumstance. "This is what I believe, regardless of the cultural context in which I find myself. I may alter my behavior according to changing circumstances, but my truth remains my truth."[4]

In a world where moral values and practices can be radically different from one place to another, this block of maintaining a constancy of identifiable core beliefs and values is the key to true stability throughout life. When it is strongly in place, TCKs are equipped to remain on a steady course, no matter which culture or cultures they live in.

Lessons from the TCK Petri Dish

Perhaps the one essential reminder here is that parents of many types of CCKs face extra challenges as they try to steer their children through the often uncharted waters of new cultural patterns before them—ones unlike their own childhood experiences. It is good to remember that in the outward complexity of our cultural mixing world, the basics of what children need and want remain the same, both for CCKs and non-CCKs alike.

~~~~~~~~~~~~~~~~~~~~~~~~~~~~~~~~~~~

CHAPTER 14

Dealing with Transition

My husband, one-year-old, and I once traveled to Portu-
gal with another couple. All the adults were over 5 feet 10
inches tall, and my friend was 6 months pregnant. We were
a group of very large and imposing people walking down the
small ancient streets. The townspeople looked at us rather
warily. Then my daughter, wearing a straw hat, sitting happily in her backpack carrier, would poke her head around
my husband's and give a big, silly smile. The warmth spread
through the street, and suddenly we felt welcomed.

Life abroad with an infant is different from life abroad
in any other stage of life. Make it work for you![1]

—*Anne P. Copeland*, from Global Baby

AS ANNE DISCOVERED, transition with TCKs often starts when they
are infants. She writes, "The fact that I moved to London with a toddler
and had a baby while there was the defining feature to my overseas assignment."[2] And think of what it did for her daughters. From their earliest moments, they were living a global lifestyle.

Another part of building a strong foundation for TCKs is making sure highly
mobile families learn to deal well with the entire process of transition. Parents
and others in the community, including teachers and school staff, can work proactively to deal with the losses inherent in any transition experience, for their
TCKs as well as for themselves. Families who learn to do this not only help their
children be able to move ahead with confidence, but also give them great tools
for living in an increasingly mobile world. We won't be able to stop these new
patterns of mobility—nor should we—but that's why it's so important to learn
to navigate them well.

~~~

In chapter 5 we discussed the common characteristics of the five stages in any transition experience: involvement, leaving, transition, entering, and reinvolvement. Keep in mind that everyone in the family will go through these stages at different rates, and it's not always a simple forward direction for anyone. It's also important for those who will be remaining behind to be involved in positive plans for the upcoming transition. No one in the family or community escapes the impact of mobility. For simplicity's sake, however, we will again offer suggestions mainly for making this as smooth an event as possible for the family who itself is leaving. Here, then, are some concrete ways parents and their TCKs can not only survive transition, but also grow in the process.

From Involvement through Leaving

The time has finally come. After carefully thinking through the pros and cons, the decision is made: the family will be moving to a new place and, for many TCKs, a new world. With that decision, each member of the family moves from the comfortable transition stage of involvement they have hopefully been in to the leaving stage. Whether this move is between countries or even to a new location in the same country, leaving is a critical stage for everyone to navigate well.

Some parents have asked us when is the best time to let the kids know. A few tell us they don't want to let their children know at all.

> After listening to Dave talk about transition at one conference, a woman came up to him and said, "Do you really believe it is better to let the kids know ahead of time? Our children had an awful time moving for our last relocation. My husband just found out we'll be changing countries again and we've decided not to tell them ahead of time. We plan to send the children to my parents in another country, go back to our home, pack up, move, then get the kids again and take them to the new place. What's wrong with that plan?"

Dave wanted to say, "Everything!!!" but he restrained himself and tried to remind this woman that no matter when the children discovered they were moving, it would be hard for them. But it would be a thousand times worse if they never had a chance to say good-bye to the world where they now lived. In addition, how would her children ever trust her or her husband again in the future any time they sent the children to visit their grandparents?

We believe that once parents know a move is on the horizon and it is okay for it to be public knowledge in the community, children should be told. Older children who can be trusted with knowledge a corporation or embassy may not yet want public about a parent's assignment may, of course, be told when the parents first know. As we said earlier, knowing in advance gives everyone a good opportunity to begin the necessary process of both closure in the present environment and proper anticipation of the new.

This leaving stage is a critical one to do well if parents want not only to make the current transition as smooth as possible, but also to help their children grow in the process rather than become stuck in some of the challenges we have mentioned already. Since denials—of parents, TCKs, or those of friends around us—and moments of special recognition, such as graduation or farewell ceremonies, don't change the ultimate reality of this leave-taking, it's essential that all involved—parents, TCKs, teachers, friends, others in the community—face and deal with the normal grief inherent in leaving a place and people we love. Doing this rather than running away from it will allow a healthy transition process to continue. We also need to look ahead realistically and optimistically. How can we do both: face our approaching losses squarely while still looking forward with hope? The best way is by making sure we go through proper closure during this leaving stage. Without that, the rest of the transition process can be very bumpy indeed, and settling on the other side will be much more difficult. *Leaving right is a key to entering right.*

BUILDING A "RAFT"

The easiest way to remember what's needed for healthy closure is to imagine building a raft. By lashing four basic "logs" together, we will be able to keep the raft afloat and get safely to the other side.

- **R**econciliation
- **A**ffirmation
- **F**arewells
- **T**hink destination

Reconciliation. Any time we face a move from one place to another, it's easy to deal with tensions in relationships by ignoring them. We think, "In two weeks I'll be gone and never see that friend again anyway. Why bother trying to work out this misunderstanding?" Children can do the same in their own ways, particularly if they have begun to withdraw emotionally from the current place.

Unfortunately, when we refuse to resolve interpersonal conflicts from the past or new conflicts that arise as we unconsciously "lean away," two things can happen. First, we are so focused on how good it will be to get away from this problem that we not only skip over the reconciliation needed for good closure, but we also ignore the total process of closure and don't move on to building the rest of the RAFT. Second, the difficulties don't go away when we move. Instead, as we leave, we carry with us our mental baggage of unresolved problems. This is a poor choice for three reasons: bitterness is never healthy for anyone; the old discontentment can interfere with starting new relationships; and if we ever move back to this same place and have to face these people again, it will be much harder to resolve the issues then. We've met some ATCKs who refuse to attend school reunions because they still don't want to meet certain people who hurt them or whom they know they also hurt. What a sad memory to carry throughout a lifetime.

Reconciliation includes both the need to forgive and to be forgiven. How that happens may vary among cultures. In one culture, it might mean going directly to the person with whom we have a conflict and addressing the issues. In another culture, it may mean using an intermediary. Obviously, true reconciliation depends on the cooperation and response of the other party as well, but we at least need to do all we can to reconcile any broken relationships before leaving. For children, it can be different from adults. If parents or others see that children have an unresolved conflict, they will likely have to try to help the child toward some sort of resolution. Perhaps simply talking with the child, seeing if there might be a time to get the child together with the friend or teacher with whom they are struggling, or finding some other way to help that child see the other person in a new light can be helpful in the long term of that child's life. It's amazing how long children can remember the particular pain of the shame from a teacher or bullying from a fellow student in a way that keeps them bound with anger for years.

Affirmation. Relationships are built and maintained through affirmation—the acknowledgment that each person in this relationship matters. Again, styles or customs of affirmation vary from culture to culture and may be expressed differently according to the age of each child, but in every culture, in every age bracket, an important part of closure is to let others know we respect and appreciate them. Here are several suggestions for ways families can do this.

1. *Have children identify who their special teachers or other favorite adults in the community are.* Encourage them to use pictures from a magazine to make a collage or have them draw a picture showing something they like best about being in this teacher's class or why this other adult is such a favorite.
2. *Encourage children to think of something they might like to give a friend as a small memento to represent a special time they have shared or that represents their special friendship.*
3. *As a family, send a note with a small gift to your neighbors to let them know what you've learned about kindness, faith, love, or perseverance through your interactions with them.*
4. *When leaving family members behind, such as grandparents, aunts, uncles, cousins, help children write specific reasons they appreciate being that person's grandchild, niece, nephew, or cousin, and then deliver the note with some flowers the children help to pick out.*

Obviously, there are countless other ways to show affirmation. The point is that acknowledging others helps us as well as those we affirm. It not only solidifies our relationships for future contact, but in expressing what they have meant to us, we are reminded of what we have gained from living in this place. Part of good closure is acknowledging our blessings—both to rejoice in them and to properly mourn their passing.

Farewells. Saying good-bye to people, places, pets, and possessions in culturally and age-appropriate ways is important if we don't want to have deep regrets later. We need to schedule time for these farewells during the last few weeks and days.

> One woman forgot to take into account that in the local culture everyone must come to the departing friend's house on the last day to bid a final farewell. In order not to offend the countless people who streamed in all day long, she visited with each one in turn. By the end of the day, her bags still weren't packed and she missed her flight!

Here are some suggestions for saying farewell in four key areas (all of which just happen to begin with *p*): people, places, pets, possessions.

- *People:* Farewells to significant people in our lives are crucial. Parents should take special care to help their children say good-bye to people with whom they have had meaningful relationships in the past as well as the present, including those from the local community who may have been caregivers. Helping kids say good-bye may include things like baking a few cookies with them to give to that special person. Brave parents sometimes schedule a party or overnight so their children can have a final chance to say good-bye to close friends. When times are planned for intentionally saying farewell, anticipating those special times can go a long way toward helping children avoid the excessive pulling away that can lead to those long-term consequences we discussed earlier.
- *Places:* Everyone has places that evoke an emotional response. It may be a spot tied to a special moment in our lives (our engagement, for instance) or where we go when we are upset or where certain events always occur. These are the places we come back to visit and show our children years later. Part of healthy closure includes visiting such sites to reminisce and say farewell. This is particularly important for TCKs who may be losing their whole world with next week's plane ride. Many TCKs we have talked to mourn for the favorite tree they used to climb years after they have left the land of their childhood. People say good-bye to places in different ways. Some plant a tree that will grow long after they are gone, symbolizing a living, ongoing connection to this part of their lives. Others leave a hidden secret message or "treasure" to look for in case they should return. No matter how it is done, openly acknowledging this time as a true good-bye is important, as

is recognizing that this stage in life and all that these places represent to us are passing.

- *Pets:* Pets aren't equally important in every culture, but they can be significant when it comes to good-byes. TCKs need to know how their pets will be cared for and who will love them. If the pet must be put to sleep, everyone who cares for that pet, particularly children, should say good-bye. Some TCKs tell us how devastated they were after parents promised their pet would be happy in a new home, only to find out months or years later that the dog was euthanized or the chicken given to someone for food.

- *Possessions:* One problem (some might say blessing!) international sojourners face is that they can rarely take all their possessions with them when they move. Parents may delight in the chance to throw out a child's dirty rock collection, never realizing how precious those rocks were to their child. Certainly, we realize part of life is letting go, but parents should talk with their children about what to take and what to leave as they pack. Everyone in the family needs to carry some treasured items to the new location. These become part of the collection of *sacred objects* that help connect one part of a global nomad's life to the next. But sometimes even treasures must be left behind. When that happens, it's important to part with them consciously. Placing a precious object in the hands of someone else as a gift or taking photographs of it are two ways to say good-bye to an inanimate but important old friend.

The celebratory rituals of farewell commonly associated with certain types of transitions, such as graduations or retirement parties, are another important part of building this raft. Taking the time for "rites of passage" gives us markers for remembering meaningful places and people and directly addressing the fact that we are saying farewell.

This normal pattern can be complicated for internationally mobile families. Many of them permanently return to their home country after the oldest child graduates from secondary school abroad. The graduating TCK goes through the rites of passage—the graduation ceremony, and the "wailing wall" afterward, where all line up and say good-bye to one another. However, the needs of the younger children for the same types of closure when they leave for the passport country are often overlooked. This can later add greatly to the younger child's sense of "unfinished business," while the older TCK in the same family is off and running once he or she gets to the homeland. Remember, *every* member of the family needs to build the RAFT during any leaving process.

Think destination. Even as we are saying the good-byes and processing the sad reality of those good-byes, we need to think realistically about our destination: Where are we going? What are some of the positives and negatives we can expect to find once we get there? Will we have electricity and running water? How will we learn to drive on the other side of the road? Do we need to take a transformer with us to keep our 110-volt appliances from burning out on a 220-volt electrical system?

This is also the time to look at our external (e.g., finances, family support structure) and internal (e.g., ability to deal with stress or change) resources for coping with problems we might encounter. What resources will we find in the new location and what will we need to take with us? Who can help us adjust to the new culture when we get there? This is the best time to find out from the sponsoring agency who will meet us at the airport, where we will stay until housing is located, and what that housing will be.

While these are primarily the concerns parents need to consider, thinking destination is equally important for children. Practical things such as maps, pictures of the next house or school, details of the upcoming itinerary, and places that may be visited along the way are all helpful tools parents can use to help children think and plan ahead. Increasingly, there are books like those Beverly Roman and others have written for preteens and young children in this leaving stage to use in this process, such as *The League of Super Movers* and *My Family Is Moving*. If at all possible, this is also a great time to try to make contact with other families or children who are in the new place or are already attending the new school so that mentors are already being put in place.

If we don't think through some of these issues, the adjustment for all members of the family may be rockier than it needs to be once we arrive at the new destination. If we are expecting too much, we'll be disappointed. If we don't expect enough, we may not use the resources available, thereby making life more complicated than necessary. Of course, we can never have a perfect picture of what life in the new place will be like, and we must always recognize that each member of the family will go through the stages of transition at a different pace, but doing our best to prepare beforehand can prevent a lot of problems later on.

After all of this thorough preparation in the leaving stage, it's time to move on into the transition stage itself.

Maintaining Stability through the Transition Stage

When people ask how they can avoid chaos and confusion during the transition process, we have to say they can't. They can, though, keep in mind that it's a normal stage and it will pass if they hang on long enough. Also, there are a few steps we can take to help us maintain some sense of equilibrium and connectedness with the past and to smooth the way for the future stages of entry and reinvolvement.

One way is through the use of sacred objects—those mementos we mentioned earlier that specifically reflect a certain place or moment of our lives. That's why the choice of which possessions to keep and which to give away is so important during the leaving stage. A favorite teddy bear pulled out of the suitcase each night during the travels from one place to another reminds the child that there is one stable thing in his or her life amidst the general chaos. At the same time, Mom or Dad may be reading a treasured book they brought along, which reminds them of other times and places where they have read those same inspiring or comforting words.

Other sacred objects are worn. Did you ever look around a group of TCKs or their parents and see how many were wearing some article of clothing or jewelry that connected them to their past? It might be a Tuareg cross hanging on a gold chain or a V-ring on a finger. Perhaps they're wearing a sari instead of a sweater. Often an ATCK's home is quite a sight to behold—with artifacts gathered from around the world, all proving that "I was there! It's part of my history." Each sacred object serves as a good reminder that the current moment or scene is part of a bigger story of that person's life.

Pictures are another way we connect with special moments and memories in our past. One ambassador asked each staff member to list what he or she would put in the one bag allowed for an emergency evacuation. Photographs headed the list for every person, far above things with much more monetary worth. Why? Because each picture reminds us of some relationship, an experience we have had, a place we have visited. Pictures add a value to our lives that money alone can't buy. A small picture album with photographs representing significant highlights of our past life and location gives us a lovely place to visit when we need a few reflective moments in the middle of this sometimes turbulent stage. Pictures can also be helpful for letting people in the new place know something more of our history.

Of course, we recognize that everyone we would like to show these pictures and sacred objects to may not see the same value in them that we do. (And often it's vice versa when they try to show us theirs!) Why don't most people particularly enjoy another person's PowerPoint or video show? Because friends who weren't there can't see anything interesting in a skinny cow walking down the middle of a road; it seems rather bizarre to them. And they certainly don't want to hear a twenty-minute story about the man with the shaved head in the back row of a group picture. For the person who was there, though, that picture or video segment brings back a flood of memories, and every detail is fascinating. That's why globally nomadic people should make a pact to look at each other's slides or home videos. It's how they can affirm their experiences!

Another thing we sometimes forget in this stage is to take time to "stop and smell the roses." Often we are flying from one spot to the next, suddenly living amid strange customs and languages. While it can be overwhelming, it can also be seen as a wonderful time of exploration. We may not feel ready to settle in yet, but surely we can at least be interested observers. There is much to learn, and to help TCKs learn, about the cultures and places in which we are living on any given day during transition.

Even if we built our RAFT perfectly in the leaving stage and enjoy observing the new world around us, transition is the stage where we often begin to mourn most acutely the loss of things and people left behind. If we think back to the grief cycle we discussed in chapter 12, up until now we have likely been in the denial and bargaining stages, maybe with some anger along the way—but even there, the anger is often directed at those we are leaving behind as part of our preparation for the upcoming separation. Transition is the stage where the sadness and possible depression can hit. We feel unbearable emptiness when we realize we can't call our best friend to meet us for a cup of coffee. We miss the comfort of knowing everyone in our factory or office by name. The permanence of the move and the irretrievability of the past stare us in the face and we wonder if we've made a terrible mistake.

During the leaving stage we knew these losses were coming, but now their reality is here. This is a critical moment and one that can affect any or all members of the family for years to come. Parents must decide what to do with their own grief as well as that they see in their children. Will they deal with it or try to pack it away—out of sight, out of mind? In particular, will they choose to comfort their children at this point or only try to cheer them up? Sometimes the chaos of the moment is so great we simply can't afford to deal fully with the reality of what we are losing, and our only choice to survive seems to be to ignore those feelings. Parents who are not willing to look at their own losses will be unable to help their children. Some children may not be able or ready to do anything but block out the past and survive at this point. That is a common means of getting through this transition stage, and that is okay in the short run. But when that happens, at some point everyone in the family must be willing to go back and do some appropriate mourning for the losses just endured. Too many people get through transition by packing away these painful feelings of loss and never taking them out consciously at a later stage. This is what winds up years later in the issues related to unresolved grief that we have mentioned earlier.

While some people try to survive the transition stage by ignoring their losses, other people, of course, seem to be able to deal more easily with the losses as they are happening. Whenever we choose to deal with the inevitable losses in our move—during this stage itself or later—it is important at some point to mourn the losses we have known even while affirming all the good that is ahead.

MOURNING THE LOSSES

But what, in fact, is mourning? How is it different from grief? A professor of philosophy, Jim Gould, says that loss always produces grief, consciously or unconsciously, and that it will come out one way or another, whether the person intends it to or not. Mourning, however, is the conscious acknowledgment of loss. Because of that, he believes those living these globally nomadic lifestyles need to develop better rituals of mourning to help in that process of dealing with grief intentionally rather than suppressing it. All the suggestions we offered for helping us build the RAFT might also be cited as these rituals of mourning.[3] Some families develop a particular ritual, such as going out to a favorite local restaurant the last night before leaving each location and always ordering pizza.

But getting through the transition stage isn't only about exploring the present or looking at our losses. It also includes the need to continue that planning for the future that we began when we "thought destination" in the leaving stage. Such planning can be something as simple as letting the children know next week we will make a Skype call to say "happy birthday" to Grandma and to let her know we miss her, or it can be helping teens figure out what subjects they will study in the new school they are about to attend. Planning ahead in such ways is realistic, and it also helps us move through the grieving process by reminding us and our children that life does go on in spite of great loss.

Entering Right

Physical arrival alone doesn't mean we have begun the entering stage. Sometimes the chaos of the transition stage remains for some days or weeks after our initial arrival. The more we have thought ahead about this time, however, and the more we are consciously aware of what we and our family will need to make a positive entry into this place, the sooner and smoother we can begin to positively move into our new life. It's important for everyone involved, however, to recognize that they don't have to wait helplessly around for the new community to reach out and receive them. There are many ways we can proactively help ourselves in this process. So how, then, can we (and the new community) move from the desire to establish ourselves in our new community to actually accomplishing it?

CHOOSING AND USING MENTORS

The key to successfully negotiating the entry stage, particularly in an international or cross-cultural move, is to find a *mentor*—someone who answers questions and introduces the new community to us and us to it. These mentors function as "bridges" and can smooth our way in, significantly shorten the time it takes for us to get acclimated to the new surroundings, and help us make the right contacts. They can also give tips for the unspoken and unseen "do's and don'ts" that are operative in this new community and culture.

The problem, of course, lies in finding the *right* mentor, both for parents and children. After all, the mentor is the person who determines the group of people all members of the family will meet, the attitude each of us will absorb about this new place, and the one from whom we learn the acceptable behavioral patterns. Ultimately, the mentor not only can affect the long-term relationships both adults and children may have to this new community but often determines our effectiveness in it as well. If we find the right one, we're in great shape.

The wrong mentor, however, can be a disaster—doing for us the exact opposite of what a good mentor would do. If our mentor is negative about the place, its people, the school, or the sponsoring organization/corporation, we begin to doubt whether we should have come and become afraid to try new things. Even worse, if the chosen, or self-assigned, mentor has a bad reputation in the community, others may put us in the same category and avoid us as well.

This issue of finding the right mentor is particularly critical for TCKs as they move into a new place. At the very time when they are in the position of being "outsiders," often those who are also on the fringes of the receiving community will be the first to introduce themselves to a newcomer. They, too, may be looking for friends while others belonging to the "in" group already have their cadre of friends nicely established and may not be interested in adding more. TCKs or any new arrivals to a school or community are, of course, so happy *someone* has reached out to them that they can easily jump into a new relationship before understanding what the ramifications of such a relationship might be.

How can any newcomer know who is or isn't trustworthy as a mentor? How can all members of the family make a wise decision at this point?

Our suggestion is to be appreciative and warm to all who reach out a helping hand during this entry time, but inwardly to be cautious about making a wholehearted commitment to this relationship before asking a few questions: Is this person one who fits into the local community or is he or she definitely marginalized in one way or another? Does this person exhibit the positive, encouraging attitudes you would like to foster in your family, or does this person make negative remarks and display hostile attitudes about almost everything?

When we take a little time to evaluate a potential mentor, we may discover that this person who greeted us so warmly is, in fact, one of those wonderful people who belong to the heart of any organization, school, or community and has the great gift of making newcomers feel almost instantly at home. That person could well go on to be the best possible mentor in the world for any particular member of the family and be a great friend. If, however, we find out that this person who is so eager to befriend us or our TCKs is a marginal member of the community, then we must ask the next question: Why do they want to befriend us?

Some are marginal simply because they, like us, are relative newcomers and are still looking to establish new friendships. While they may not yet be members of the inner circle, they have learned the basics of how life is lived in this place and can be most helpful. In fact, they often have more time to spend orienting newcomers than those whose plates are already full with well-defined roles and relationships. Relationships that start like this often turn into lifelong friendships.

If, however, we find out that the first person who approaches us, and particularly our TCKs, so invitingly has been intentionally marginalized from the community, we need to be cautious about adopting this person as a mentor. Such people are often in some kind of trouble within the community. Perhaps they rebel against the accepted standards of behavior, break laws, or defy teachers, and they often want to recruit naïve newcomers for their own agenda.

Besides using our common sense in situations such as we have just described, there are other ways to try to find good mentors. We can make use of any active mentoring programs already in place. Some agencies or corporations set up "matching families" for those coming to their community. One potential problem is that an organization may have a mentoring program for the adults in the family, but the children's need for a mentor is forgotten. In such cases, parents may need to be more proactive and ask those in the human resources or employee care departments of their organization if they can give the names of possible families to contact in the next posting. Many international schools have set up a "big brother/big sister" program, with good mentors already identified, to help new students through their first few weeks at school. Getting involved with such things as parent/teacher groups can be a way for parents to meet other parents and help to find informal mentors if no formal mentoring programs are available.

One thing to note, however. In communities with chronically high mobility, we have noticed two interesting, though rather opposite, responses to newcomers. Some, like those just mentioned, have a regular routine to help new members get oriented. There are maps of the town with the key places to shop marked and instruction guides for dealing with the local host culture—all tucked in a basket of goodies. One person is specifically assigned to take the new family around, and the whole system of orientation goes like clockwork because it has happened so many times. It's great when your family relocates to such a community.

On the other hand, members of other highly mobile communities are so tired of seeing people come and go, they basically don't do much at all for the newcomer. Their thought process goes like this: "What's the use? These people will just be gone again," or "Why bother getting to know them? I've only got three months left here myself." Such an attitude makes it more difficult, of course, for newcomers, who can then begin to feel very angry and withdraw from others too. But with some understanding of why others may seem cautious, and with some patient persistence to reach out to new acquaintances, or by inviting families with children of like ages over for an evening, in time it is possible even in these communities to find a way into a positive sense of belonging to this new place.

Most of our discussion on this entry stage applies to any kind of move. But there are extra stresses recognized by experts around the world for those trying to enter a completely new culture—which is the nature of most transitions for third culture families. Lisa and Leighton Chinn, a couple who work with international students, have outlined four stages of cultural stress that occur during this phase: fun, flight, fight, and fit. It's important to acknowledge these extra stages, because they often happen in spite of all we have done right to prepare for our move and can make us feel that none of our other preparations mattered. The process can go something like this—sort of a second transition cycle within the larger first transition process.

As we have looked ahead, we have developed a sense of anticipation and excitement for our new assignment. We decide it will be *fun* to explore the new environment, learn its history, and enrich our lives through meeting new people. The first few days after arrival, we busily engage with all we meet, feel excitement that we can actually answer the greetings in this new language we tried to study before we came, and all seems well. We think, "What fun!" A few more days pass, however, and things aren't quite as exciting. We don't like not knowing how to get to the store on our own because we haven't learned yet how to drive on the "wrong" side of the road, we're tired of not being understood past simple greetings by those around us, and we wish we could go "home"—back to that place where we knew how to function and where we fit. This is the *flight* stage.

Soon, however, we get tired of feeling so useless or out of place and begin to get angry. After all, we used to fit. We were competent individuals where we used to live so it can't be our fault that we feel so lost and insecure, and we begin to blame everything and everyone in this new place for our discomfort. If they would only do things "right" (meaning the way we used to do them), everything would be fine. Internally, and sometimes externally, we begin to *fight* with the way things are being done here—perhaps even becoming angry at our mentor who is doing his or her best to teach us these new ways.

Knowing these reactions might happen doesn't necessarily stop them, but, again, knowledge helps us at least make more appropriate choices. In this case we might choose not to be quite so vocal about all we despise in our new situation!

These are the moments we need to remind ourselves that entry also takes time, to remember that six months from now we can presume that somehow we will have learned to drive here, discovered where the stores are for the things we want to buy, and most likely have made new friends by then. At that point, once again we will *fit*.

Reinvolvement Stage

The light at the end of the proverbial tunnel is that in any transition, cross-cultural or not, a final, recognized stage of reinvolvement is possible. We settle into our new surroundings, accepting the people and places for who and what they are. This doesn't always mean that we like everything about the situation, but at least we can start to see *why* people do what they do rather than only *what* it is they do. We've learned the new ways and know our position in this community. Other members of the group see us as one of them, or at least they know where we fit. We have a sense of intimacy, a feeling that our presence matters to this group, and once more we feel secure. Time again feels present and permanent as we focus on the here and now rather than hoping for the future or constantly reminiscing about the past.

Lessons from the TCK Petri Dish

In all transitions, we gain as well as lose. While all CCKs may not have the international mobility that TCKs know, everyone alive goes through big and little transitions all the time. Perhaps one more paradox of the TCK experience is that learning to deal in healthy ways with the losses of transition can become a great asset in a TCK's life, both for themselves and for others. Having language and concepts to understand this basic process gives further clarity to situations that would otherwise seem completely unrelated.

> ATCK Latasha told us that during her bout with breast cancer, knowing about the transition cycle was key in helping her deal with it. She realized with the initial news of the diagnosis that she was in the "leaving" phase—moving from life as it had been to life in the world of chemo and radiation cycles she didn't yet know. As she faced the prospects ahead, she saw how she needed to deal not only with her potential loss of life, but the many hidden losses also entailed in such a time as this: the loss that she could not be involved in the day-to-day activities of life with her friends as she was used to doing; the loss that her record of near-perfect health was now forever gone; and the loss of her sense of identity—that when others saw her bald head, they would see "cancer patient" rather than Latasha.
>
> She found this insight extremely helpful as she went through the different feelings of her treatment phase of chemo and radiation. She could name this as the transition stage—the old world was gone and what lay ahead remained unclear. Survival was the goal for each day, knowing another stage was coming. At the end of her treatments, she realized she had moved into the entry, or perhaps reentry, phase. Life had gone on without her in her former world; how would she find her way back in? "With intentionality," meaning it was up to her to reach out to others as well as expecting them to reach out to her. She did so and feels totally reinvolved at this stage.

Latasha's story demonstrates what we mean when we say learning to deal constructively with the challenges of the TCK experience can translate them into strengths for our lives as well. As not only TCKs but also others continue to understand this basic human process, we can understand why we no longer have to shut down our emotions or shut out relationships. Instead, all of us—TCKs, CCKs, adults of all backgrounds—can risk the pain of another loss for the sake of the gain that goes with it, because we know how to get from one side to the other. Learning to live with this kind of openness affects all areas of life in a positive way and does, indeed, turn this challenge into one more strength.

CHAPTER 15

Meeting Educational Needs

By the time I was nine, I was already used to going to school by trans-Atlantic plane, to sleeping in airports, to shuttling back and forth, three times a year, between my parents' (Indian) home in California and my boarding school in England. Throughout the time I was growing up, I was never within 6,000 miles of the nearest relative—and come, therefore to define relations in non-familial way.[1]

—*Pico Iyer, from "Living in the Transit Lounge"*

THIRD CULTURE FAMILIES FACE A VARIETY OF CHOICES when it comes to deciding how to educate their children, and every option has distinct advantages and disadvantages. How can parents know which one is best for each particular child?

Unfortunately, parents often face this major decision with little or no awareness of the different types of opportunities available for schooling in a cross-cultural setting, let alone the pros and cons of each method. Yet, for many TCKs, their experiences in school dramatically shape how they view their childhood and whether they look back on it with joy or regret. Because making the right choice for schooling is so crucial for TCKs, we want to look at this issue in depth.

As we mentioned earlier, before parents accept any cross-cultural assignment, it's important they ask the sponsoring organization about its current educational opportunities and policies. These can vary greatly from one group to another. Few, if any, agencies now require families to send children to a boarding school as in the past. But there may be other written or nonwritten expectations: Are parents expected to homeschool the children? Are all children required to attend the local international school? Are they likely to attend a local school?

Once parents know the answers to these questions, they must decide whether the organization's policies will or won't accommodate their children's educational needs. If a family feels that an agency's policy won't work well for them, they are generally better off to seek a career with another sponsor or corporation rather than try to force the organization to change its policy—or perhaps worse, to compromise the family's needs.

If parents discover an organization gives complete freedom of choice to its employees regarding their children's schooling, there are still important questions to ask: What, in fact, are the available options? What language and curriculum do local national schools use? What language and curriculum does the local international school use? Who will pay for the extra costs of schooling (including travel expenses for children attending school in other countries to come back for vacations), since some options are very expensive?

Making the Best Choice

There is no perfect schooling formula that guarantees a happy outcome for all TCKs. There are, however, some underlying principles about the educational process that can help parents make the best choices possible.

Some parents fear taking their children into a cross-cultural setting because they believe their children will miss out on too many educational opportunities offered in the home country. But the educational process for any child includes more than school; it includes *all* learning, in every dimension of a person's life. Everyone acquires information and masters skills by a variety of formal and informal means.

One great advantage TCKs have is the wealth of learning opportunities available to them from their travels, cross-cultural interactions, and the third culture experience itself. When TCKs move through the *suk* in Sanaa, eat in an Indian friend's home in Mumbai, or watch a murky brown river flow through the greenery of a Brazilian or Vietnamese jungle, they are learning in the most dynamic way of all—through the five senses. This hands-on education in geography, history, basic anthropology, social studies, and language acquisition is a great benefit of the TCK experience and more than replaces some of the deficits in equipment or facilities that might be present in an overseas school.

Parents must also remember that in terms of preparing their children for life, they themselves are the primary educators. Schools can't substitute for the home in building values, developing healthy attitudes, and motivating children in positive directions.

Brian Hill, professor of education at Murdoch University in Australia, suggests seven basic outcomes parents in cross-cultural settings should look for from their children's educational experience. The experience should enable them to maintain a stable and positive self-image while learning new things; acquire survival skills appropriate to their own culture; identify and develop their personal creative gifts; gain access to the major fields of human thought and experience; become aware of the dominant worldviews and value orientations influencing their social world; develop the capacity to think critically and choose responsibly; and develop empathy, respect, and a capacity for dialogue with other persons, including those whose primary beliefs differ from their own.[2] Note that this list is another way of looking at how a child can develop a strong and healthy sense of personal identity. Parents should evaluate a school in terms of how well it will help meet these larger goals of the educational process.

EDUCATIONAL PHILOSOPHIES DIFFER AMONG CULTURES

Parents must examine the total approach to education in any system of schooling, not merely the academics. Styles of discipline, teaching, and grading can vary widely from one culture to another. These differences can have an enormous impact on children. Those who always make straight As and a few Bs in one system are devastated when they suddenly bring home mostly Cs with only one or two Bs after they switch school systems. In Britain, 50 percent is passing, 70s and 80s are considered great, and scores in the 90s are practically unheard of. In the United States, 50 percent is failure, but As are given to those with 94 percent and higher. An American child going to a British school can panic when she sees these lower marks. She knows if her transcript is filled with 70s and 80s and it is sent to universities in the U.S. without interpretation, she may never be admitted.

Corporal punishment is a common practice in certain places, while it would be unthinkable in others. Some school systems stress learning by rote. Others use only problem-based learning, where students must personally seek out the answers to each assignment. In some cultures discussion and other forms of student participation are encouraged, or even required. In others, this type of behavior is considered disrespectful.

> In one Western-based international school, Asian children told their parents the American teachers didn't know anything about the subjects they were teaching. The parents asked to talk with the principal about his incompetent staff. In the end, it turned out that when the Asian students asked questions, the teachers would often ask them in return, "What do *you* think?" or "How would *you* work this out?" The teachers believed they were trying to teach their students how to think, not only to give rote answers. The Asian students and parents felt if the teacher knew the information, they wouldn't have asked the question. After all, it was the teacher's job to impart knowledge. For them, amassing

information was the key ingredient required for a good education. When teachers asked students questions, it seemed to the Asian parents that these teachers were playing games rather than educating their children.

Ways of motivating students vary from culture to culture too. In some places, external methods are emphasized. Homework is assigned and graded each day. Every six weeks parents are notified of their child's progress, or lack thereof. Instant rewards and punishments are the major means of encouraging students in these systems. Other school systems rely far more on internal motivation. Students are assumed to be responsible for their own learning, daily homework is neither assigned nor checked, and class attendance is optional. Only the final exam matters.

We have seen this single difference between motivational philosophies cause great consternation for TCKs and their families. When a student who is used to doing homework assignments every night goes to a school with no daily assignments, he or she often has trouble knowing how to organize the study time necessary to cover the assigned work before the end of the semester. Parents may wonder why their child seems to go out socializing every night with seemingly little regard for school work. Since, however, no reports come home to tell them otherwise, they presume all is well. Only when the final exam comes and the TCK fails do they—or their child—know something is wrong.

Conversely, a student who is used to working independently may see no reason to do the daily homework assignments; they seem trivial. Perhaps he or she also sees no reason to attend class regularly; studying in the library seems more important. Only when the first reports come home with failing grades does it become clear that things like homework and class attendance matter in this new setting.

In considering a particular school, parents must ask for an explanation of the philosophy of education, the methods of teaching, and the policy toward discipline and then decide if this school is a good match for their child. Even when an educational option seems like a good one from the parents' view or has been great for other children in the same family, some of these differences in the philosophical or psychological approaches to education can cause enough stress for a particular TCK that a change to a school with a different method of teaching is justified.

SCHOOL TEACHES MORE THAN ACADEMIC SUBJECTS

School is one of the principal means whereby one generation communicates its culture and its values to the next. As long as everyone comes from the same culture, we hardly notice this process and what's taught is accepted as "right."

In international schools the transmission of cultural values and expectations takes place as it does in any other school, because there is no such thing as value-free education. The difference is that teachers and peers, who come from many countries and cultures, along with the curriculum itself, may represent value systems that vary markedly from that of the parents of any given TCK. Parents who forget this are often surprised to discover that the cultural values and behaviors of their children's teachers and peers have influenced their children far more or in different ways than expected.

> One Korean father told us how shocked he was during an exchange with his son. The son had attended an American-oriented school in an Asian country. As the Korean community in that country grew, they started their own school. The Korean parents believed the American school wasn't preparing their children to take the exams necessary for them to continue school in Korea. They also felt their children were forgetting Korean culture.
>
> When the father told his son he would soon be changing schools, the son refused. "No, I'm not. I've attended the American school all my life, my friends are there, and I'm going to graduate from there."
>
> This conversation distressed the father—not because his son refused the improved educational opportunity, but because he dared to disobey. "When I was my son's age, I would never have considered resisting my father," he said. "No matter what I felt, I would have obeyed without question."

For good or ill, educating this Korean student in a school based on the American values of independence, free speech, and individualism had deeply affected a family's cultural heritage.

SCHOOLING SHOULD NOT MAKE IT IMPOSSIBLE FOR THE CHILD TO RETURN TO THE HOME COUNTRY

Many children, particularly those whose mother tongue is not English, face even more cultural influences and differences in curriculum in their educational process than the historical Western-based international school student of the past. In those days, most TCKs were Westerners from English-speaking countries attending English-speaking schools. Now this has changed. The new degree of cultural layering can make it extremely difficult—or even impossible—for some TCKs to return to the educational system in their home country. But it isn't only the difference in school systems or curriculum that can pose problems.

> Judith Gjoen, a Dutch TCK from Indonesia, was educated
> in American schools in Malaysia and now lives with her
> Norwegian husband in Oslo. She is a practicing counselor
> who has expressed particular concern about TCKs who
> return to their passport culture wanting to continue their
> education but lack proficiency or confidence in using their
> mother tongue. A young woman from a Nordic country
> observed that her speaking, reading, and writing ability
> in her mother tongue was fine for home and social use, but
> her school language was English, the language of her high
> school education. She finally had to pursue her university
> education in the United States. This, of course, further alien-
> ated her from her home country.

Parents, educators, and agency administrators have a responsibility to provide the opportunity for TCKs to learn their native language so that they have the
option of returning to their passport country for further formal education and
settling down there, if that's what they choose. As mentioned earlier, the International School of the Hague has begun special after-school groups for many of the
mother tongues represented in their multinational school population. After they
have identified the various languages present in their school and faculty population, they pair up teachers or other students with new students who share their
language to help during their orientation and transition into the school community. Other schools are beginning to take more proactive roles in trying to help
students be able to return to a local school when they repatriate.

However, there's another potential barrier to TCKs acquiring fluency in
their own language. Sometimes the TCKs themselves resist. Children want to be
like their peers. If everyone else around is speaking French, why take more time
away from socializing or be labeled as different just to learn another language?
School-age children are not able to look ahead to long-term consequences. Most
don't think about life after secondary school. Parents and educators need to be
sensitive to this possibility and try to help their TCKs see how learning their
own language is an expansion of their world rather than a limitation. One added
bonus for the mother tongue program at the International School of the Hague
is that this approach makes learning a mother tongue not only something to be
valued, but also something that is normal.

Different Schooling Choices Are Available

Having said all of this about what education is, one fact remains: school is, in
fact, important; it's the place where we learn things that can't be assimilated by

pure observation. We do need to learn how to read and write; we do need to know the history of our world and country if we are to learn from and build on the past; we do need to know how atoms and molecules work if scientific research is to continue. The question then is, "Which type of schooling is best for my child?" The next question is, "Which of our options best fit those criteria?" Answering these questions usually results in a pretty good fit for the student's needs. Parents can then make intelligent, informed, and sensitive decisions about the schools, and then monitor the school experience and decide if it is a good one for their child.

To help parents make wise choices, let's look at specific options generally available to third culture families. Although the variety may seem a little confusing at first, these choices give parents the necessary flexibility to help meet the needs of each individual child. The most common methods for formally educating TCKs include home and correspondence schooling, online schools through the Internet, satellite schools, local national schools, local international schools, boarding schools, and preuniversity schooling in the home country. The following sections discuss some of the pros and cons of each of these options.

HOME AND CORRESPONDENCE SCHOOLING

Pros	Cons
Child lives with parents	Lack of parental teaching skills
Individualized instruction	
	Children may fall behind if so
Moral and spiritual values of parents taught	Parent-child stress
Parent- and home-centered	Lack of peer contact
Child can continue schooling in home country without interruption	Lack of healthy competition
Can use curriculum of choice	

Figure 15-1 Pros and Cons of Home and Correspondence Schooling

An increasing number of internationally mobile families use various methods of homeschooling, particularly for younger TCKs. Some parents create their own curriculum. During home leave, one mother went to the local public grade school in Chicago, found out what textbooks they used, ordered those books online, and made her own lesson plans from them for each of her four school-age children.

Other parents combine materials offered by several homeschooling groups to design their own curriculum. Still others use a syllabus offered by a specific correspondence school, including DVDs. In some of these cases, the lessons are monitored by the parents but graded by teachers back home.

SCHOOLS ON THE INTERNET

In recent years, online schools have added another dimension and option for those who have to, or choose to, school at home. In these programs students log in online and, in real time and through the miracles of teleconferencing, can listen to the teacher speaking from another continent and can interact with fellow students who may be on five other continents. This can be particularly helpful for families who live in remote areas of the world—as long as they have satellite dish connections or some other means of high-speed Internet. The positive here is that there are definite schedules the child has to meet, classes are taught by professionals, and the parents are no longer the primary tutors. Students can make friends with classmates even though they may not meet in person. Some online schools even offer virtual graduations to add to the sense that this is, in fact, an actual school.

Pros	Cons
Child lives with parents	Lack of physically present peers
Small class size	
Child can continue schooling in home country without interruption	May be more expensive than other home schooling options
Internet classes include virtual classmates, discussion, real time teacher	
Teaching responsibility with teacher, more like physical classroom; parents not teaching outside their skill level	

Figure 15-2 Pros and Cons of Schools on the Internet

Some parents have successfully put together a smorgasbord of educational options by combining modified homeschooling and correspondence courses with online or national schools. A growing cooperation between counselors from local and international schools with parents who are homeschooling for various reasons is another positive development for many globally mobile families.

For any type of homeschooling or correspondence and online schools, parents must have access to educational tools, technology, and other resources in order to do a good job. One compelling reason for working with counselors from an online, local, or international school is to make sure the parents have access to standardized testing. It is important for parents using any of these homeschooling methods to know the content and sequencing of the curriculum to ensure it will be compatible with the child's next educational step. Standards required in a more structured school setting must be maintained.

Keeping to a time schedule is also important for homeschooling. We've met TCKs who saw no reason to be on time, or present, for their classes when they began university. They disdained such requirements as "too rigid." In their experience, if interruptions to planned schoolwork happened in the morning, it was no big deal. They would do it that afternoon, or perhaps the next day, maybe on the weekend—occasionally, never. Of course, interruptions happen in any life, but this lack of structure should not be the main pattern.

The greatest benefit to homeschooling is, of course, that kids remain with their parents. This is important, particularly in a child's early years. Some ATCKs who presumably did "just fine" as six-year-old boarders struggle as adults with attachment issues not only to parents but to their spouses and children as well. Another benefit—especially to those with erratic home leave or frequent relocations—is that the children can maintain continuity in school without having to jump from one system to another in the middle of the year.

Homeschooling, however, isn't always the best option—even in its most creative form. First, TCKs may be isolated from peers—particularly those TCKs raised in remote areas. This may not be a significant problem during early childhood, but it can be a serious problem during the teenage years when peer approval seems more crucial than parental support.

Second, the dynamics in some families simply aren't suited to this type of schooling. Perhaps the parents have neither the natural nor the professional skills to properly teach the academic subjects. One or both parents may be so disorganized that instruction is haphazard or never takes place at all. Some kids chronically refuse to do anything their parents suggest, causing constant friction and confusion in the home.

In those situations, the benefits of homeschooling in any of these ways may not be worth the frustrations. That doesn't mean the parents or children have failed. It only means that homeschooling isn't the best option for this particular family.

SATELLITE SCHOOLS

Pros	Cons
Living at home with parents	Labor-intensive for sponsoring agency
More chance for interaction with peers than homeschooling	Still may have limited social opportunities
Trained teacher	Inadequate equipment for certain subjects
Externally organized curriculum	High teacher attrition
Parents still closely involved	

Figure 15-3 Pros and Cons of Satellite Schools

In the 1980s, a model for satellite schools was introduced as another option for some TCKs. These are usually small groups of students who have clustered together into a slightly more formalized setting than the individual home. In those early days, the children might have gone to a base from outlying areas for a five-day program and then gone home for the next week or two as they completed their homework assignments with parental help. Now it is more likely the sponsoring agency sends a teacher to a specific locale for a few families. Classrooms often resemble the old-fashioned, one-room schoolhouse. Other satellite schools depend primarily on DVDs or interactive computer programs. While an adult supervises the proceedings, the teaching itself takes place through these electronic tutors, but not in real time as the newer online programs offer. In certain situations, these schools may also use correspondence courses.

Satellite schools usually have a good teacher/student ratio, with each child receiving individualized attention. They provide more socialization than a strictly homeschool setting, and the TCKs are still able to live at home with parents.

LOCAL NATIONAL SCHOOLS

Pros	Cons
Child lives with parents	Religious/philosophical differences from parents
Cross-culture relationships	
Language acquisition	Total cultural identification with host culture—loss of own cultural identity
Good education in many places	
Relatively low cost	Unacceptable philosophy of education
Strong exposure to host culture	Tension or rejection due to nationalism
Cultural immersion/ assimilation more possible	Competes with host nationals for available places to attend school

Figure 15-4 Pros and Cons of Local National Schools

National schools may be one of the best educational options in some countries, enabling children to become immersed in the culture, learn the language quickly, make friends in the locality, and become truly bicultural. Often national schools cost far less than the international schools. In fact, in the United States, they're free. TCKs can remain at home while having strong peer relationships. More and more third culture families successfully and happily make this choice.

However, there are special issues to consider as well. If school is taught in a language different from a child's mother tongue, the TCK must know enough of the local language *before* entering the school to function comfortably. We know of several sad cases where kids were put in classrooms before learning a word of the local language. Two weeks of absolutely no communication (not even the ability to ask for directions to the toilet) is an eternity to an eight-year-old. Parents must make certain their children have at least elemental language skills before the first day of school.

If the primary school language is not the parents' mother tongue(s), parents need to decide how they will deal with this reality. Sometimes those in English-speaking countries forget that globally nomadic families with non-English backgrounds have extra challenges, particularly when their mother tongue is not one of the world's main language groups. That challenge is how to keep their children not only fluent in *speaking* their mother tongue, but also in being able to do academic work in it. This can be especially true when the children physically look like the majority/dominant culture. As children want to blend in and be socially acceptable, many do not want to learn their mother language or use it lest they be "different." It's also a huge amount of work for both parents and children. Many families eventually give up even trying, and TCKs who are raised in these English-speaking worlds resettle there almost by default.

> Erik and Ria Verrijssen are one couple who have success-fully faced these challenges. The Verrijssens are from Belgium, and Erik works for a large multinational corporation. Their three children have grown up in multiple countries (Belgium, Italy, Poland, and the United States) and are now living in Atlanta, a city in the heart of the southern U.S. The challenge they faced was how to send their three children (Hendrik, An-Sofie, and Jeroen) to the local private schools but keep a high level of fluency in Flemish and French. Ria augmented the local schools' curriculum with daily language lessons in Flemish when the children came home. Although the children objected, sometimes strenuously at the time, all tell her now they are grateful for her hard work in helping them maintain oral and written fluency in their mother tongue.

Parents should also understand the basic philosophical and methodological underpinnings of this local system, as stated earlier in this chapter. Another matter to consider is the degree of animosity to the child's nationality in the host culture. If negative perceptions exist, a TCK might be the designated "outsider" and find the school situation intolerable. At that point, even if parents ideologically want their children to assimilate to help in the overall immersion of their family into this new culture, it might be wise to look at other options.

Finally, there is this issue of assimilation. While one benefit of attending local schools is that it helps TCKs become part of the surrounding community faster, some parents, however, are not prepared for how quickly and completely this might happen. When the child's behavior or language starts to be more like the host culture's than the parents', it can cause much consternation. Suddenly the parents realize the child has little sense of connection to their home culture compared to what he or she feels toward this new place. What does this do to the integrity of family identity? How will this affect their TCK's ultimate sense of cultural identity?

> Dave Pollock was confronted with the assimilation issue at a seminar on TCKs at the United Nations, where none of the attendees was from North America. To start out he asked them why they had come. After a period of silence, one father said, "Most of us are here to find out how to keep our children from becoming too American." The other participants laughed and nodded in agreement.
>
> Dave replied, "Well, I have some bad news and some good news for you. Whether you knew it or not, when you decided to become a globally nomadic family and move to the United States (or any other country), you decided that your children would become third culture kids. That means they will be influenced by the culture they live in and become in some degree bi- or multicultural; it's inevitable. Now the good news: it doesn't have to ruin their lives. In fact, it will add a lot to them. It's okay to be a TCK."

Parents must be prepared for this. There are many positive things about TCKs who identify closely with the local culture, but sometimes the cultural immersion is so complete that the TCK chooses to never repatriate. While there's nothing inherently wrong in this choice, it can be a painful one for a TCK's parents because they may feel their child is rejecting them along with their culture. It can make decisions for where parents will live in retirement more difficult as well. In their minds, they had always assumed that one day they, their children, and their grandchildren would again be "home" and life would be as it was for their parents and grandparents. Now they aren't sure where to live. It's unfair, however, for parents to encourage the great positives of in-depth cross-cultural relationships throughout their child's schooling and then object when that same child wants to marry and settle down permanently in the host country. Interestingly, however, in the end many parents come to value the world that opened to them in ways that might never have happened if their TCKs hadn't jumped so fully into this new place. In fact, they're often quite proud of their globally competent offspring. Still, the possible long-term implications of attending local schools need to be thought through at the beginning of the TCK experience, not the end.

LOCAL INTERNATIONAL SCHOOLS

Pros	Cons
Academically high standards	Expensive
Excellent facility and equipment	Potential lack of preparation for school in home country if curriculum/language are different
Enrichment and specialized programs	
Potential continuity with schooling during leave in home country	Economic imbalance among students
Usually home with parents	
Good preparation for reentry if curriculum is based on home country's system	

Figure 15-5 Pros and Cons of Local International Schools

International schools are another popular option for TCKs. A significant problem arises, however, in trying to identify what the term *international school* actually means. In her master's thesis, "Some of the Outcomes of International Schooling," Helen Fail raises these issues:

> Are there certain characteristics which define an international school, and if so what are they? Is it because children from several nationalities attend? If so, then many schools in Britain could be described as international. Is it determined by the curriculum? If so, then only the schools offering the International Baccalaureate would qualify. There are many schools overseas offering a U.S. or U.K. curriculum or another mixture which would presumably [result in their being] rated as national schools overseas. It may well be that many schools overseas consider themselves and indeed call themselves international yet never consider that while teaching an international curriculum to a group of students from many different nationalities, the teaching faculty is 95 percent British or American and inevitably they perpetuate certain national and cultural values.[3]

As international educators continue working on this matter, undoubtedly the term *international school* will be more precisely defined in the future. Probably no two international schools are alike, given the diversity of the cultural and educational backgrounds among those who administer them. For our discussion here, we'll include a broad spectrum of schools under the term *international school* and loosely define it as meaning any school that has students from various countries, and whose primary curriculum is different from the one used by the national schools of the host country.

So what are particular elements to consider when thinking of sending a child to an international school? First, cultural framework. Many such schools historically have their grading, style of teaching, basic curriculum, and philosophy of education rooted in a particular culture. This can be fairly obvious if the school is designated as "The British International School of Prague" or "The American School of the Hague." Certainly, many schools that began with a specific cultural focus have expanded in significant ways to accommodate the changing multinational student population. No longer are students primarily from three or four Western countries; many schools now have 40 to 60 nationalities in large urban centers in Europe. Most schools have embraced the new diversity and work to accommodate the many backgrounds of their students. Some, however, still see themselves as mainly serving their primary community. They believe if people come to their school, they understand the cultural base and have tacitly agreed to that by enrolling a child in this system. Parents can become frustrated later when they feel their voices are not being heard, so this is something to investigate ahead of time. Jill and Roger Dyer write about the disadvantage Australian TCKs face when they take placement tests at many supposedly international schools that are, in reality, based on American standards in testing and curriculum content.

> Why are such [placement] tests invalid? Firstly, such aptitude testing is rarely carried out in Australian schools.... There has long been a belief among Australian educators that no scores are conclusive because of the enormous range of variables involved.... Secondly, there is no doubt that the U.S. tests are biased in content. Small children may be asked to complete a sheet by filling in the initial letter of a word represented on the page by a picture. One example of this is of a window with flowing material covering much of the glassed area. The Australian child would automatically write "C" for curtains and be marked incorrect, as the required answer is a "D" for drapes. Further evidence of testing which requires cultural understanding is a general knowledge test for primary school children asking what is eaten with turkey at Thanksgiving...the answer required is cranberry sauce.[4]

The second thing to examine is curriculum. Whatever their historical roots, international schools are now incorporating broader choices in their subject material, including the International Baccalaureate degree and the International General Certificate of Secondary Education. Languages such as Japanese, Chinese, or Russian may now be offered, when before only the more standard French, Latin, Spanish, and English were available. Many schools offer different choices in history courses, including the history of the host country. In an effort to make it easier for TCKs from non-English speaking countries to repatriate, an increasing number of international schools use a non-Western-based curriculum. Parents must look at the whole picture of any so-called international school to make sure their child's needs will be met by the variety of subjects offered and the philosophy or cultural base of education practiced there.

These preceding issues aside, there are several significant benefits of international schooling. High on the list is that children usually remain at home, allowing the parents to have a more active role in school activities and in monitoring their children's progress. In fact, the very availability of group activities similar to those in schools back in the home country is another advantage. One of the greatest blessings is the diversity of backgrounds among students. When ATCKs look back on their international school experiences, many say they value most what they learned from their relationships with peers from many different nationalities. These global friendships opened the door to knowledge and understanding for a much larger worldview.[5]

Another important benefit offered by international schools is their general understanding of the internationally mobile experience. Many international schools have a 30 percent or more turnover rate each year as families are transferred in and out. Students understand what it is like to be "the new kid on the block" and typically extend themselves toward the newcomer. Administrators, teachers, and counselors also understand the transition experience. Doug Ota, a guidance counselor at the American School of the Hague, and his team have developed a comprehensive program that includes students, parents, and staff. The foundation of this program began initially in the 1990s when Shell Oil funded a pilot program designed by Barbara Schaetti to evaluate how a good approach to transition could be accomplished by a systemic approach as well as an individualistic response alone. More schools are implementing such models. Indeed, when parents have to choose between two or more international schools (not an uncommon situation in European and Asian capitals), they might want to factor into their decision which school provides ongoing, institutionalized transition programming. The school that offers transition activities to facilitate the adjustment of arrivals and departures and that integrates intercultural skill building and cultural identity explorations into the academic curriculum is probably the school to choose.[6]

The major drawback of international schools is their great expense. If parents are working for an agency that doesn't pay educational costs, the tuition may be prohibitive.

BOARDING SCHOOLS

Pros	Cons
Academically good	Isolated from "real life"
Parents don't have to double as teachers	Early separation from parents
Usually closer than a school in the home country	Living away from parents
	Separation from local culture
Peer group relationships	Individualized care difficult
Good preparation for reentry if based on home country curriculum	Potentially different religious/ philosophical values from parents

Figure 15-6 Pros and Cons of Boarding Schools

Many boarding schools around the world originally developed when strong formal educational programs of any kind were severely limited in many of the countries where third culture families worked. In those early days of international mobility, when missionary parents began a hospital in remote jungles or government officials moved to faraway lands to administer colonial regimes, few educational options were available for their children. Generally, the choices these families had were to homeschool their children or leave them with relatives or a boarding situation in their homeland.

In the early years of the twentieth century, however, various mission and colonial agencies founded boarding schools in the host countries as an attempt to help TCKs remain closer to their parents. The schools catered to students primarily from Britain or North America, and the curriculum was generally either British- or American-based. Children from other countries had to adjust as best they could.

Much of this has changed and is still changing. Now many of these same boarding schools have students from a broad spectrum of the international population, and they have students and teachers from the host country as well. Host country parents may want to send their children to a primarily English-based school to increase their chances of being competitive in the global marketplace. While there are many good things about this, these children live a very TCK-like experience as they change cultural worlds on a regular basis, and parents need to understand that as well. Some highly mobile families or those in dangerous assignments still choose to use boarding schools back in the passport country, particularly for the high school years.

Some obvious benefits of these boarding schools are the opportunities students have to make close friends with their peers, to have healthy competition in sports or other areas, and to have trained teachers and a committed staff caring for them. In addition, children attending boarding school in their host country are usually closer to parents than they would be if left back in the home country.

The negatives mainly have to do with the separation from parents and home. In the past, many children left home to go to boarding school at five or six years of age and were separated from their parents for long periods of time. This had been a common practice in Britain for years, and these schools were held up as proof that children survived well in such settings. Unfortunately, as adults some have had to deal with deep feelings of abandonment stemming from these early patterns of separation.

Another drawback for boarding schools is that it's almost impossible for parents to monitor what is happening on a day-to-day basis. In former days, many times parents didn't know until long afterward if their child was having academic or personal problems or difficulties with a staff member. However, in today's world of instant messaging, e-mails, Skype, and the like, this is improving, but it can potentially happen even now. Some ATCKs feel they were raised by older students, or even peers in the boarding school, rather than by adults. In the extreme, there has been and is the risk of child abuse when any child is vulnerable as they may be when away from parents in such situations. While certainly not the norm, mistreatment occurs often enough to be of legitimate concern to parents.

Our suggestions for parents considering the boarding school option are to take into account the child's age and temperament, the character and reputation of the school, how often they will be able to see the child, and whether their child's communication with them is unhindered (some schools in the past have monitored their students' contact with parents).

As new findings continue to stress the importance of attachment and of strong bonding with parents during a child's early years, and after listening to so many adults struggle to come to terms with early separations, we believe it's not wise with so many other options available to send young children—particularly those as young as five or six—to boarding school unless there are absolutely no other alternatives. It is simply impossible to measure how that kind of separation affects the children, or which ones will struggle with the effects of separation later on and which won't.

While it's good to include children in all discussions regarding their schooling, the decision about boarding school is one area in which this type of inclusion is vital. The feeling of *abandonment* expressed by ATCKs seems most often to come from those who say they were "sent off." When parents include children in the decision-making process, acknowledge the pros and cons of each schooling option, and listen carefully to the children's concerns and preferences, it makes a long-term difference. Children whose opinions are taken into account see that their thoughts and feelings matter; they do, indeed, feel valued.

PREUNIVERSITY SCHOOLING IN THE HOME COUNTRY

Pros	Cons
Education compatible with higher education	Extended separation from parents
Reentry adjustment minimized	Lack of personalized care
Educational/enrichment opportunities	Cultural influence without parental guidance
	Loss of cross-cultural advantage and language acquisition

Figure 15-7 Pros and Cons of Preuniversity Schooling in the Home Country

As we mentioned, leaving children with relatives or at a boarding school in the homeland used to be a common practice for third culture families. In fact, the normal practice for internationally mobile families until the late 1950s and early 1960s involved leaving TCKs in the homeland for secondary school, which often meant four or more years of separation from parents—all without benefit of e-mail, instant messaging, or Skype. We know many now older ATCKs who never saw or talked with their parents even once during that four-year stint.[7]

Although sending preuniversity TCKs to school in the home country while parents remain overseas is no longer a common practice, it remains an option. Some families feel that nothing else suits their needs. Perhaps the parents take their first overseas assignment while a teenager has only a year to go to finish high school. That child doesn't want to switch schools and the corporation says the assignment can't wait. Relatives may offer to keep the teenager for the year. Perhaps the TCK prefers living with relatives at home rather than going to a boarding school overseas, which was why Courtney left Saudi Arabia and returned to the United States to live with her grandparents. She felt if the only other option was to go to a boarding school where her American expatriate peers made up most of the student body, she would rather be with her grandparents. There can be any number of legitimate reasons for this choice.

The major benefit, of course, is that an early start in the school system of the home country makes it easier for TCKs to continue successfully in that system through university. But such a benefit must be weighed against the trauma of leaving their lifelong friends overseas (unless those friends are also moving) before the normally accepted time of secondary school graduation. Also, this question remains: How does changing cultures and facing all the issues of re-entry during the height of identity formation in the early teen years affect TCKs compared to those who make the same switch a few years later? Some questions for researchers to consider are: Do TCKs who stay through high school in the international scene with the friends and life they have known move on with a more integrated sense of themselves as "internationals"? Is it possible, developmentally, that while they will still go through cultural adjustments when repatriating, they have had the opportunity—much as those who make a cross-cultural move initially as adults—to explore their abilities, their sense of belonging, in a context they know? When they change cultures at repatriation, do they have more capacity to see it as one more new experience rather than a demolition of all they have presumed themselves to be? We would love to see further discussion on these issues.

For some TCKs, of course, it may be essential to return home before attending university. Those who face competitive exams in their midteens may find this the only real option if they wish to pursue certain careers. We've noticed a major difference in schooling patterns among Australian and New Zealand TCKs as compared to Americans. Most Americans can easily return to the United States at age seventeen or eighteen and go directly to university, but TCKs from "down under" generally return to their home countries by the age of fifteen so they can prepare for the exams that determine which courses they will take at university. When TCKs do need to repatriate before university for any reason, it's helpful for them to find ways to keep in touch with friends left behind. Some have even gone back to participate with their original class in high school graduation exercises. Depending on the circumstances of their early leaving, this can help them have good closure with the past if that is still needed.

The major drawback of schooling in the home country is the great distance from parents. In these days of e-mail and Skype, communication is certainly far easier than in the last century. Nevertheless, an ocean apart is still pretty far to be away. With increased ease of travel, however, for those who can afford it, parents and children often make more frequent trips back and forth compared to former years.

It's obvious that there are many good choices for educating TCKs and statistics show that, as a group, they do well academically. A survey of 608 adult missionary kids conducted by MK CART/CORE (a research organization composed of ten mission agencies) resulted in these statistics:

- 30 percent of the respondents graduated from high school with honors
- 27 percent were elected to the National Honor Society
- 94 percent went on to university-level studies
- 73 percent graduated from university
- 25 percent graduated from university with honors
- 3 percent were Phi Beta Kappas
- 11 percent were listed in *Who's Who in American Colleges and Universities*[8]

Another survey on ATCKs confirms that a strikingly high percentage of TCKs go on to postsecondary school education. In 1993, a study of 680 ATCKs done by John and Ruth Hill Useem and their colleagues showed that while only 21 percent of the U.S. population as a whole has graduated from a four-year college or university, 81 percent of the ATCKs they surveyed had earned at least a bachelor's degree. Half of them went on to earn master's or doctorate degrees.[9] Undoubtedly, with thoughtful planning and wise choices, the educational process for TCKs has every chance of being a rich one indeed.

Lessons from the TCK Petri Dish

CCKs of many different backgrounds may also face serious questions regarding their schooling options, particularly if the schools around them differ in language or culture from the parents' primary culture(s). They may not have or choose to use some of the options mentioned in this chapter, but all parents must remember how critical their choice of educational options will be. We hope that some of this discussion will help non-TCK families also know what things to consider as they make their choices too.

CHAPTER 16

Enjoying the Journey

I am from Belgium, where the clouds are usually soaked in rain,

I am from Italy, where the clouds are always cleared by sunlight,

I am from Poland, where the sky is as dark as coal,

I am from Mozart, whose music charmed peoples' hearts and woke their souls,

I am from my dreams and nightmares, where my imagination takes over,

I am from Egypt, whose mysteries haunt peoples' minds,

I am from the ocean, where the waves calm my thoughts,

I am from the mountains, where the echo calls my name,

Most of all, I am from my family, where my heart truly belongs.[1]

—"I am from..." by Hendrik Verrijssen

BELGIAN CITIZEN HENDRIK VERRIJSSEN WROTE THIS POEM at the age of 12. In these few lines, he captures the incredible wealth of his experience, the challenge of defining his roots geographically, and the comfort of defining them relationally. He gives evidence that while mobility may interrupt the traditional patterns of developmental flow and relationship building, globally mobile families can reach the same goals of helping their TCKs develop to their fullest potential and maintain relationships through less traditional, but equally positive, patterns of family living. Where do we start?

Have Fun!

Never forget: one of the best aspects of a TCK lifestyle is the fun it can be. In his book *Living Overseas,* Ted Ward emphasizes the importance of enjoying the adventure—of *living*![2] Having fun in the journey is another great way to tie the many elements of a TCK's life together into a cohesive whole that is essential for building a strong sense of identity.

Unpack Your Bags and Plant Your Trees

Without knowing he had a name for his TCK experience, Ruth's dad, Charles Frame, gave her solid, lifelong advice.

> "Ruth, wherever you go in life, unpack your bags—physically and mentally—and plant your trees. Too many people never live in the now because they assume the time is too short to settle in. They don't plant trees because they expect to be gone before the trees bear fruit. But if you keep thinking about the next move, you'll never live fully where you are. When it's time to go, then it's time to go, but you won't have missed what this experience was about. If you never eat from the trees, someone else will." And he followed his advice by planting trees all around their home in Kano, Nigeria. Twelve years after going back to the United States, Ruth made her first trip back to Kano. As she picked and ate an orange off one of his trees, she knew he had been right.

For any member of a globally nomadic family, following this simple piece of advice can make all the difference in whether it is a positive experience or not. It means you have made a choice to embrace all the possibilities and live with an openness to all the opportunities this life affords rather than to live in a self-protective mode. As parents model this, TCKs get the picture and will do it themselves.

TOUR WHEN TRAVELING BETWEEN COUNTRIES

Stopping off in various countries while traveling between home and host countries is another experience that adds fun to the third culture lifestyle. Such stops expand the world of TCKs and they create lifelong memories. Courtney had this to say about her travels:

My memory is much bigger than most of my friends' because of all the exciting places my parents took me on our trips between Saudi Arabia and America. When we went to England or Germany, for example, knowing I loved art, my mom would take me to the museums while my sister and dad went off on other excursions. I learned so much by absorbing the cultures we encountered; we would take tours and soak up the information the guides told us.

My parents may not realize that the most profound thing they did for me was to take me to Dachau. I must have been about 11 or 12. We walked the grounds; we looked at everything; I cried. My parents did not protect me; they exposed me to everything—including the crematoriums, gas chambers, photos. When you read about World War II and the concentration camps, I can't imagine how you can truly understand it without seeing it. I just stood there, overwhelmed, and thought, how is this possible? It was so big.

I am filled up when I think of all that I've seen and touched, and how much I want to return and touch them all again.

EXPLORE AND BECOME INVOLVED IN THE SURROUNDINGS

When families arrive overseas, parents shouldn't forget the plans they made beforehand to get to know their host country. Ironically, the richness of their lives can become so routine that TCKs and their families forget to notice it. Learn about the country's history, geography, and culture. Families should pretend they're tourists once or twice a year and plan trips just to see the sights. Courtney's parents also helped her to explore their host country—Saudi Arabia. "My parents often took us out into the desert to look at various natural treasures such as sharks' teeth, sand roses, and arrowheads. It was exciting to imagine this place under water millions of years ago." These may seem like simple memories, but they've left Courtney with a deep sense of connection to her past.

As a corollary, a common regret we hear from ATCKs is they never really got involved with the surrounding culture when they were children. Whether it happened because they lived on a military base, went off to boarding school, or played only with expatriate friends, many consider this a loss. As adults, they realize they could have learned so much more and wish they had studied the language or taken time to learn how to cook the wonderful local dishes they enjoyed when they went out or simply found a way to make friends among those from the local culture.

Keep Relationships Solid

Over and over TCKs echo what Hendrik says—that the ultimate place of belonging and home comes in relationships, not place. These are the pieces of life that cannot be taken away when they are built well, for they are the places of the heart.

DEVELOP FAMILY TRADITIONS

Traditions bind people and groups together. They are visible markers of shared history and celebrate a unity of thought, purpose, or relationship. Every nation has them, every ethnic group has them, and, hopefully, every family has them. Often a family's traditions evolve without special planning. Uncle Fred pulls out his mandolin at every reunion and family members old and young sing along. No one has consciously decided this will be a tradition, but the family gathering wouldn't be the same if Uncle Fred and his mandolin weren't there. These are the moments that build a family's unique sense of identity and belonging.

Third culture families have at least as much need for traditions as other families do—maybe more. But, because they aren't always at the family reunions to hear Uncle Fred, they may have to do a little more conscious planning. It's important to develop at least some traditions that are transportable and replicable in whatever culture and surroundings the family might be. These traditions may be as simple as letting each family member choose the menu for his or her birthday supper every year or as complicated as making a piñata stuffed with candy for a particular holiday once a year.

Developing traditions in cross-cultural settings isn't just important—it's fun! As new ideas gleaned from different places are incorporated, traditions also become a way of marking family history. In Liberia, a hot dog roast on the beach defined Christmas Eve for some expatriates—not a traditional custom in most snow-covered lands, but a nice one to carry back home (even if the hot dogs must be roasted in a fireplace!) as a distinctive reminder of the family's history.

Build Strong Ties with Community

TCKs usually grow up far from blood relatives, so finding substitute aunts, uncles, and grandparents wherever TCKs live can be very important in creating "extended family." Sometimes these people will be host country citizens; sometimes they will be within the third culture community itself. Parents can foster such relationships by inviting these special people to join in celebrating the

TCK's birthday, allowing their child to go shopping with them, or in other ways appropriate for the situation. This "created" extended family gives TCKs the experience of growing up in a close community, even without blood relatives. As ATCKs remember their childhood, some of these relationships rank among their fondest memories. And don't lose touch with this "family" when you move. As much as possible, continue this thread of connection to help TCKs feel that their life is a continuous process, not one broken into many pieces.

BUILD STRONG TIES WITH EXTENDED FAMILY

Relatives in the home country (or wherever they live) are another important part of a TCK's life, and relationships with them need to be fostered. A great way to cultivate these relationships is by bringing a grandmother, grandfather, aunt, uncle, or cousin to visit. A visit not only helps TCKs get to know their relatives better, but also lets relatives see TCKs in their own environment—the place where these children do, in fact, shine. It also builds a place of shared history with extended family that TCKs may otherwise miss. In addition, TCKs love to return "home" and be able to talk to family members who know what they're talking about. Even if relatives cannot make a trip to see them overseas, it's important for TCKs to maintain contact with their relatives as much as possible through Skype, Facebook, instant messaging, e-mail, faxes, telephone, and pictures. This type of relationship building goes a long way to creating a sense of continuity throughout life.

Developing closeness with relatives at home becomes especially important if and when the time comes for TCKs to repatriate while parents continue living overseas. These relatives' homes can be the places where TCKs go for school breaks, vacations, and weekends when parents are away.

One reminder here: the time to plan for this interaction with extended family starts at the beginning. This contact also helps keep children fluent in the mother tongue of their parent(s). Here's what happened to one family who didn't maintain this contact.

> I spoke to my parents-in-law, who are German and do not speak English, about how they felt about having two grandsons who only spoke English for many years. Now both boys speak reasonable German, but that is a fairly recent change. They are now both teenagers, so Oma and Opa have had 10 years of little or no real communication with their "foreign" grandsons.[3]

When this happens, everyone loses—so don't forget language learning and/or teaching as part of your plan if this is needed.

BUILD STRONG TIES WITH FRIENDS

Friends are an enormous blessing for many TCKs. Indeed, many TCKs thrive in international schools and communities where there is no given norm for race or nationality. In many places, public transportation systems make it easy to form social gatherings at a favorite cybercafe on weekends. As they move from country to country, TCKs can keep up with friends in ways never before possible. Yet this here-and-now communication system can affect new connections. TCKs in a new place may spend so much time keeping in touch with friends from the "old place" via e-mail, instant messaging, Skype, or Facebook that they don't make the effort to develop new friendships in their schools or community. Initially, parents should not be alarmed at such behavior. It is one of the "new normals" in today's world. However, if this pattern persists for a long period and their children refuse to engage in the local scene, parents should find ways to encourage face-to-face contact in the new surroundings. They might invite another family over who have children of similar age, or find an area of particular interest, such as a sports team or choir, that the child could join.

In the end, however, as TCKs move on through life and become ATCKs, it is often reconnecting with friends from the past that validates the TCK experience and proves that the third culture world and experience wasn't a dream. Attending school reunions and returning to visit the home or homes of their childhood are all ways TCKs and ATCKs can maintain connections with the various pieces of their lives. Such friendships are a gift that tops the list for many ATCKs when they look back at their past.

Return to the Same "Home" during Each Leave

Whenever practical, third culture families should return to the same place each time they go on home leave. Children who change countries every two or three years as well as those who stay in one host country their entire lives need the sense that there is at least one physical place in their passport country to identify as home. When staying in the same physical house isn't possible, families should try to relocate nearby so that TCKs can keep the same school, church, and friends. It's also helpful when visiting friends or relatives in other places to stay long enough to establish a basis for the relationship that can be built upon during the next leave.

While it's good to foster these relationships in the home country, families shouldn't spend their entire leave visiting people. When every evening is spent with the adults chatting happily in one room and the TCKs and children from the host family eyeing each other warily in another, and when every night is spent in a different bed, this overload of travel can be stressful. But these trips can also be fun when parents include fun, kid-friendly activities. Wise parents make time for nights in motels, camping trips, or other private times during their travel to reinforce their sense of being a family in this land as well as in the host country.

Acquire "Sacred Objects"

As we have mentioned before, artifacts from countries where they have lived or visited eventually become the TCK's portable history to cart around the world in future years. It's important to take back meaningful, portable objects from each place TCKs have lived, or even visited. These help to connect all the places and experiences of their lives. During her childhood, ATCK Jennifer acquired a set of carved ebony elephant bookends, a lamp (whose base included more elephants), feather paintings, and other ebony carvings to hang on the wall. At university and in the 16 locations where she has lived since her wedding, when the bookends are in place, the paintings and carvings hung on the wall, and the lamp turned on, she's home.

One German TCK, Dirk, summed up best what we are trying to say. When we asked him what he thought of his experience as a TCK, he said, "The thing I like best about my life is living it!"

That's what it's all about—living and enjoying the world of TCKs. As parents help their children do that, they are building into their TCKs' lives a solid sense of who they are as individuals, as TCKs, and giving them a deep sense of relational belonging, a connection to many geographical sites, and the freedom and courage to fully participate in life no matter where their feet land. It's a good place to be.

Lessons from the TCK Petri Dish

Perhaps the application is simple: whatever our life circumstances, wherever we live, whatever opportunities we have, no matter our cultural interactions or not, "unpack your bags and plant your trees." The specifics of how we do that may be different, but the principle is universal for those who want to live life fully and with as much joy as possible. Even CCKs who find themeselves away from home because of political unrest or other situations that force them to leave their homelands tell us that by living fully one day at a time they found blessings despite the tears. And this principle applies, even during re-entry—our next topic!

~~~~~~~~~~~~~~~~~~~~~~~~~~~~~~~

CHAPTER 17

Coming "Home": Reentry

Culture shock is a peculiar thing. It feels as if all your
guideposts have been turned upside down, as though the
words you read were unexpectedly printed backwards, as if
the air you took for granted with every breath was suddenly
scented in a strange and unfamiliar way. I looked around
at the people I went to classes with: I looked like them; all
of us wore jeans and T-shirts, we spoke the same language,
though some of us had different accents. We had similar
interests, similar callings. We were intelligent, we were
young, we were finding our paths, defining our interests. Yet
the very way the other students walked in the world, viewed
their place in it, and approached others made me feel like
a stranger, and there were times of intense longing for the
familiarity of home.[1]

—*Nina Sichel, from* Unrooted Childhoods:
Memoirs of Growing Up Global

A ND NOW WE HAVE COME FULL CIRCLE. After all these years of
careful planning to make the most of their years in a host culture, to
deal positively with the transitions along the way, to make good school
choices, and to enjoy the journey among many worlds, the time has finally come
for the family, or at least the TCKs themselves, to go "home." As we said at the
beginning of this book, one of the factors that distinguishes the TCK experience
from a true immigrant is the full expectation that after living for a significant
period of their developmental years outside their passport culture, there will
come the day when TCKs make a permanent return to that country and culture.

~~~~~

Oddly enough, for many TCKs this is one of the most difficult transitions they go through, no matter how many other moves they have already made. Commonly called *reentry*, for a great number of TCKs this process more closely resembles an entry.

Why is reentry so hard for so many?

Reentry Stresses

Some reasons for reentry stress are simply extensions of the many factors we have already talked about, particularly the normal challenges of any cross-cultural transition: the grief of losing a world they have come to love, the discomfort of being out of cultural balance once more, and the struggle to start to find a place of belonging in a new place with new people. There are also some very particular and additional stresses TCKs face during this transition to their home culture, however, and they are worth examining carefully.

UNREALISTIC EXPECTATIONS

Expectations of their "dream world." In today's world, most TCKs go back and forth between home and host cultures at fairly regular intervals. When they tell us they "know what it's like" to live in that passport country because of that, they forget that going for vacation is different from living somewhere longer term. When TCKs return for a limited time, relatives plan special events and parents may indulge their children (and themselves) with various "goodies" they have missed overseas—a favorite ice cream flavor or a trip to Disneyland. It's easy for TCKs to begin to think of all this attention and these kinds of privileges as normal for life in this country. When it turns out they have to settle in and no one is treating them any more special than anyone else, it can be a shock.

Expectations of "sameness." One of the most basic reasons for reentry stress relates to the unconscious expectations of both the TCKs and those in their home culture of how they will relate to one another. As we discussed in chapter 4, many TCKs have been recognized as foreigners while living in their host culture. Some have lived there as hidden immigrants, and a few fit into either the adopted or mirror category. When TCKs return to their passport culture, however, almost all are hidden immigrants. Now everything Gary Weaver talked about in his model of the iceberg and how that relates to cultural expectations and stress starts to make even more sense. People at home take one look at these returning TCKs and expect them to be in the "mirror" box illustrated in Figure 4-3—persons who think and look like themselves. Why wouldn't they? After all, these TCKs are from the same racial, ethnic, and national background as those "at home" are.

TCKs look around them and they, too, often expect to be in the mirror box. For years they've known they were "different" but excused it because they knew they were Asians living in England, Africans living in Germany, or Canadians living in Bolivia. That justification for being different is now gone, and they presume they will finally be the same as others; after all, these are their own people. Wrong. Take another look at Krista and Nicola, our look-alike TCKs who let their host culture peers in England and Scotland know how eager they were to return to their home countries where they knew they would finally fit in and belong.

> When Krista first returned to the United States, she felt euphoric at finally being "home." It didn't take long, however, before Krista realized to her horror that she couldn't relate to her American classmates either. Somehow she was as different from them as from her English peers.
>
> The same thing happened to Nicola when she returned to England. After literally kissing the tarmac when she disembarked from the plane in London, a strange thing soon happened. Nicola found herself increasingly irritated with her English student peers. Their world seemed so small. Internally, she began resisting becoming like them, and within a year virtually all of her friends were international students and other TCKs. She wondered why she could never completely fit into the world around her, whether it was Scottish or English. Both Krista and Nicola's disappointment was greater because they had always presumed if they could only make it "home," they would no longer feel so different from others.

Conversely, TCKs aren't doing much better in their opinions of new-found peers. When TCKs saw themselves as true foreigners in Romania, they never expected their local friends to know where Alberta was on a Canadian map. Now they can't believe how dumb their friends in Alberta are because they have no idea where Romania is.

REVERSE CULTURE SHOCK

How many TCKs have we met who assure us they will have no problem with reentry because they have, indeed, made trips back and forth every year with nary a hitch? In fact, they tell us they love it and can't wait to get back and settle in permanently. They have kept up on the latest fads and styles, and they know all the music friends are listening to. All will surely be well. When we try to talk about reverse culture shock—going through the same cycles of culture shock or stress many adults feel when going to a new country for the first time—most TCKs, and often their parents, assure us it will not be so. Again, the very fact that it isn't expected can make it worse.

Many TCKs have similar experiences to those of Krista and Nicola, where all seems well at the beginning of reentry. Relatives and old friends welcome the

TCKs warmly, while the school bends over backward in its efforts to assess how transcripts from some exotic foreign school relate to the local curriculum. Soon, however, unexpected differences begin to pop up. Classmates use slang or idioms that mean nothing to the returning TCKs. Everyone else is driving a car; they only know how to ride a bike. If they do drive, they learned to drive on the other side of the road. They never had to pump their own gas when they could still call it *petrol* and others understood what they meant. Friends, relatives, and classmates are shocked at the TCKs' ignorance at these most common practices necessary for everyday living. If they were true immigrants, no one would expect them to know all these things. But because they are presumed to be in the mirror box, those in the home country begin to peg them as "strange" or, at least, slightly stupid.

Reentry might not be quite so difficult if the unexpected differences were merely in some of these more obvious ways. But deeper levels of cultural dissonance lurk beneath the apparently similar surface. When friends ask a TCK whose parents worked in Uganda with the AIDS patients in refugee camps to join them at McDonald's for a hamburger, all that the TCK can think about is how many people could eat for a whole day or week in Uganda for the amount of money this one meal cost. Even worse, he watches people throw out leftover food and can't help expressing his shock and horror. The friends who took him out for lunch feel this TCK is ungrateful at best, condemning at worst.

And so the problems may continue to mount. TCKs who have grown up in a culture where there's a commitment to honesty and respect accompanied by orderliness and quiet find entry into a confrontational, loud, self-centered home culture quite offensive. Those who've grown up in a boisterous, activity-centered, individualistic culture may find people from their own country docile and self-effacing. Often TCKs begin to realize they don't even like what is considered their home culture. And those in the home culture may soon realize they're not so sure they like the TCKs either. But no one stops to think through how these reactions are related to the cultural expectations they had for one another in the first place. They still presume their inside selves are supposed to match their outside selves in a way they would never expect with friends in another country or culture. Despite expectations to the contrary, never forget that reentry is, in fact, reverse culture shock. Soon the fun stage is gone and the fight and flight stages appear.

Common Reactions to Reentry Stress

We have looked before at the three common styles of behavior TCKs often use when changing cultural worlds: adapting as a chameleon and basically trying to hide the difference, becoming a screamer and making sure to define the difference, or retreating as a wallflower to hope others don't notice the difference. Most TCKs we know pick up at least one of these personas during reentry and that is okay. It's normal and gives them an opportunity in different ways to assess the situation and decide what choices they will make for longer term responses. But in the process of reentry, we have also seen some other behaviors that are understandable but perhaps not so necessary if we can help TCKs find better ways to cope. Here are some common ones.

ELEVATED FEARS

Fear of being disloyal to the past. For some TCKs, it seems they unconsciously fear that allowing themselves to repatriate totally would mean being disloyal to their host country. "If I allow myself to like it here, it may mean I really didn't like it there," or "If I adjust and fit in, I may lose my memory of and commitment to return to that place where I grew up." Such fears can make them lose the delight in their present, which is as much a part of their life experience as their past has been. They haven't yet learned to live in the great paradox of the both/and-edness of their worlds.

Fear of losing their identity. When the foundation of the cultural ground beneath them is badly shaking, even those who thought they had a clear sense of personal identity may begin to shake with it. At that point, all they may feel they have left is this memory of who they were, the life they had before, and that there was once a place they felt as true "home." "If I let go of the place and the people where I have always identified most and fit in best to align myself with my home country and culture, will I lose some important part of me?" This can be a hard time for parents, who can easily feel their children are rejecting what is a precious part of the parents' identity—being a member of this community or nation.

EXCESSIVE ANGER AT "HOME" CULTURE AND PEERS

At times, it seems TCKs can be culturally tolerant anywhere but in their own culture. When people move to a new host culture, they usually keep quiet if they have strongly negative opinions about that culture. At most, they only express them to fellow expatriates. These rules seem to change, however, on reentry. Some TCKs appear to feel quite free to express every negative opinion they can possibly think of about their home culture, no matter who is around. While chronic put-downs may be an unconscious defense for the TCKs' own feelings of insecurity or rejection, such remarks further alienate them from everyone around them. But, like it or not, they *are* a member of this group by birth and citizenship. In affirming one part of their experience and themselves, they reject another.

A SENSE OF ELITISM—TRUE OR PROJECTED

We talked of this in general before, but reentry is a key time to think about TCKs becoming disdainful of those who do not share their experience. This is a troubling behavior we often see at this time and can carry on for years. While understandable, it goes against all we would consider to be the gifts of this up-bringing. The idea in our definition that TCKs relate on experiential lines rather than traditional lines seems to turn into the reality that "I can *only* relate to other TCKs." Perhaps this is a subtle way of screaming, "I'm not like you so don't expect me to be," but it can lead to a certain type of at least projected arrogance that further isolates the TCKs from many rich friendships they might otherwise have.

Another form this may take is when TCKs feel so upset that no one wants to know their story but forget that perhaps they have not stopped to ask those at home more about their own stories either. In some discussions, it seems TCKs almost assume no one who didn't live overseas even has a story to share.

DEPRESSION

While we mentioned that the "wallflower" response of withdrawing to assess the scene is certainly a common response during reentry, we also want to say that at times these behaviors can reveal or, ironically, mask depression. Common withdrawal patterns that can initially be within normal and then move toward true depression might include TCKs having a hard time getting out of bed, or sitting in their rooms and watching TV all day rather than joining any activities at school or church. Withdrawal can have less obvious forms, however. Some students retreat into their studies and earn straight As—and who can fault them for that? Others spend hours practicing their favorite instrument and winning every musical contest they enter. While everyone congratulates them for their honors, no one realizes this is another form of escape or even depression.

While these behaviors—including anger or depression—may be an initial coping mechanism, if any continue for six months to a year in an unremitting form, getting some outside help may be needed. The sad thing is for a few TCKs, when they find out that even at "home" they don't fit, the depression can become a serious and a life-threatening issue at times. Psychiatrist Esther Schubert, an ATCK herself, has done research among TCKs and reports that suicide rates go up among TCKs after their first year home when it seems they give up hoping they will ever fit in.[2] For them, it's the ongoing struggle to fit in that leads to despair rather than simply the initial reentry. This, of course, is not the common pattern, but one of which to be aware. If TCKs or ATCKs are reading this and feeling this despair even now, please seek some help from trusted friends or counselors.

Helping in the Reentry Process

While there are no foolproof ways to ensure a perfect reentry, it's an important time and everyone involved should pay attention to it, whether you are the TCK,

ATCK, parents, relative, school personnel, or friend. How TCKs do or don't cope with the reentry experience can shape their lives for years to come. The basic key for all concerned is to first understand what the normal process is about. Normalizing this part of the TCK experience is as important as it is for so many other facets. Barbara Schaetti, an American/Swiss ATCK who did her Ph.D. dissertation on identity development among TCKs/global nomads, offers this advice.

> Introduce your children from their earliest years abroad to the terms "global nomad" and "third culture kid." They may not be interested at the time, but when they start searching for how to make meaning of their internationally mobile lives, they'll know there's this particularly relevant subject that people have written and spoken about.[3]

It's also helpful to approach the reentry process by talking with others who have already been through it, attending seminars, and reading the growing number of books available for third culture families, including *Homeward Bound* by Robin Pascoe[4] and *The Art of Coming Home* by Craig Storti.[5] Having said that, here are some practical steps to help TCKs get through this process in a healthy rather than a harmful way.

Prepare for reentry before leaving the host country. Rosalea Cameron, an Australian ATCK, did her dissertation research on TCKs and writes in great detail about the impact of mobility on relationships and identity development within that context. She also looked for factors that contributed to developing leadership skills among TCKs, and she discovered a major positive link between TCKs who had managed to keep a sense of continuity between the different phases of their lives and those who developed into leaders.[6] Hopefully, before the family leaves the overseas experience, each member has built a strong RAFT (chapter 14) and made concrete plans to keep the thread of connection going between where they've been and where they will be. This is vital for making a smoother way in during reentry, as TCKs can affirm the both/and-edness of their lives when they realize they can maintain connections with the past as well as make new friends in the present.

Remind TCKs that the foundation stones of their lives can never be taken away. When TCKs fear losing the past by moving on to the future, remind them that a building set on a firm foundation doesn't lose that foundation when it gets bigger. No one can ever take away their experiences or depth of understanding or breadth of how they see the world. Others around may not always recognize these foundational stones, for some may lie deep where they are not instantly visible, but they are there. The fact that others don't yet see them can never remove one brick.

Remind TCKs that foundations are meant to be built on. While no one can take away any foundation stone, foundations without a building on top aren't very functional. Placing new bricks, perhaps of some different colors and textures, makes the whole building stronger, more useful, and beautiful, but they don't replace the foundation. To move ahead in life and grow in and into each phase is never a negation of the past, but rather an affirmation of how solid that past has been—solid enough to support a lifetime of building an ever-growing edifice on it.

Remind everyone this is the time a mentor can be helpful. Since reentry is actually the entering stage of the larger transition experience they are going through at this point, don't forget this is when TCKs most need a good mentor, as discussed in chapter 14. Reentry is the key period when TCKs are most vulnerable to being swept up in a group of friends they would never have chosen under normal circumstances, and they can get into drugs, alcohol, or other behavior they previously would have spurned. A good mentor can be a positive role model and lead them in the other direction too.

Parents must remember it's okay when their children don't share the same sense of national identity as they do. This may seem like a small point, but this can be a source of great stress in a family if the TCKs are rejecting, at least for a while, identifying with the home country. Parents need to remember once more that when they decided to move to another culture, they also realized (or should have!) that their children would likely wind up with a broader sense of cultural or ethnic identity than they might have. Again, it's helpful if parents can understand this is an expansion rather than an exclusion of their worlds.

Parents must remember that they have the ultimate responsibility for helping the children through reentry. This is such a basic fact that it almost seems silly to say, but, believe it or not, we've seen TCKs arrive at universities with no clear idea of where they will go for long weekends, during school breaks, or even during summer vacations. It seems as if parents have shipped them back home while they remain in another country in the rather vague, blissful assumption that everything will work out by itself—perhaps relying on other relatives to take care of their children, even when those relationships have never been nurtured.

It's not enough to presume that relatives at home will automatically pitch in to take care of a "homeless" TCK. We can't state this point strongly enough. Any time parents send their children back home (and also to a different country altogether for university as sometimes happens) while they themselves remain overseas, parents are still responsible for making sure their children are protected and cared for. It's their absolute responsibility to make sure their children have a designated "home-away-from-home."

Remember it's okay for families to customize their approach to reentry depending on their circumstances. One family's story shows how creative some parents can be to fulfill both their parental roles, keep their children ready throughout their expatriate journey to repatriate at some point, and still accomplish their career assignment as well. We mentioned Ria's attempts to help her children stay conversant in their mother tongue of Flemish in our chapter on education. Here's the rest of their story.

All through their years living abroad, Ria continued to help her children learn Flemish. When it came time for university, the two older kids chose to return to Belgium and enter university with others who had been raised in Belgium. But the Verrijssens soon realized they had to make some radical decisions to help their children adjust to their passport country.

The Verrijssens bought an apartment near the university in Belgium so the siblings could stay there together, and they decided that Ria would travel back to see them every six weeks. This frequent traveling, along with Erik taking side trips to them whenever his business travel took him into the region, meant the kids got the right support in addition to all the other support they enjoyed from Ria's and Erik's family and friends in Belgium.

While this obviously cost the family much in terms of both money and time, it made this transition back easier for their children. After one year, both of the Verrijssens who were in university felt settled in their "new" world. The parents had made some radical decisions and found creative ways to address the reentry issues their kids faced. Because they can relate to their passport culture in this deep way, it can now be their choice whether they stay in Belgium or return to some international career.

Of course, not everyone can do this. However, a strong extended family can help the process greatly, especially if both the relatives and the TCKs already feel comfortable and at home with one another. If it's possible for TCKs to attend college near their relatives, this can help ease them through reentry.

If no extended family is available, close friends can help. But if there is no safe harbor available for their TCK, parents should think seriously about staying home themselves until their child is secure in his or her new life. This may cost the parents of such TCKs a few years of their careers, but failure to do so may cause their children lifelong harm because of mistakes these TCKs make or the abandonment they feel as they try to adjust to a world they have never known.

Remember a "journey of clarification" later on can be helpful. Ultimately, one of the best things to help TCKs resettle in their home country on a long-term basis is to provide an opportunity for them to revisit the host country where they feel most deeply rooted. It's easy for that past experience to become so idealized or romanticized in the transition to their home culture that it grows to larger-than-life proportions. Going back can help put it into perspective. Going back does something else as well. It connects the past and present worlds of TCKs and reminds them that their past is not a myth of their imagination or totally inaccessible. In addition, such a journey reminds them that things never stay the same, and to see in ever clearer light that ultimately the past is now their foundation for the future.

How Reentry Becomes a Plus

While this discussion of what happens during reentry and what we can do about it are hopefully helpful, we want to conclude this chapter with a basic concept we believe can help TCKs and ATCKs understand a bit more about their overall story and assist in reentry as well.

We've talked a lot in this book about personal and cultural identity. We expanded the cultural iceberg in chapter 11 to show how basic human identity precedes culture, ethnicity, or race, for these are the attributes all humans share at the moment of birth. When, however, our friend Barb Knuckles first saw the expanded iceberg (Figure 11-1), she said, "If you leave the list of what it means to be a person at the bottom of the iceberg, you still can't see the real person because you still have to go through all the differences looking for that person. But if you flip your iceberg, you will see the person first. Once you see this fundamental likeness all people share, it's safer to explore who the other person is in the deeper layers of culture as well because you have a place underneath that is still there."

So what's so special about that? The irony is we have really come full circle. TCKs have unwittingly been flipping the cultural iceberg for years! Look at Figure 17-1.

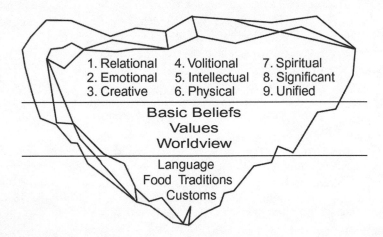

Figure 17-1 The Flipped Iceberg
(© 2006 Barbara H. Knuckles/Ruth E. Van Reken)

Think about it. Of the countless TCKs we've asked, "What is the greatest gift of your experience?" most will say, "Having the opportunity to meet people of many cultures and getting to know them." While the world is trying to figure out what to do with "diversity" based on traditional models that are primarily defined by many of the externals of the cultural iceberg, most TCKs have lived a life where, indeed, they saw the person first and the details of race, culture, or economics second, third, or not particularly at all. Why is it that the same person who sat around a village fire in Papua one day with a tribal friend can fly to a resort in Bali the next day to meet another friend who works for the World Bank? How is it Barack Obama can live in the White House and be equally comfortable with the friends he met as a community organizer in Chicago?

Why is it that TCKs so often seem to relate across what would typically be profoundly distinct social, cultural, and racial lines? In the previously cited situations, these are not all fellow TCKs relating only to each other. These are people from very different backgrounds, language, and experiences in true relationship. How can that be?

When a TCK sits by the fire in the village and asks his friend questions about his life, the two are connecting as people. In sharing their stories, both are meeting the fundamental needs of relationship—being known and knowing others. The details of the stories are different but they understand the shared emotions of gladness when stories of success are told or sadness when stories of a child's death emerge. TCKs on tour on the Masai Mara understand how much joy their tour guide has when he successfully finds them the animals they want to see. Why? Because, as a person, this guide also wants to know the satisfaction of a job well done. While the TCK's life may be very different in detail from all these friends— that TCK isn't a village person, a guide on the Mara, or a banker who can afford to invite friends to Bali, and none of these others is a TCK—yet they have related deeply at the human level despite the amazing differences in their stories.

So how does this relate to reentry? Simply this: TCKs who have related to people quite different from themselves so comfortably need to remember a couple of bottom-line lessons they have learned from their cross-cultural life experiences when they return home.

1. *People from the home culture are persons too.* They want relationships, they feel, they can create and think like others around the world. Again, their circumstances may be different, but their shared humanity is not.
2. *People from the home culture also have a story.* Once TCKs and ATCKs understand this, instead of waiting around to be asked their own fascinating story, they can take the initiative to ask those in the home culture about *their* lives. Just as it was in any other culture, through the stories of those who live in a community, we learn about the history and culture of that place, not only about that person.

3. *People from the home culture can understand the emotions of your story even when they don't share in the details.* CCKs must remember that others may not have all the hooks upon which to hang and retain every interesting detail of their exotic story (or vice versa), but as they tell it over time and from the perspective of what they felt as they experienced various situations, new friends can make that emotional connection even when they don't remember every detail.

4. *People all around them have lived far more similar stories than they may have yet recognized.* Part of the beauty of expanding to look at the world of CCKs is to see how many people are, in fact, living similar lives of cross-cultural interactions, mobility in different ways, and in worlds their parents never knew, under different labels. Some have been doing it for generations without recognition. Again, the details may differ, but there are intense places of specific shared connection in these stories, and deep friendships can be formed here as well as with local friends or other TCKS.

When TCKs (and all others) see this most fundamental fact of the human likeness they share with others, they don't need to fear losing their sense of identity, no matter where they are, reentry or not. And then, in the mystery of life, they can look without fear at where they also differ from others, for we also have a need to be unique! The beauty of the flipped iceberg is that we can see both our likeness to and our uniqueness from others. That, in the end, is a pretty strong place of finding our identity!

While many TCKs look back on their reentry period as one of the more stressful parts of their TCK experience, they still wouldn't have missed much of what they learned from the process. Often they emerge from reentry with an awareness of how their own culture works and operates in ways those who have never left may never see. This awareness can help them decide, perhaps more proactively than they might have otherwise, which values of their own culture they want to keep or let go of. Most also come to appreciate the special gifts they have received from each culture that has been part of their lives, including this one finally known as "home."

Lessons from the TCK Petri Dish

One of the first "aha" moments for Ruth regarding the expansion of the TCK concept to the larger area of CCKs came when listening to members from an immigrant community try to understand what was "wrong" with their first and second generation U.S. born children. These immigrants were trying to raise their children within the cultural values and practices of their homeland, but when these children returned on vacation to visit their grandparents, they didn't seem to fit in. Relatives in that country berated the parents for not raising their children "right." At this point Ruth realized for the frist time a major difference between immigrant communities of old, who landed on their adopted shores expecting never to return to their homeland again, and today's immigrant experience. In the first case, assimiliation and integration into the new culture were the highest priorities. To make it, they had to fit and blend in the new land. The option to return, even for short visits, usually wasn't part of the equation. In todays' world, however, immigrants easily travel back and forth between their present and past worlds, just as traditional TCKs do. This means immigrant CCKs may frequently experience being hidden immigrants in their former homelands. Certainly, these realities also apply to many of the other groups, including international adoptees who might try to go and visit their birth countries, where they will look alike but not be alike in the deeper layers of their values and worldviews. Minority CCKs or borderlander CCKs, who function in the dominant culture by day but return to their ethnic subculture each evening, tell us they go through reentry on a daily basis! Refugee families who try to return to their passport country after the violence ceases report very similar types of responses, especially from the children born or raised during this time away.

But we also believe that many CCKs of all groups experience close interpersonal interactions between highly diverse cultural groups at the most fundamental parts of life. This may be one of the greatest gifts CCKs have to offer others in our changing world—demonstrating that it is possible to move beyond old stereotypes and boundaries to meet the real people behind who we might otherwise assume them to be based on the visible aspects of our world and theirs.

CHAPTER 18

How Sponsoring Organizations Can Help

In all my travels, conversations, and research, I've discovered that the only people who had relatively easy identity encounter experiences related to growing up globally were those who had been introduced to the terms "global nomad" and "third culture kid" while still living overseas, or those who were offered repatriation services upon coming "home" and heard the terms that way (or at least subset terms like "missionary kid," "oil brat," "military brat," and so on.[1]

—Barbara F. Schaetti, Ph.D.

IN ADDITION TO PERSONAL AND PARENTAL CHOICES that can help TCKs thrive in their experience, the policies and the programs (or lack thereof) of sponsoring organizations weigh heavily in the equation. Even if parents and TCKs do everything we've suggested to maximize the TCK experience, CEOs and human resource managers of international organizations need to realize that their personnel policies have a profound effect on the employee's family—for example, a company asking its employee to move in the middle of a school year or an organization only paying for one type of schooling. At home, employers rarely have any influence on the schooling and living choices of their employees, but in cross-cultural situations the ramifications of corporate and organizational decisions filter down through the family of every employee affected by them.

Administrative decisions based solely on the interests of the international organization are shortsighted. Agencies should consider family needs as well as corporate needs when planning to send an employee overseas for at least two reasons.

1. *It's for the long-term benefit of the company.* Eighty-six percent of moves fail due to stresses on the family.[2] Given the high cost of preparing and sending families overseas, premature ending of assignments affects the sponsoring organization's bottom line. When agencies help employees meet their family's needs—whether for schooling, travel, or home leave—parents who work for the agencies are far more likely to stay with the company longer and be more productive. Since the cost of sending an employee overseas usually costs two to five times that employee's annual salary,[3] agencies benefit financially if they can keep their seasoned, internationally experienced employees from departing prematurely.

   Keeping employees with strong cross-cultural skills also helps an agency's performance in relationship to the host culture. New people trying to learn those skills are bound to make more professional and social gaffes that hinder their effectiveness in a strange culture than someone who has already gone through the process of cross-cultural adaptation. After all, there are lessons about crossing cultures that only time can teach.

2. *Sound family-aware corporate policies are not only good for the corporation or agency, but also are good for the family.* In 2008, Robin Pascoe, a true pioneer in spousal and family issues for expatriates, did a survey of 656 expatriates living in 62 countries and representing 44 countries. She writes, "In serving family needs, it's not only a company's bottom line which is at stake in areas such as attracting and retaining good employees who are productive and loyal and will not walk out the door to the competition upon repatriation. The family system—the relationships between partners and their relationships with their children—is also put at risk when a deployment is handled badly or with indifference."[4]

   When corporate or organizational decisions are made with families in mind, the family feels protected and cared for, a relationship that any organization should wish to cultivate as part of the organizational or corporate culture. With each family member having space to grow and develop, parents can make decisions only they are qualified to make—decisions that will help their children effectively use their cross-cultural heritage. In turn, the organization or corporation is able to retain these highly qualified parents as now well-contented employees.

How Agencies Can Help Prior to the Overseas Assignment

Dave Pollock talked for years about the "flow of care" organizations and corporations need to put in place once they begin sending families overseas. It begins before they go. In the "Family Matters!" survey, Pascoe compares the reports from surveys done among headquarters of international organizations with responses from the employees and their families related to preassignment preparation. While most of the companies felt they did predeparture training, almost two-thirds of the employees who took this survey said they had no help offered. The survey found that only about 20 percent of the accompanying spouses received help, 12 percent of the working partners had predeparture training, and only 6 percent had assistance for the entire family. Since nearly 70 percent of the respondents listed family reasons, including marital breakdown and children's education, as the top reasons for failed assignments, it is important for corporations and sponsoring organizations to work hard in this area of support for families.[5]

One of the most important steps an organization can take for its overseas employees is to make sure the employees know the schooling options they will have well before the date of departure. Corporations and organizations must make their policies and practices regarding educational costs and choices clear. Of those surveyed, 50 percent said they were offered a trip during that period to go to the new location, see the schools, and consider their housing, and they felt this preparation was extremely helpful.[6]

A second valuable step is to plan a preassignment orientation. This training should include tips for living in a new culture as well as for transition itself. Some international agencies are doing an excellent job of this, offering workshops for both the employee and the employee's spouse and children. Other agencies, however, still think only of the employee and make no preparation for the intercultural adjustments the employee's family will inevitably face. Such agencies should seek outside help from cross-cultural training consultants and organizations.

Finally, and perhaps even more important than the two preceding strategies, organizational managers need to gather information on how often and why personnel are transferred to new locations. Since many challenges of the TCK experience are so closely tied to high mobility, administrators must look for ways to minimize the frequency and severity of the transition cycles. For example, why do embassy personnel change posts at least every two years? Is it always because of staffing needs, security reasons, or is it simply tradition? Similarly, when a business decides to send a person overseas, is it essential that the employee go in the middle of the school year? Sometimes moves can't be avoided, but other times, with creative thinking, perhaps they can. Simple matters like examining the options for moving a family during a school vacation or after a child graduates can make all the difference as to whether a family thrives or barely survives in a cross-cultural lifestyle. At the moment, there seems to be a trend for short-term assignments, with families remaining in the passport country. Serious consideration needs to be made on how this may affect the long-term family dynamics as well as how it fits into organizational staffing needs.

How Agencies Can Help During the Third Culture Experience

An agency's responsibility to the family's well-being doesn't end after the final plans for departure are made or good-byes said. To increase a family's chances of success abroad, the agency should have a plan in place that includes the following components.

1. *Have an entry team or a designated employee to welcome new employees on-site.* This was at the top of the list when Pascoe asked her respondents what the sending company or organization could do to help the families.[7] Each agency should have a formal plan for introducing new people to both the host and expatriate community as quickly as possible. It's important for newcomers to know the people they need to contact locally for business connections as well as for the practical issues of life that long-time residents take for granted. We know of one young couple who went overseas where, after their initial welcome at the airport, were left on their own to figure out how to get their driver's licenses, find someone to install a phone, and even locate a doctor when a family member became sick. It was three months before they met anyone who explained to them where they could buy meat they could actually chew. The problem there was that the home office presumed that families in the overseas branch would take care of properly orienting new arrivals but had no formal plan in place to make sure that was done.

   Sometimes people are assigned to a post where they are the only employees from their particular home country. Those from the local culture may work hard to make the newcomers feel welcome and introduce them to local customs and stores, but it is helpful during this time if newcomers can find others from their home culture as well. These people are the ones who know the types of products the newcomers can substitute for things they have been accustomed to using at home. They are also the only ones who might think to explain, for example, that a siren going off in bad weather means a tornado may be approaching. Local residents are so accustomed to these things that they don't think to explain it or realize these new friends have never been around tornadoes before.

2. *Help employees evaluate schooling options using the compiled list put together before departure.* Agencies should never insist on one particular method of schooling for their families. As we've said, parents must have freedom to consider each child's personality and special needs when making this critical choice.

   Agencies must also take into account the additional costs of education for expatriate children. Part of the employee's salary and benefits should include helping with those costs. In the home country, educational expenses for children are rarely discussed when negotiating a job contract, but schooling is often a complex and costly issue for expatriates, especially in certain countries.

3. *Establish a flexible leave policy.* Policies for leave vary from agency to agency. Some insist their employees remain onsite for four years, followed by a one-year home leave. Others have a cycle of sending people overseas for eleven months, then home for a month. Between those two ends of the spectrum lie other alternatives. There are pros and cons to each—both for the sponsoring organizations and the families. Wise administrators are willing to negotiate mutually beneficial leave packages if the standard policy for that organization doesn't work for a particular person or family.

4. *Make provision for children who are attending school in the home country to visit parents during vacations.* Traditionally, many sponsoring organizations have paid for TCKs to return home for vacations if they were away for schooling through secondary school, but once those children returned to their home culture for university, those benefits ended. It's during those post-secondary years, however, that many major life decisions are made, years when parental support and guidance are crucial. Many organizations lose valuable employees whose children are at this critical life crossroads; many employees would rather resign than be separated from their children for long periods of time—particularly if the parents are in a situation where they can't afford to pay personally for frequent trips.

   We believe there is a fairly simple answer. Paying for children who are attending school in the home country to visit their parents for vacations should be a normal benefit for those working with international organizations. That policy change alone would likely prolong the careers of many of their employees, and it would also go a long way to reducing many of the most challenging aspects of this globally mobile lifestyle.

5. *Support international community efforts to provide ongoing expatriate family services.* Factors contributing to the relative success or failure of an overseas assignment include the degree to which a sponsoring organization provides ongoing assistance abroad. Barbara Schaetti, a consultant to the international expatriate community whom we quoted earlier, suggests that the challenge for a company lies in how to provide such assistance in every

one of its international locations. She notes that, historically, most have re-
lied upon their network of expatriate spouses. Support has been limited to
paying membership dues to international women's clubs and contributing
funds to international school parent/teacher association programs. Some
companies are taking a more proactive approach and contracting with International Employee Assistance Programs (IEAPs) to provide expatriates
with access to confidential mental-health services on demand. Others are
underwriting spouse-managed information centers and organizations, such
as Lilly LINK for spouses of the Eli Lilly employees in Indianapolis, Indiana.
They also may provide access to the Internet so that spouses in diverse locations can keep in contact. Still others sponsor events such as Families in
Global Transition, where families and those who work with them meet for
continuing exploration of how best to support globally mobile families.

6. *Help families prepare for repatriation and organizational reentry.* Not only do
companies lose valuable employees during the posting abroad, but disap-
pointing statistics indicate that almost half of all expatriate families leave
the company within one year of repatriation.[8] Repatriating, or returning
home, is frequently more difficult than moving abroad in the first place.
Many, especially corporate employers, have been out of the loop while they
were overseas. Their old job has been filled by someone else, their career is
off track, and the company doesn't know what to do with them or how to
use the international and cross-cultural skills they've acquired. Also, while
overseas these employees may have had a good bit of autonomy as decision
makers or leaders, but at home their position is subordinate and it is hard for
them that their opinions are no longer valued.

Unfortunately, agencies and employees who prepared well for the original cross-cultural transition forget to prepare equally carefully for the transition home. Ideally, before the family leaves the host country, a formal or
informal briefing should be provided by people who have experienced this
type of transition before. Families should be reminded it is as important to
build the RAFT we discussed earlier during this transition home as it has
been prior to a transition anywhere else.

The military has a great model for preparing both the deployed spouse
and the family at home before they are reunited. Before the reunion, all
members of the family—the serviceperson at the place of deployment and
the family members at home—go through training on the common challenges reuniting families often face. This training helps them prepare better
for the inevitable readjustment they will face as a family, despite the joys of
being reunited.

7. *Offer reentry seminars for both parents and TCKs soon after repatriation.*
Several organizations sponsor week-long seminars every summer for TCKs
who are returning to their home country, and some agencies hold debrief-

ing seminars for the adults. Recently, some groups have begun offering programs for the entire family. Some agencies include support for their TCKs to go to reentry camps offered in different places around the globe.

How Agencies Can Help Their TCKs in the Long Term

Because so many TCKs grow up with a strong sense that friends from the sponsoring agency or their international school are a part of their extended family, belonging to this group becomes part of their very identity. It may be the one place outside their family where they have a deep sense of belonging. They want and need to stay connected to this support system in some way.

Helping TCKs and ATCKs stay connected to one another and their past is beneficial for those directly involved as well as for the organization. Think of how advantageous it would be for a company if these children brought their cross-cultural skills back to it when they are ready for their own careers. Here are some ways administrators can play a vital role in helping TCKs who have grown up in their communities continue to thrive—ways that can also help in the healing process for those ATCKs who still need help adjusting.

1. *Support an alumni newsletter.* A growing number of agencies and international schools already help their TCKs and ATCKs maintain a sense of connectedness by helping them put out a newsletter. This forum not only distributes information, it also gives them the opportunity to discuss relevant issues from their past, to offer suggestions for the present, and to stay part of the "family."

2. *Use the experience of TCKs and ATCKs.* It's ironic to see an organization bring in "experts" about a particular subject or country while ignoring the wealth of knowledge and experience of their own ATCKs.

> One ATCK sat through a meeting where a medical facility to be established in Brazil—modeled after one in the United States—was being described and discussed. She knew from the beginning that it wouldn't work because the philosophical concepts on which the project was based were very different from those that shaped Brazilian thinking. When she attempted to raise a few questions, she was disdainfully put down. Three years later, after vast sums of money had been spent on the project, it folded, a complete failure.
>
> In New Zealand, one organization asked Ruth to speak about using the resources of the ATCKs in their organization. She asked how many ATCKs there were in the audience,

and invited them to come forward and form a panel. As they fielded the questions from fellow employees, Ruth never had to answer another question. The fact was they had this resource right among themselves and never thought to tap into it. Sadly, the ATCKs didn't seem to recognize all they had to offer either.

Perhaps all prophets are without honor in their own country, but agencies shouldn't overlook the great resources they have in their ATCKs.

3. *Apologize for past organizational mistakes.* Unfortunately, as a direct result of poor administrative decisions from the company or sponsoring agency, some TCKs suffered the consequences. Some policies on relocating families, for example, have caused needless separations. An unfortunate choice of a caregiver in a boarding school may have done harm to some children. The errors may not have been willful, but they did happen. Even though those who made the decision may have since left the organization, it helps the employees—and the TCKs who were hurt by those policies—to know that the system itself is taking responsibility and that someone representing that system or organization is willing to apologize for past mistakes and, where needed, offer restitution.

4. *Support a TCK's "journey of clarification."* Some agencies already offer a trip back to the host culture during or immediately after university for all of their TCKs who grew up overseas, even if the parents are no longer abroad. As mentioned before, going back to their roots and validating past experiences helps TCKs move on more smoothly to the next stages of life. But when the agency itself is willing to pay for such a trip, the journey becomes even more healing. TCKs receive the important message that they do indeed belong to a community that cares for them—not one that discards them at a certain age with no concern for the impact growing up as a member of that overseas community had on them. It's another way of validating the value of their heritage and inviting them to build on it rather than disown it.

International organizations must face the fact that they bear responsibility not only to their individual employees, but also to their families once they begin to give employees international assignments. Too often administrators have blamed failures totally on the person who didn't succeed rather than looking at the part their agency or corporate policies and decisions may have played in the matter. We're grateful for the growing awareness among companies and sponsoring organizations of their role in helping cross-cultural families be successful.

Lessons from the TCK Petri Dish

Another simple reality: While families are hugely important in every child's life, so are the community and the various organizational systems around them—and none more so than for CCKs of all backgrounds. These groups may include the local Indian Community Center, Chinese Church, Girl Scouts or Boy Scouts. While all CCK families may not belong to as strong a sponsoring organizational system as traditional third culture families often do, these other types of civic, community, and religious communities can also give a great deal of support to CCKs and their families during many of the stress points of this journey. Adoption agencies can make all the difference in whether parents have a positive or negative experience during international adoptions by their policies and attitude toward those they serve. Local schools that have programs in place to welcome the child who just moved from a refugee camp overseas will change that child's life forever. In today's mobile world, there are many ways organizational and educational institutions can be helpful in creating positive environments for those who come to them and those they serve. It's important for leaders in these groups to also recognize the vital role they play. We've talked a lot about what we can do for current TCKs, but what about those who are already adults? That's our next discussion.

CHAPTER 19

It's Never Too Late

I remember when I was at school and struggled with unresolved grief. My health began to deteriorate because of this unresolved emotional baggage, and for two years I suffered from chronic pain. I couldn't even use my hands without having pain—it was every student's nightmare. Especially if you're the type of student who spends most of his time chatting with his friends around the world.

To make matters worse, I still didn't know where I belonged, I was confused about my cultural identity, and I felt I had no real purpose. It was a really dark period in my life.

But I'm really lucky I discovered and learned a few little things that would change the course of my life.[1]

—Brice Royer, developer of *TCKID.com*

IN SPITE OF THE GROWING EFFORTS TO HELP current TCKs better understand and use their cross-cultural experiences, many ATCKs, like Brice, have grown up with little assistance in sorting out the full effect of their third culture upbringing. No one understood that help might be needed, let alone what to do if it were.

Even so, as Brice also expresses, many ATCKs have successfully found their way through the morass of conflicting cultures and lifestyles, come to terms with the inherent losses, and developed a positive sense of identity. They have learned to use their heritage in personally and/or professionally productive ways.

Unfortunately, we have also met many ATCKs who continue to be so confused or wounded by the challenges of their childhood that they've never been free as adults to celebrate the benefits. Depression, isolation, loneliness, anger, rebellion, and despair have ruled their lives instead of joy. Some ATCKs may outwardly continue to be successful chameleons, but inwardly the questions "Who am I?" "Where am I from?" and "Why can't I seem to move on in life?" still rage. They can't figure out why they've always felt different from their peers.

Other ATCKs believe they're just fine, but spouses, children, friends, and coworkers know better. There is a shell around them that no one can penetrate—even in the closest of relationships. Some of them grew up in organizational systems where extended periods of separation from their family seemed so normal at the time that they never considered how these separations might have affected their lives. Others went through periods of war or conflicts in their host country with or without their parents being present. TCKs have experienced emotional, mental, physical, and spiritual abuse, or at least trauma, as they have traversed their worlds, but because these worlds vanished with one plane ride, they have never been able to sort things out—the experiences and their contexts simply disappeared. Often ATCKs are stuck in one of the stages of unresolved grief without realizing it. All they know is that they are trapped in some place or behavior from which they can't break free.

So what can they do now? Is it too late for wounded ATCKs to put the pieces together? When they have been stuck for a long time in a self-destructive lifestyle, is it possible for them to learn to use their past constructively rather than be bound by it? The answer is, simply, yes. It's never too late to deal with unresolved grief, identity issues, or other challenges related to the TCK lifestyle.

But how does healing occur? Obviously, ATCKs and their parents can't go back and relive their transitional experiences or undo the separations. The years of family life lost are irretrievable. In fact, most ATCKs can't recover any of their hidden losses. They can't reclaim the sights, sounds, or smells that made home "home" as a child. They can't stop the war that displaced them or the abuser who stole their innocence. What they *can* do, however, is learn to put words to their past, name their experiences, validate the benefits as well as the losses, and ask for help from their families and others. They can learn to name the gifts they have been given and are often unconsciously using productively in one way or another. One ATCK wondered why she had always felt drawn to work with the homeless when her family had often lived in beautiful homes around the world. As she understood her own story better, she could continue her work in ways she hadn't considered before.

What ATCKS Can Do

NAME THEMSELVES AND THEIR EXPERIENCE

For many ATCKs, simply putting a name to their past—"I grew up as a third culture kid"—opens a new perspective on life. Discovering there are legitimate reasons for their life experiences and the resulting feelings not only helps them understand themselves better, it also normalizes the experience. Some who have spent a lifetime thinking they're alone in their differentness or wondering "What's *wrong* with me?" discover they have lived a normal life after all—at least normal for a TCK.

Somehow the concept of normality is very liberating. It doesn't solve every problem, but it gives permission for a lot of self-discovery and frees ATCKs to make some changes they may not have thought possible. For example, rather than remaining eternal chameleons and continuing to try fitting in everywhere, they can focus on examining who they are, where they do fit, and where they can best use their gifts. If ATCKs can understand such questions as why they chronically withdraw before saying good-bye to others, they can purposefully choose to stay engaged in relationships until the end.

> Since one ATCK discovered withdrawal was her consistent pattern before moving, she now tells her friends a month before the departure date, "I want to let you know what a great friend you've been, because I might not be able to tell you at the end. I also need to tell you that I've hurt a lot of people by acting like I don't care when it comes time to say good-bye. I'm going to try not to do that, but if I start to withdraw, you let me know." And her friends do.

This simple acknowledgment both helps others understand this ATCK's potential behavior and helps her remain emotionally present in relationships both before and after she leaves.

For other ATCKs, discovering they have a name—that they are adult third culture kids—and are members of a group whose membership extends around the world finally gives them a feeling of belonging. Instead of feeling their history is a piece of life's puzzle that will never fit, they now see it as the key piece around which so many others fall into place.

NAME THEIR BEHAVIORAL PATTERNS

Once ATCKs realize their past has undoubtedly influenced their present life and their choices, it's time for them to make an honest assessment. Are there certain lifelong, repetitive behaviors (such as chronic moving or failure to allow intimacy in one relationship after another) that they have always excused as "That's just the way I am"? Is their anger, depression, or other behavior often out of proportion to its context?

After looking at such repetitive cycles, ATCKs need to ask themselves some questions: Is this behavior related to a confusion of identities? Is it related to one of the expressions of unresolved grief? Is it totally unrelated to anything except a personal or family matter? If it seems to be a personal matter, how might the influences of cross-culturalism and high mobility have added to that stress?

NAME THEIR FEARS

Often a major barrier to healing is fear—fear of facing the pain, fear of taking a risk again, fear of rejection. This fear is hidden behind such statements as "I don't see any reason to look back. Life is to be lived in a forward direction." Or "That TCK stuff is bunk. I'm just me, and my life experiences have nothing to do with the way I am. I'd have been the same no matter where or when I grew up."

It is scary to go back, but it can be helpful to realize that no matter how badly a certain situation hurt, they have already survived it and that situation is now past. Facing the pain will hurt for a bit, but it can be grieved and dealt with in the end. Not facing it may well continue to drive the ATCK into far more pain-producing behaviors than they can currently imagine.

NAME THEIR LOSSES

After deciding that healing is worth the risk of pain, it's important for ATCKs to look back and try to identify some of the losses they haven't been fully aware of before. Journaling is one effective way to do this, answering such questions as these:

Did you properly say good-bye to a country you loved dearly?
What ever happened to your pets?
Where is your amah now?
Have your relationships with your siblings ever been restored?
What do you need to do to heal parental relationships?
Have you rediscovered your role in a group?

Some use other means rather than journaling to look at these questions: combining the many pieces of their life into magnificent artwork; decorating homes with symbols of the past places and people; writing stories or poems. All of these can help to put into form things so deeply loved that have simply disappeared with seemingly no way to retrieve them.

Having named the losses, it's not too late to go back and do the work of grieving that should have happened as the losses occurred. We have been astounded at the severity of losses some ATCKs have experienced in their childhood: death in the family while the TCKs were away at boarding school; sexual abuse they never told anyone about; wars that uprooted them in the middle of the night. So many of these have been covered over with no proper period of mourning or comfort to deal with the losses. Many ATCKs have simply disassociated themselves from the pain, but the grief merely surfaces in the other forms mentioned earlier.

If ATCKs dare to face the losses in their lives, to acknowledge and grieve for them, they will discover that proper mourning takes away the power for those losses to drive their behavior in ever more destructive ways. What are some ways to do that grief work?

The methods are as many as the ATCKs who create them. Some have literally gone back to the sites where they grew up and planted a tree as a lasting connection, found their past amahs and friends, or carried back a rock from the sea. Others continue the journaling or artwork in which they first named the losses. Some go on Facebook and begin to reconnect with friends from these days.

In any type of community, whether online like *Facebook.com* or *TCKID.com*, or through reunions or, in the past, such conferences such as Global Nomads or Global Reunion—both of which were organized for ATCKs of all backgrounds— ATCKs can offer great support to one another. One class reunion from an international school concluded their weekend together by bringing a large fishnet in the middle of the room. They brought many types of cloth, string, pieces of wood, paper, buttons, and other random articles. Each ATCK had to create a montage of some sort representing his or her life story. From where they sat around the edges of the net, they then wove that montage into the fishnet toward the center. After it was completed, each ATCK explained the meaning behind his or her creation. Not only was it wonderful to tell the story in a community who cared, but visually seeing where they were together in the center of the fishnet at the end was an incredibly powerful experience for the participants. Other groups have invited attendees to bring their sacred objects and tell their life story that way. What this does, of course, is not only validate the past journey, but also provide a way of normalizing the experience by relating it in the context of others who understand.

When the pain has been severe, good friends who listen and support well are essential, but there are times when professional help may also be needed. Some ATCKs have had severe trauma, perhaps in an unplanned evacuation or from sexual, physical, or emotional abuse. These things can happen in any background and require extra help. In the past, it was often difficult to find someone who understood the underlying theme of the TCK experience. Sometimes ATCKs felt more misunderstood when their counselors weren't familiar with the nontraditional places grief might be coming from. Hopefully, this is changing, but we have also seen ATCKs proactively give their therapists information on this part so they could know what might be "normal" and what issues might be tied to other events in the ATCK's life.

One word of warning: we've noticed that when ATCKs first acknowledge some of their hidden losses, part of the grief process is a newly found or at least newly expressed anger at various people whom they feel are responsible for those losses. Lots of ATCKs (to say nothing of the people they're angry at) are so upset by this phase that they back off from going further. Don't give up on the process if this begins to happen! The angry phase *can* be a very difficult period of the healing process for everyone involved, but remember it is a normal stage of grief, and it can be worked through to a stage of resolution as the ATCKs (and those around them) persist and give the healing process time.

NAME THEIR WOUNDS

Even retrospectively, it's important for ATCKs to name not only their losses, but also the ways in which they have been hurt and how they have hurt others. Why is this important? Everyone has been hurt by other people, and each of us has hurt others. Some of the wounds, whether intentional or not, have been significant, and they must be acknowledged to be dealt with properly.

Once we have identified a wound, then we have to make a critical decision. Will we hold on to our anger forever or will we forgive the ones who have hurt us? Some ATCKs we have met are living lives bound by bitterness. They have turned their pain into a weapon with which they beat not only the offender but themselves and everyone else as well. It seems that the hurt becomes part of their identity. To let it go would be to leave them hollow, empty. The problem with that is that the anger and bitterness destroy as much as, or more than, the original wound. Many are unwilling to forgive because they feel the offender will "go free." They believe that saying "I forgive you" means "It doesn't really matter what happened."

Forgiveness is not something lightly given, bestowed without looking at what the situation cost the person who was wounded. Without forgiveness, however, the offended person's life continues to be ruled by the offender. It's important to acknowledge the offense, but forgiveness is making a decision to let go of the need and desire for vengeance—even if the offender never has to pay. Forgiveness is the only thing that ultimately frees the wounded one to move on to true healing.

None of us is perfect. Healing also involves looking at how we ourselves have knowingly or unknowingly hurt others and asking their forgiveness. It's amazing to listen to stories of rage against parents, siblings, relatives, friends, and administrators in the sponsoring organizations from ATCKs who seem to have no perception that they are doing similar damage to their own children. Some who complain of emotional abuse or separation from parents one moment are yelling at their children the next. Some who complain of abandonment in their childhood are workaholics who may not send their children away to boarding school but still never seem to have time for them.

Until and unless we are willing to acknowledge our own sins and failures against others, true healing is stymied, for we will have to continue living in our self-protective modes, shutting out any who would dare approach us and mention our offenses against them. We need to identify specific places where we have wounded others, and when we recognize the offense, we need to be the first ones to go and ask for forgiveness, not waiting for them to approach us. Doing this both heals important relationships in our lives and frees us from having to defend and protect ourselves. Instead, we can begin to live more openly and with greater joy.

NAME THEIR CHOICES

Dealing with the past in a healthy way frees us to make choices about the future. We are no longer victims. Each of us must ultimately accept responsibility for our own behavior, regardless of the past. That doesn't mean that we're responsible for all that happened to us. A sexually abused child isn't responsible for the abuse; a child who felt abandoned is not responsible for the parents' choices. But as adults, we *are* responsible for how we deal with our past, how we relate to those around us in the present, and what we choose for the future. ATCKs must ask themselves several questions as they sort through their past in order to get on with their future: Will I forgive? Will I retaliate? Will I succumb to the message that I am worthless? Will I look at what it means to be a person and realize that it's okay to think, to create, to have emotion? Will I dare to find ways to express these parts of myself?

The choices ATCKs make in response to these questions can make all the difference for those who feel bound by the past but are longing to move on to freedom in the future.

We started this final chapter focusing on what ATCKs can do for themselves because, in the end, how they deal with their history and how they can best use it is ultimately their responsibility. They can heal and find fulfillment in life even if others never understand their background. However, those close to the ATCKs can be immensely helpful if they try to understand the struggle and freely give their support during the time of healing.

How Can Parents Help Their ATCKs?

We have been saying throughout this book that family relationships are key to a TCK's well-being while they are growing up. This is also true for ATCKs who are still struggling with the challenges from their TCK experience. Parents can often be partners with their ATCKs during this healing process. If parents can be supportive and understanding rather than defensive or threatened for themselves or their organizations when ATCKs are sorting through the past, they can help open the way to much faster healing for their adult children. Support throughout an ATCK's healing process is the greatest gift a parent can give. The following sections discuss some specific ways that parents can help.

LISTEN AND TRY TO UNDERSTAND

This may seem simple, but it's not. ATCKs sometimes turn against their parents when they begin verbalizing their feelings about the past. When the accusations rage, parents often try to defend themselves with the facts: "We *didn't* send you away for six months. It was only three." "We never *made* you wear those hand-me-down clothes. You *wanted* to."

However, the facts aren't the main issue here; the issue is how ATCKs *perceived* the event. For them, the separation *felt* like six months. In other words, they really missed their parents. When they were laughed at for their attire, they *felt* they'd had no choice in what to wear. Like everyone else in the world, the ATCKs' perceptions of reality have been shaped by the emotional impact of their experiences. That emotional reaction is real, and it's far more important at this point for parents to deal with those perceptions of certain events and the feelings behind them than to argue about the facts. Arguing the facts only proves to the ATCK that the parents never understood anyway—and still don't.

Sometimes parents not only argue with the facts ATCKs bring up during this time but also with the feelings ATCKs express. For example, the ATCK tries to express how lonely he or she felt when leaving for boarding school and the parent replies, "You never minded going off to school. Why, you smiled and waved and always said you had a great time there." Or the ATCK talks of how hard it was to leave the host country and the parent interjects, "How can you say you were heartbroken to leave Port-au-Prince? You always told us it was too hot and you couldn't wait to get back to France." Perhaps nothing will shut down communication faster between parents and their ATCK than such a response, because no one can tell another person what they did or did not feel. Outer behavior often masks inner feelings. That's why it is critical that when ATCKs try to tell their parents, even years later, what they were feeling as they grew up, parents need to listen and accept it. This kind of acceptance opens doors for far more fruitful discussion between parents and ATCKs than trying to prove this isn't what the ATCKs felt.

Parents may be stunned when suddenly confronted with feelings their ATCKs have never expressed before—especially when the ATCKs are in their thirties and forties. These feelings may not be easy for parents to hear, but it's important for parents to keep in mind that life has stages, and that often children can't fully deal with or understand what is happening at a certain time in their lives. Many TCKs, like people from any background, in all sorts of situations, do experience the cycle of "grief, despair, and detachment" John Bowlby talks about. When children face any trauma, they can first feel grief, which then turns to despair when it seems the situation can't be changed, and then detachment—

moving to a place virtually outside the feeling.[2] Hopefully, they will look at it later when it is safer to examine the full impact of a situation. For many ATCKs, this is likely the first time they have allowed themselves not only to name it, but to feel it and grieve whatever these losses might have been.

Children basically have to deal with life's traumas in a survival mode—whether it be someone calling them a bad name, their own physical handicap, parental divorce, major separation from either or both parents, abuse, or death. Some kids escape into fantasy. Others block out the feelings of pain with denial or rationalization. Compulsions may be another child's attempt to control the pain. It's not the *how* that's significant; it's the fact that children have to survive, and they must use everything at their disposal to do so.

As life proceeds, however, the pain remains until finally the day comes when adults decide to face their inner wounds.

> Many people have asked Ruth how she remembered so many details of her childhood to include in *Letters Never Sent*. She always explains, "I didn't remember; I reexperienced those moments. But as an adult, I had words to describe the feelings I felt but couldn't explain as a child." After one such discussion, Faye, another ATCK who had been through a similar process of retracing her own childhood, challenged Ruth. Faye said, "I don't think we reexperience those feelings. I think we allow them to be felt for the first time."
>
> On further reflection, Ruth agreed. She realized that when she was six and the lights went off at bedtime her first night in boarding school, she felt an immense sense of isolation, aloneness, and homesickness that threatened to squeeze her to death. To give in to that much pain would surely have meant annihilation. So, like most kids, she tried everything she knew to dull the pain, to control it somehow. Ruth's solution involved "trying harder." She prayed with great attention to style—carefully kneeling, giving thanks in alphabetical order for everyone and everything she could think of—so God would stay happy with her and grant the requests to see her family again that she would sneak onto the end of the prayer. She tried to meticulously obey all the rules at school so she wouldn't get in trouble. Keeping track of the details of life took a lot of focus and attention away from the pain.
>
> When she picked up her pen at age thirty-nine and wrote, "I want my mommy and daddy" as part of the letter her six-year-old self would have written if she'd had the words, Ruth felt that same horrible squeezing in her chest that she'd known as that six-year-old child. This time,

however, she didn't need to put it away or work against it. She had already survived it and could allow herself to feel the anguish all the way to the bottom of her soul in a way she couldn't have when it actually happened.

This pattern of midlife clarification of the past seems to be common for many ATCKs, but it's a process that brings great consternation to some parents. It's helpful for parents not only to accept that ATCKs may need to deal with their emotions many years after the events themselves, but also to see that their ATCKs' attempts to share feelings with them—though initially some may be expressed in anger—are because the ATCKs still want and need their parents to understand what they felt during their moments of separation or other experiences of childhood. Consciously or unconsciously, the ATCKs desire to be in a closer relationship with their parents or they wouldn't bother trying to communicate these feelings. After all, these are the only parents the ATCK will ever have.

COMFORT AND BE GENTLE

Offering comfort is a key factor in any grieving process—even when that process is delayed by decades. Remember, comfort is not encouragement. It is being there with understanding and love, not trying to change or fix things.

One ATCK took courage and finally wrote his parents some of the things he had felt through some of the early separations from them as a child. His mother wrote back, "Thank you for telling us how you felt. As I read your letter, of course I cried. I wish I could give you a big hug right now. I'm sorry we didn't know then what you expressed now or we might have made some different decisions—but we didn't. I love you and trust your story will help others."

Obviously, the first piece of comfort came with the acknowledgement that his mom understood the feelings he had expressed. The second came with the words, "I wish I could give you a big hug." Then his mom expressed her own sorrow with a simple acknowledgment that as parents they had not realized what he was feeling. His mother never denied his feelings, nor did she wallow in self-blame or defensiveness. Instead, she blessed her son. Parental listening, understanding, comfort, and blessing are huge, wonderful steps in the healing process that parents can provide for their children—even when those children are now adults.

DON'T PREACH

Almost all parents find it difficult not to preach, but for parents who have often spent their lives serving in causes they see as greater than themselves, this may be especially hard. Take, for example, parents of adult missionary kids who have spent their lives dedicated to a religious cause, or military parents who have given their all to defend a particular country. There is probably no greater anguish a parent can feel than when their ATCKs reject the system for which the parents have stood—particularly when it is the faith or freedom they have gone halfway around the world to share or defend. Often, the sense of urgency to convince their children to believe in what they themselves believe grows as parents watch their ATCKs fall into increasingly self-destructive behavior: "If they'd just get their lives right with God, they'd be fine." Or "If Suzy would just enlist, the Marines would shape her up."

To that we would respond with a "yes, but" answer. Yes, what the parents desire for their children is valuable, but ATCKs who suffered within a religious system must first sort out their pain in terms of who God actually is compared to the rules and culture of the religious system that seeks to represent God. Until then, preaching, or worse, words of spiritual reprimand, will only fuel the anger. A lecture on what a great country this is and why they should be grateful to be part of it may all be true, but not helpful for a military ATCK trying to understand the many nuances of his or her story. All ATCKs need, at some point, to differentiate between what parts of their experience are basically "normal" for being a TCK and what parts are particular to their family structure or the organization under which the parents worked.

Is there never a time for third culture parents to talk forthrightly with their ATCKs both in response to the accusations that are being made as well as the destructive behavior parents see? Of course there is. When parents have listened and understood what their adult child is feeling, there *is* an appropriate time to express their own feelings and beliefs. But it must come as a sharing of who they are and their perspectives rather than as a denial of what the ATCK has shared or is feeling.

FORGIVE

Sometimes parents need to ask their ATCKs for forgiveness. They have made mistakes too and shouldn't run from acknowledging them. If their ATCK has been extremely hurtful and rebellious toward them, parents will also have much to forgive. This can be very difficult, particularly if their adult child is not yet acknowledging how badly he or she has hurt them. But if parents are able to forgive and ask for forgiveness, it can be a major factor in their adult child's healing process.

ASSUME YOU ARE NEEDED

Parents should assume their adult children still need and want them as part of their lives.

They may tell parents not to bother coming for a birth, graduation, or wedding, saying "It isn't that big a deal," and these ATCKs probably believe that's how they really feel. But it makes a big difference—even to those who don't think they need their parents any longer—when parents make the effort to remain involved in a caring way in their children's lives as adults. Sometimes those years together as adults finally make up for the separations of the past.

What Friends and Other Relatives Can Do

Sometimes friends and other relatives can help ATCKs take the first major step in the healing process because they stand outside the emotionally reactive space occupied by the ATCKs and their parents. What can they do for the ATCKs they love to help in the healing process?

LISTEN TO THE STORY AND ASK GOOD QUESTIONS

Many ATCKs feel their childhood story is so far removed from their present lives that they have nearly forgotten it themselves. Few people cared to know more than the cursory details when they first returned from their third culture experience, and they quit talking about it long ago. To have someone invite them for lunch, ask to hear about their experiences, and then actually listen may be such a shock to some that they seem to at least temporarily forget everything that has happened to them. But persist. When friends or relatives initiate the conversation and clearly express their interest, the ATCK knows it's bona fide. It may even give them the first chance they've ever had to put words to their experiences.

Questions such as these can also help the process: "How did you feel when you said good-bye to your grandma?" "What was the hardest thing about returning to your home country?" "What did you like best about growing up that way?"

These kinds of questions prove the friend is listening closely enough to hear the behind-the-scenes story and may even challenge ATCKs to consider issues they never stopped to think about before.

DON'T COMPARE STORIES

Friends and relatives shouldn't point out how many other people have had it worse. Generally, ATCKs already know they've had a wonderful life compared to many others. That has often been part of their problem in trying to understand their struggles.

Most ATCKs will first relate the positive parts of their story. They won't tell the difficult aspects until they feel safe and comfortable with the listener. Once they do begin to share the darker times, don't try to cheer them up by reminding them of the positives. Both sides of the story are valid.

COMFORT IF POSSIBLE

Sometimes friends are the first to ever comfort an ATCK. There are ATCKs with amazing stories of pain who came through an uncontrollable situation such as a political evacuation under heavy gunfire, or simply an insensitive remark that has cut them deeply all their lives. For ATCKs who went through political stress and resulting physical danger in days gone by, few had any debriefing teams. People celebrated their survival but never addressed the trauma. That unthinking remark may not be known by others, but it forever seals them inside to that place of "I'm too stupid to figure out what's happening." When a situation like that comes out, it's helpful for the listener to take a moment and say, "That must have been incredibly scary," or "I am so sorry that happened to you. If you were ten years old, that would have felt terrible." The ATCKs may reveal terrible things that have been locked up as their secrets throughout life, once someone begins to truly listen. If you feel overwhelmed by the story they tell, you can still find ways to acknowledge their loss or grief even as you realize they might need to discuss the events and feelings with a professional counselor at some point.

One point to bear in mind is that, initially, comfort can sometimes be hard for the ATCK to accept. Many feel as if admitting to any pain is the same as disowning their parents, their faith, or the organizational system in which they grew up. Sometimes ATCKs become angry when others try to comfort them, because they refuse to admit they might need it. So offer comfort, but don't push if they aren't ready to receive it.

How Therapists Can Help

We don't presume to tell therapists how to counsel ATCKs, since professional therapy is outside our domain. We hope, however, that we can help therapists understand the problems specific to the TCK experience, such as where TCK grief often comes from, where the early attachments between parents and children might have been broken, and how TCKs' concepts of identity and worldview have been affected by cultural and mobility issues. Our goal is to help therapists understand the basic life patterns of the third culture experience so they will be better prepared to assist their TCK clients. Hopefully, a careful reading of this book by therapists will have done that. An interesting occurrence when we have given seminars for therapists is that after our presentations, our audience begins to redefine the topic by explaining it back to us and one another from therapeutic models such as attachment theory, triangulation, or post-traumatic stress syndrome with which they are already familiar.

After attending a conference on TCK issues, one therapist said, "We used to think that if a child was adopted at birth, that child would have no different issues to deal with than a child born to the adoptive couple. Now we know anytime a client comes in who was adopted, there are certain questions to ask.

"It seems to me the TCK issue falls in that category. Being aware of this experience can help us ask better questions when we realize our clients are TCKs or ATCKs."

RECOGNIZE HIDDEN LOSSES

Therapists who understand the nature of the third culture experience may be the first to help ATCKs identify the hidden losses that are part of the TCK experience, but that TCKs themselves are often not aware of. The Cycles of Mobility chart (see Figure 19-1) can be a useful tool in this process. Many ATCKs do not recognize the degree to which separation has been an integral part of their lives and how it has contributed to feelings of loss and grief.

Instructions: Make a time chart of the separation patterns for the first eighteen years of the ATCK's life, using different colors to fill in the spaces for when and where he or she lived. For example:

Blue   = *time living with parents in the home country*
Green   = *time living with parents in the host country #1*
Purple   = *time living with parents in the host country #2*
Yellow   = *time living with parents in the host country #3*
Brown   = *time spent away from parents in boarding school in the host country*
Pink   = *time spent away from parents in boarding school in the home country*
Orange   = *time living with anyone other than parents or boarding school*

This chart can be modified to fit the specific situation of each ATCK. What's important is for the therapist—and the ATCK—to see the overall patterns of mobility: where the transitions between various cultures happened, what ages they occurred, and so forth. As the times of transition, separation, and loss become obvious, therapists may discover the roots of some of the issues they see in their ATCK clients. This insight can help them aid their ATCK clients in recognizing the areas that need healing.

Therapists should also help their ATCK clients carefully think through the issues regarding the impact of culture on a TCK's developmental process. Some of the feelings ATCKs struggle with may, in fact, be largely a result of cultural imbalance.

	1	2	3	4	5	6	7	8	9	10	11	12	13	14	15	16	17	18
January																		
February																			
March																			
April																			
May																			
June																			
July																			
August																			
September																			
October																			
November																			
December																			
Age in Years																			

Figure 19-1 The Cycles of Mobility Chart
(© Lois M. Bushong)

RECOGNIZE THE IMPACT OF THE SYSTEM

One major factor that many therapists of ATCKs overlook or fail to understand is the powerful influence of the military, mission, business, or other organizational system under which these ATCKs grew up. Often the ATCKs' anger or hurt stems directly from policies that either controlled their lives on a daily basis or took away choice when it came to schooling, moving, and so on. On the flip side, ATCKs who were used to being protected or nurtured in that system (for example, the perks like free medical care or inexpensive housing) may not know how to cope comfortably in a larger, less structured world where they are expected to depend more on themselves. Therapy is sometimes stymied if issues are dealt with only in the context of family relationships rather than understanding the operative system that often superseded family decisions.

RECOGNIZE THE PARADOX

Often ATCKs are defensive in therapy when asked about the painful parts of their past. They don't want to negate the way of life that is the only one they have known and is a core element in their identity. Corporate kids may feel they are discrediting the many privileges they have known if they say there was anything hard about the experience. Missionary kids may have trouble acknowledging the pain because they feel that to do so will negate their faith. It is hard for many to know how much of that system they can examine, and potentially give up, without renouncing what they value in the process.

Acknowledging the paradoxical nature of their experience may be particularly important in relationship to a client who attended a boarding school. These ATCKs may have so many great memories of the camaraderie experienced there and friendships made and maintained through the years. How could there be any negatives? In addition, for some TCKs who were boarding students for as long as twelve years, their identity is deeply tied into the boarding school experience. To acknowledge anything but the good would threaten their entire sense of self. But young boarding students feel unprotected; a six-year-old child going to boarding school may actually experience something akin to becoming an orphan. How can ATCKs acknowledge the loneliness they felt without seeing it as a denial of the good they have also known at school? For these, or any ATCKs who grew up in strong systems and feel closely identified to that system, questioning system policies can be such a threat to their core identity that they may refuse to continue with the therapy they need.

That is why those working with ATCKs must never forget to recognize— and help the ATCKs recognize—what we have tried to stress time and again. Looking at the TCK experience from the perspective of the adult TCK will reveal many paradoxical realities. Therapists must affirm the positive elements as well as identify the stress points to give their ATCK clients the permission they need to look at all sides of their past experiences. It's also helpful to remind them once more that if there hadn't been so much good to lose, there often wouldn't have been so much grief at its passing.

Lessons from the TCK Petri Dish

Looking at the impact of childhood experiences on our adult lives is an important part of each person's journey in moving to a fuller understanding of who we are, ATCK or not. But when we meet CCKs from the other types of cross-cultural experiences we mentioned in chapter 3, we see that many face the same types of specific issues mentioned here. Certainly their own hidden diversity—that place has been shaped by their various cultural worlds—remains unseen by others who judge them based on old models of culture and ethnicity. Even more frequently, we see that there may be other types of unrecognized losses stemming from the specific nature of their cross-cultural upbringing. One bi-racial ACCK said she realized she never had a mirror for understanding who she was because she didn't look like her mother or father. ACCKs who were raised in refugee camps feel they lost the wonder and innocence of childhood. Domestic ACCKs never realized they, too, lost a sense of cultural balance when moving from one place to another. Without language and understanding, these ACCKs also had no way to process what they were experiencing. For all parents and therapists of ACCKs, realizing the way they themselves may have grown up in more monocultural environments and how this is different from how their ACCKs have been raised means that the same lessons we list above regarding careful listening are critical. We are indeed facing a "new normal" in this world. The more we all understand the changes taking place, the better we can move ahead with confidence and hope, not with fear or rejection.

Where Do We Go from Here?

In the years since the first edition of *Third Culture Kids,* we've been encouraged to see the end of apathy and the beginning of real awareness that there are some valid issues to deal with in this particular lifestyle of children growing up among many cultural worlds. Sponsoring agencies are developing new strategies for taking better care of their families. Schools throughout the world are making changes in curriculum and approaches to teaching that will make it easier for students from any country to fit back into the school system of their home country. Parents are making careful, thoughtful decisions that take into account their own TCKs' needs. Everywhere we see ATCKs taking ownership of their past so that they may use it well.

But we also concluded our first edition saying that we hoped this book would be a beginning for all of us to consider what some of the ramifications of globalization might be for children everywhere. We are encouraged to see that vision growing as well. And this phase has just begun. We believe various disciplines such as developmental psychology, sociology, counseling, and education need to begin a comprehensive, multidisciplinary dialogue on how global changes are challenging traditional models in each discipline by studying patterns of development or identity based on those who grew up primarily in the more monocultural communities of the past. We believe those who have grown up as CCKs of all backgrounds can contribute enormously to the discussion.

And so we have now reached both an ending and a beginning with this edition: the end of sharing what we have already learned from and about TCKs and ATCKs, and the beginning of watching the rest of this story unfold—wherever it grows. But, after all is said and done, we repeat what we said in our first edition: it's a great gift to grow up among many cultural worlds. It's been wonderful to know, love, and work with so many who have had this experience. Without all who have shared their lives and stories with us, this book could never have been written. We are grateful indeed. And we wish each of you, our readers, much joy in your own journeys as well.

Let the conversations begin!

Epilogue

By Ruth E. Van Reken

WHEN I HEARD THE SAD NEWS of David Pollock's impending death in April 2004, I felt as though I was just about to lose half of my brain. For so many, the size of Dave's heart is what they remember most. Time and again at his memorial service, individuals spoke of how, when they met him, Dave's undivided attention made them feel as if they were the most important person in the world. And at that moment, they were.

I, too, have no question of the size of Dave's heart. When I sent him the journaling I did at age 39 trying to figure out my own journey, not only did Dave respond, but he worked out a way for me to attend the first conference on these topics in Manila and encouraged me to publish my writings in what became *Letters Never Sent*. But what I also came to value beyond measure was the size of Dave's mind.

Rarely have I known someone with his capacity to listen patiently while someone explained an idea, then bounce it back and forth and synthesize it into a form that had shape and could be crystallized into usable form as The Big Idea (e.g., the Pol/Van Cultural Identity Box). It was through countless conversations such as this with TCKs and their families around the world; with people like Ruth Hill Useem, originator of the *TCK* term; her co-researcher, Ann Baker Cottrell; Norma McCaig, founder of Global Nomads; and others in the field that he formed his TCK Profile and The Transition Experience models. Now, with Dr. Useem having died a few months before and Norma passing away in 2008, I wondered: With these leaders gone, what would happen to this topic they pioneered with such passion?

And then I had a mental image of Dave at the top of a long, vertically ascending, single-file line of people rising toward the sky—almost as if those in this line were climbing an invisibly suspended stairway to the stars, each person tucked in behind the one ahead. The line wiggled and wove its way up, until it abruptly collapsed because the leader who held us together—Dave—was gone. For a moment, it seemed all was lost. But suddenly I saw something else. In that collapse, everyone in the line was flung far and wide. And then this verse (John 12:24) came to mind: "Except a seed of wheat fall into the ground and die, it abides alone. But if it dies, it springs forth and brings forth much fruit." In that moment, I realized that the seeds Dave had gathered from others and replanted in so many lives had and would continue to take root in countless places around the globe. Instead of dying, new life and growth would spring up everywhere. Updating *Third Culture Kids* at this time, with the hope of sharing more of Dave's growing vision as well as my own, is my way of distributing those seeds.

I hope that, whether you are reading this book for the first time or the tenth, you will find seeds of potential here to take and replant where you live. And together we will see what is yet to be. Yes, we've only just begun.

Adult Third Culture Kids Survey Results

A Historical Overview of Mobility Patterns for TCKs and Their Long-Term Impact on ATCKs

People often ask, "Is it fair to look at adult TCKs and project their experience onto current TCKs when conditions for third culture living are so different (and presumably better) than they were during the first half of the twentieth century?"

That's a valid question, and in our early days of working with TCKs we wanted to find an answer. Were the long-term effects of both benefits and challenges of the third culture experience valid for current and future TCKs or simply fading products of an earlier day and way of life?

In 1986, the few surveys that had already been done among TCKs mostly reflected the benefits of the experience but seemed to miss any major discussion of the challenges. We soon realized that because boarding schools and universities were the easiest place to access this population, every survey that had been conducted among TCKs picked up mostly missionary kids, and all were teenagers or in their early twenties. That raised the next question: Did the "positive only" nature reflect that the younger TCKs didn't face the issues of former generations, or did it reflect another possibility—that young people often don't have a full perspective on their life experiences and perhaps haven't yet started to deal with some of the long-term ramifications of their experiences? Certainly we had found a pattern among the many ATCKs we had talked to. Most had not begun to deal consciously with issues relating to their TCK experience until their mid-to-late twenties—or even into their thirties. Armed with this information, we decided to do a simple survey ourselves.

In 1986 we gathered 800 names of ATCKs from a variety of sources—personal contacts, referrals by friends, and alumni lists of various TCK boarding schools. Most of these prospects were adult missionary kids, so our sample pool in parental occupational orientation closely reflected that of the initial surveys we had seen. All were postuniversity ATCKs, and the 282 who responded ranged from twenty-two to seventy-five years of age.

The questionnaire focused on two major issues:

1. *What were the patterns of separation from family, home, and host countries—both in kind and amount—during the first eighteen years of the ATCK's life?*
2. *How did the respondent think these separations had affected him or her?*

The results were revealing. We not only learned the ways many ATCKs felt their lives had been affected by these patterns of separation, but a vivid picture of the changes occurring in the third culture community emerged as well. The findings painted a clear historical picture of the TCK world as well as showing changing trends.

When we began noticing some significant differences in certain statistics among ATCKs of the pre- and post-World War II eras, we decided we could best compare the past and present world of TCKs by dividing our respondents into two major categories: those born before 1947 we called the "older ATCKs"; those born in 1947 and later we called the "younger ATCKs." To study the data more precisely, we broke these two larger groups down into subgroups representing all the respondents born within five-year spans. Each of the following graphs and discussions is based on this framework.

Our first clue about the changing patterns in the third culture world came when we graphed the place of birth. In every five-year group of the older ATCKs—those born during or before World War II—the majority were born in the host country (see Figure A-1). It was the opposite for every five-year age group of TCKs born after the war: the majority of these younger ATCKs were born in their home countries.

There are undoubtedly several reasons for this marked difference. In the prewar years, most missionaries (the major group from which our sample came) went overseas for at least four years at a time—some much longer. It could easily take six weeks to three months on an ocean freighter before they arrived at their destination.

In those early days, many mission boards didn't accept people over thirty years of age, feeling that by the time anyone older than that learned the language in a new country, they would be too old for useful, long-term service. Agencies also believed that only younger people could better stand up to the health risks involved in overseas living. This meant people went overseas in their early twenties, often before the birth of their children. When babies came later, they were born wherever their parents were—usually in the host country.

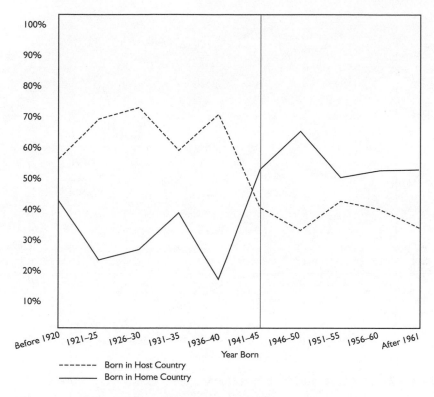

Figure A-1 Place of Birth—Home or Host Country

In the post-World War II era, children were and are still being born wherever parents are, but patterns for how and when people engage in international careers are vastly different from before. Long, uninterrupted stints in faraway lands are less common now than they used to be. Because people can travel by jet rather than ship, it means they come and go between countries far more easily. Leaves or furloughs are scheduled more frequently. Women who choose to do so can fly home for the delivery of their babies rather than stay in a host culture that may have less adequate facilities. Short-term assignments are also possible because the business or mission started by the lifelong pioneers of earlier days is now well established. It's easy to identify a place where people can plug in to meet a specific need of the moment. For these reasons, and doubtless others, more TCKs are being born in their home country now than formerly.

The next difference between the older and younger ATCK groups became clear when we looked at how many had been separated from their parents for a significant period of time before the age of six. Many ATCKs born just before

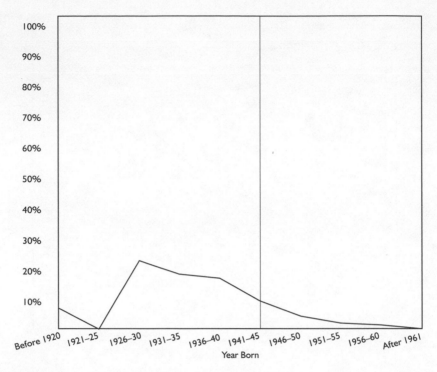

Figure A-2 Those Separated from Parents for a Significant Period before Age Six

and during World War II were in this category (see Figure A-2). There were two common reasons children were left in the home country at an extremely early age while parents went overseas.

1. *Children weren't allowed to travel overseas during the war because of the risks involved.* In 1944 this ban on children traveling across the ocean meant Ruth Van Reken's parents faced a major dilemma when they discovered Ruth's mom, Betty, was pregnant while they were preparing to go to Africa for the first time. They could either go while Betty was pregnant, not go at all, or wait in the United States for the baby to be born and then go on to Africa, leaving the baby with caregivers until the war was over. Ruth's folks chose to cross the ocean while her mom was still pregnant. (Sadly, the ship that carried them to Europe was torpedoed and sunk by enemy fire on its return trip to the U.S.; there were obviously good reasons for the ban on travel for children.)

2. *Even before the war, many parents chose to leave their young children at home for educational purposes.* Others left their children behind because they feared the disease and other perils they might face in an overseas post such as West Africa, which in the colonial era was called "the white man's grave."

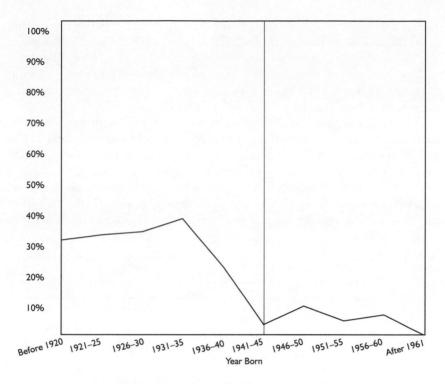

Figure A-3 Those who Lost a Family Member to Death before Respondent Was Eighteen

During their first eighteen years of life, the older ATCKs surveyed had suffered a much higher mortality rate in their immediate family than had the younger ATCKs (see Figure A-3). Before antibiotics and antimalarial drugs became available, death rates were high for expatriates in many tropical countries. When an article came out in the early 1990s in *Christianity Today* discussing the children's graves at a mission station in Nigeria, Ruth realized she'd known every one of those children personally except for two. They'd either been her friends, or she had babysat them, or they were the children of her parents' close friends. Death was a sad, but common, occurrence among the expatriate community in those earlier days.

Aside from the TCKs mentioned in Figure A-2, who were left at home for fear of war or disease, most separations for TCKs occurred because of schooling. Figure A-4 reflects some interesting possibilities regarding educational patterns. The higher number of total years away for the oldest ATCKs likely reflects not only time away in boarding school overseas but long stretches in their home country as well.

The graph stays relatively steady until we see those born after the war, in the 1950s and 1960s. Suddenly, the total number of years away drops. The trend toward homeschooling and the more varied options offered by satellite schools and by local national and international schools are likely reflected in these statistics.

The greatest difference between the older and younger ATCKs, however, is in the average longest period of time TCKs went without seeing their parents at all during those same first eighteen years of life. These figures tell a remarkable story.

In the older group, the average length of time for not seeing parents even once was 3.6 years. The normal pattern for most missionaries in those days was four years overseas and one year back in the home country for furlough. With few American or British secondary schools available overseas, many TCKs stayed in the United States, Canada, or England and went to boarding schools or lived with relatives in the home country during their teenage years. Meanwhile, parents returned overseas for the next four-year stint. With slower transportation

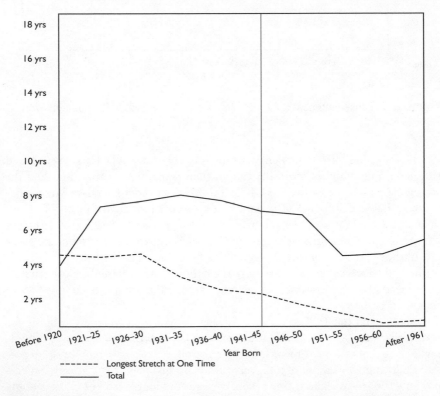

Figure A-4 Total Years of Separation from Parents before Age Eighteen and Longest Single Stretch of Time without Seeing Parents Even Once in First Eighteen Years

and the high costs involved for travel, TCKs rarely visited their parents overseas during those four-or-more-year stretches.

The average length of time the younger TCKs went without seeing parents once was only eleven months. Quite a change.

A quick look at Figure A-5 shows how common these long separations were for older ATCKs. They were accepted as a normal and inevitable part of an international, or at least a missionary, career. The dramatic lowering in this pattern of extended separations for the younger ATCKs (among those born in 1956 and later, not one ATCK during the first eighteen years had gone a full year without seeing parents at least once) clearly reflects several points. Like Figure A-4, this decline no doubt reflects the trend toward homeschooling and the more varied options offered by satellite schools and by local national and international schools. These figures also reflect the trend for sending children who are in their home country back to see their parents in the host country during the school vacation periods.

The rising average age when TCKs permanently reentered the home country clearly reflects the increased availability of international schooling options

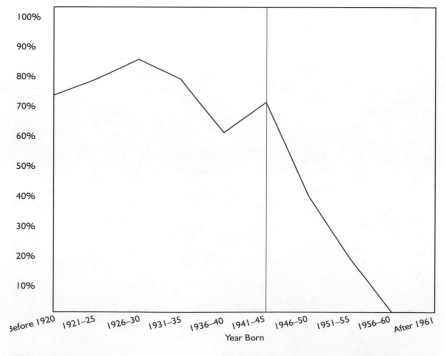

Figure A-5 Percent of Those Separated from Parents for Longer than One Year at a Time before Age Eighteen

around the world (see Figure A-6). Instead of returning at age twelve or thirteen for secondary school in the home country as the older ATCKs did, the great majority of younger TCKs stayed in the host country until an average age of almost seventeen. They only returned to the home country for college.

After looking at the notable differences in type, amount, and patterns of separation experienced by the older and younger ATCK groups, we expected to find that the issues TCKs from previous generations faced weren't relevant for today's culturally mobile kids. We presumed there would be a significant difference in how the older and younger groups responded to our question of how the separations had affected them—with the older generation saying they had been hard and the younger group barely noticing them.

The specific question we asked was, "How do you feel the cycle of separations affected you?" Here are some of the replies.

"Don't know."
"Hard to communicate and make friends."

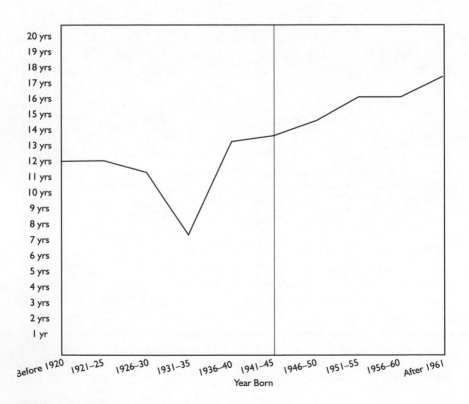

Figure A-6 Age at Permanent Return to Home Country

"I am sympathetic with those who have to be separated from loved ones."

"Have never made intimate friends."

"Because of internment by Japanese, I was spared separation. [Apparently this ATCK was in internment camp with the parents.] My brother, who was separated, was affected."

"Am very interested in people and their needs."

There were three basic types of response: positive, negative, and both. Positive responses were judged as those that included such statements as "It made me more independent," although we have no way to assess if that is a healthy independence or the isolation we talked about in chapter 7. We judged as negative those remarks that included *only* challenges with no benefits listed. Here's one example: "I have become very protective emotionally. I do not let others get close emotionally. I find it very hard to communicate in an intimate relationship for fear of rejection. It has crippled my marriage." A major recurring theme in many of the remarks reflected the ATCK's fear of intimacy because of the fear of loss.

The responses we marked as "both" included replies such as this respondent's: "I struggled with depression for years but now find my own struggle gives me greater empathy for others." None of these were listed in the negative responses.

To our surprise, in spite of all the differences in separation patterns between older and younger ATCKs, 47 (40.1%) of the 117 respondents in the older group said the chronic cycles of separation had a negative impact on them and 62 (39.2%) of the 158 in the younger group said the same thing (see Figure A-7). A mere 1 percent difference!

How could this be? With further reflection, and many intervening years to test our hypothesis, our conclusion was, and remains, that it is the *cycles* of separation and the loss itself that affect TCKs and ATCKs—not merely the longevity or amount. Though TCKs may now return from boarding school every three months instead of being separated from parents for four years, these children still know, and internally stay prepared for, the fact that they will soon be leaving again. If TCKs see grandparents and relatives back home more often than before, they know it's not a permanent settling down. In fact, some ATCKs who experienced the long periods of separation from parents adjusted to it much as they would to death. Perhaps they experienced less of the *cycle* of separation by staying with the same relatives in one place rather than saying "hello" and "good-bye" to parents every three months—although other types of losses are certainly inherent in such prolonged separations between parents and children. It was Figure A-7 that made us begin to look more carefully at the hidden—rather than the obvious—losses we discuss in this book.

Surely there is much more research to do in this whole area. While other surveys have been done in the intervening years on ATCKs as well as TCKs, many

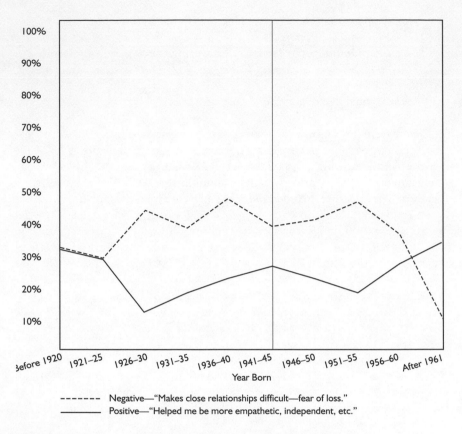

Negative—"Makes close relationships difficult—fear of loss."
Positive—"Helped me be more empathetic, independent, etc."

Figure A-7 Impact of Multiple Separations on Relationships

questions remain unanswered. Perhaps because this is such a highly paradoxical experience, it is hard to measure the both/and-edness in any quantitative survey. For those interested, we would suggest that any survey designed for TCKs and ATCKs take into account the inherent paradoxes and leave room for open-ended responses as well as those designed to gather statistical data

Comparing Third Culture Kids and Kaigai/Kikoku-Shijos

Momo Kano Podolsky was born in Japan and spent 11 years as a TCK in England and France. She received her Ph.D. from the University of Toronto, and has studied the kaigai/kikoku-shijo phenomenon since 1985. Momo has worked extensively with Kakehashi (the western Japanese association of kikoku-shijo parents) while associate professor at Kyoto Women's University (2001–2008), and is currently the program coordinator for the Harney Program in Ethnic, Immigra-tion and Pluralism Studies at the University of Toronto.

THE TWENTIETH CENTURY IS OFTEN referred to as the "era of mass human migration." People moved from one country to another on an unprecedented scale in pursuit of better economic and social opportunities or to flee from war and persecution. For some, migration was not a matter of individual choice, but rather mandated, as discussed in this book, by their employers and job requirements.

The theme of expatriate children has been studied thoroughly all over the world, and these children have been the subject of intense scrutiny in Japan for the past four decades. There they are known as *kaigai-shijos* while they reside abroad due to their parents' work and as *kikoku-shijos* upon their return to Japan.

Like most TCKs, kaigai/kikoku-shijos experience *temporary* (if lengthy) stays overseas during their formative years and eventually return to their passport country. They are thus distinguished from immigrant children, who in principle are destined to live permanently in their host society.

Unlike TCKs, whose parents may be military personnel or religious missionaries, the overwhelming majority of kaigai/kikoku-shijos are children of corporate employees. Kaigai/kikoku-shijos have long been treated as a specific group of children worthy of government support in Japan, whereas TCKs are still in the process of becoming known by the general public as a distinct category of child migrants.

Who are the kaigai/kikoku-shijos? When and how did they emerge as a major social phenomenon in their home country? What impact does their presence have on Japanese society? This appendix focuses on the societal factors that influence the children's experience rather than on the nature of the experience itself. It also discusses the need for a "cross-pollination" between various approaches of understanding the children's experiences in order to shed further light on the issues faced by kaigai/kikoku-shijos and third culture kids.

Kaigai/Kikoku-Shijos and the "Making" of a Social Phenomenon

DEMOGRAPHIC DATA

According to 2007 data from the Ministry of Foreign Affairs of Japan, there are now over 740,000 Japanese long-term expatriates and temporary overseas residents worldwide. Of those, 59,000 are school-age dependents (kaigai-shijos) who are concentrated in three geographical areas: Asia (38 percent), North America (32 percent), and Europe (19 percent). Table A-1 shows the shifts in numbers of long-term expatriates and kaigai-shijos over the past 35 years, in 5 year-periods, from 1971 (when kaigai-shijo data was first collected) to 2006. This historical shift in their numbers and geographical distribution mirrors the trends in Japan's economic activities overseas.

The number of kaigai-shijos more than doubled between 1971 and 1976, and then rose by approximately 10,000 for each period thereafter before hitting a plateau of 50,000 in 1991. Their number stagnated for the following decade, showing a slight decrease along the way, before rising again in the twenty-first century. Similarly, the overall number of long-term expatriates showed a sharp increase from 1971 to 1976, between 1986 and 1991, and again after 2001.

TABLE A-1

Shifts in long-term expatriate and kaigai-shijo populations (1971–2006)

	1971	1976	1981	1986	1991	1996	2001	2006
Long-term expatriates	83,939	150,068 (+134%)	204,731 (+36%)	251,545 (+22%)	412,207 (+63%)	492,942 (+19%)	544,434 (+10%)	735,378 (+35%)
Kaigai-shijos	8,662	18,092 (+108%)	30,200 (+66%)	39,393 (+30%)	50,773 (+28%)	49,740 (−2%)	50,793 (+2%)	58,304 (+14%)

Source: Ministry of Foreign Affairs of Japan, Annual Report of Statistics on Japanese Nationals Overseas (www.mofa.go.jp/mofaj/toko/tokei/hojin/index.html).

The first increase in the number of both long-term expatriates and kaigai-shijos can be explained as much by a move by Japanese corporations to establish overseas branches, thereby boosting the size of their expatriate staff, as by a worldwide relaxation of regulation regarding immigration and foreign funds transfer. The second increase coincides with the so-called "bubble economy" that Japan experienced in the mid-1980s, understandably bringing about the proliferation of overseas bureaus and personnel. The latest spike in the number of overseas nationals is mostly accounted for by an increase of Japanese corporate expatriates in Asia, especially China.

The only period during which the two numbers are not synchronized took place in the 1990s: while the kaigai-shijo population remained at around 50,000, the overall number of corporate expatriates continued to increase. This was at the time of the "Heisei recession," when companies maintained their overseas operations by sending employees without their families in an effort to cut relocation costs.

Let us now turn our attention to kikoku-shijos (kaigai-shijos who have returned to Japan at the end of their parents' assignment). Statistics kept by the Japanese Ministry of Education, Culture, Sports, Science, and Technology suggest that there were approximately 1,500 kikoku-shijos in 1971. This number increased to 5,900 by 1977 and reached the 10,000 mark by 1985. This trend should be understood as part of a cumulative process: although some kikoku-shijos may leave again for another posting overseas, many of them remain in Japan to form an ever-increasing pool of returnees. This demographic trend, which started four decades ago, is at the root of the emergence of kaigai/kikoku-shijos as a conspicuous social phenomenon.

KIKOKU-SHIJOS AS "EDUCATIONAL ORPHANS"

As early as 1966, the Japanese government was aware that children who returned from an overseas sojourn presented a challenge to the highly centralized national school system. According to the first large-scale government survey conducted that year, close to half of the returnees of middle-school and high-school age were entering a grade below that which they would normally attend, in order to make up for the (Japanese) school years that they had missed. The study also found that only 40 percent of the minor dependents accompanied their working parent (i.e., the father, in virtually all cases) if he was posted in Africa or Asia, while 70 percent did so if the overseas mission took place in North America or Europe.[1]

Two areas of concern were thus identified, which interestingly overlapped with the geographical location of the overseas posting: (1) children who had accompanied their parents abroad (mainly to North America and Europe) had trouble reintegrating into the school system upon their return to Japan, and (2) in the case of a posting in less-industrialized countries, parents felt there was a need for better schooling opportunities if their children were to accompany them overseas. The government set out to address these concerns based on two separate strategies: establishing a system of reentry for the kikoku-shijos, while assisting the kaigai-shijos by building full-time and part-time Japanese schools in areas where parents requested them.

The trickle-down effects of these ministerial decisions were not felt immediately, however. Kaigai/kikoku-shijo education specialist Gunei Sato conducted a thorough analysis of newspaper and magazine databases, and found that most articles written during the mid-1970s through the 1980s dealt with frustrated and concerned parents of kaigai/kikoku-shijos advocating on their children's behalf.[2]

The first of these articles was authored in 1975 by journalist Junji Kitashiro (himself an expatriate parent). In his inflammatory "Open letter to the Minister of Education, Culture, and Science," Kitashiro claimed that the government had failed their duty toward kikoku-shijos, making them "educational orphans (*kyouiku kimin*)." Sato argues that such rhetoric set the tone for a public perception of kikoku-shijos as "poor children in need of rescuing," a perception furthermore shared by educators as well as government officials and reflected in their policies.

KIKOKU-SHIJOS AS "SYMBOLS OF INTERNATIONALIZATION"

Sato's analysis goes on to show that media reports on kikoku-shijos abruptly changed in the mid-1980s: not only had the number of articles increased dramatically, but they were painting a much more positive picture of the returnees. With the historical signing of the Plaza Accord in 1985, the Japanese yen suddenly found itself almost at par with the U.S. dollar, prompting a tremendous enthusiasm among businesses and public alike for overseas expansion. International travel, foreign real estate buying sprees, and establishment of factories and plants outside of Japan all were manifestations of that enthusiasm—which would eventually lead to the wild era of its bubble economy.

However, it was not enough for the Japanese to venture outside of their borders. There was intense pressure exerted by U.S. politicians on the Japanese government to "open up" and to "internationalize." Although this pressure was mainly aimed at Japan's economy to ease its trade barriers to help decrease the United States' huge trade deficit, the term *internationalization* became a country-wide slogan that the Japanese took to heart. It is in this social atmosphere that kikoku-shijos, with their overseas upbringing and (presupposed) language and intercultural communication skills, came to be seen as the perfect symbol of a future Japan was aspiring to.

One crucial characteristic in media coverage during this period was that kikoku-shijos themselves, and not their parents, made appearances and talked about their experiences. The public now saw firsthand those internationalized youths on television, expressing themselves with confidence and maturity, and the perception dramatically shifted from the negative "deficient Japanese" image to that of a "new elite."

Sato points out that a deliberately skewed sample of returnees was behind the formation of such an image, as the majority were students of prestigious universities, had come back from North America or Europe, and had attended local or international schools.[3] Conveniently overlooked was the fact that only a small percentage of actual returnees possessed such a background.

The turnaround in public perception can also be attributed to a much-improved system of reintegration for kikoku-shijos: a large network of schools all over Japan accepted them and provided special academic and counseling support. Indeed, many private schools rushed to accommodate returnee students in order to qualify for government grants, and boasted their increased kikoku-shijo enrollment as proof of the school's commitment to "internationalization."

Fewer cases of kikoku-shijo maladaptation, bullying, or discrimination were heard of, and in an ironic twist, claims were raised that the special treatment kikoku-shijos enjoyed amounted to "reverse discrimination" toward home-grown Japanese students. It was argued that the otherwise extremely competitive university entrance system was made unduly easy for kikoku-shijos, who were admitted under separate criteria and therefore gained an unfair advantage over students who had toiled all the while in their home country.

THE KIKOKU-SHIJO STEREOTYPE AND ITS CONSEQUENCES

It should thus be reasonable to conclude that economic and social trends contributed to the construction of a certain image of kikoku-shijos during the 1970s and 1980s. Although initially negative, the image underwent an abrupt shift toward a more positive version, and subsequently stabilized in the eyes of the general public to the point that we can safely speak of the existence of a *kikoku-shijo stereotype*.

Kikoku-shijos are almost always perceived as being fluent speakers of a foreign language (i.e., English), having a profound knowledge of the host society and culture, and resulting in some type of "emancipated" personality. Few people realize that approximately one-third of all kaigai-shijos attend a full-time Japanese school and live a secluded life away from the host population, or that a great number of Japanese children in California are classified as "Limited English Proficiency" students even after several years of residence.

Another common perception is that kikoku-shijos enjoy special privileges in regards to entrance exams into prestigious schools. The Japanese Ministry of Education did establish special kikoku-shijo provisions for national university admissions and encouraged private schools all over Japan to follow suit. However, with the recent influx of foreign workers, the ministry has allocated resources formerly dedicated to kikoku-shijos in favor of more needy, non-Japanese speaking children. Kikoku-shijo education grants were officially ended in 2003, and many schools have since tightened their admission standards and are reluctant to take in any but the most accomplished students.

At the conclusion of his media analysis, Sato forewarned that a deeply engrained stereotype (as positive as it may be) can lead to the oversight of individual differences and actual needs among returnee children. Not least of the serious ill-effects is that teachers and school administrators put unduly high expectations on a returnee student as to their foreign language (i.e., English) or intercultural communication skills. Many cases of students who hide the fact that they lived overseas are testament to the stress caused by such mismatched expectations. Sato points out that this tendency to hide one's kikoku-shijo background is prevalent among, but not exclusive to, children who attended a full-time Japanese school while abroad.

Currently, the kaigai-shijo population is greatest in Asia, a region where traditionally the overwhelming majority of expatriate children attended the local full-time Japanese school. In recent years, however, the proportion of Japanese school students among kaigai-shijos in Asian countries declined from approximately 90 percent to just over 60 percent, while attendance of local international schools has soared.

Interviews of kaigai-shijo parents in Asia revealed that they are themselves very much influenced by the "bilingual, bicultural kikoku-shijo" stereotype constructed over two decades ago and wish for their own children to emulate that image. Sending the children to an international school where English is spoken is therefore considered a more desirable and fancier alternative to the full-time Japanese school, even though the latter may ensure a smoother transition into the Japanese school system upon return.

Consultants in the field of kikoku-shijo education worry that selecting an international school over a full-time Japanese school may backfire on two fronts. First, schools in Japan are no longer so eager to accommodate any returnee student just to appear "internationalized"; as a matter of fact, children who attended full-time Japanese schools (and thus do not need any remedial support) are now the more welcome type of kikoku-shijos. Second, attending an international school for a few years does not ensure a child will become a fluent speaker of English or gain competence in academic subjects taught in English. It could thus be argued that parents may be risking the consistency of their children's education for fewer returns than hoped for.[4]

Comparing Third Culture Kids and Kaigai/Kikoku-Shijos

SOCIETAL FACTORS

Why has Japan paid so much more attention to expatriate and returnee children compared, for example, to the United States, whose organizations arguably send out a larger number of expatriates than any other country in the world?

With the influx of foreign workers that started at the turn of the century, the population of Japan is becoming more diverse in terms of its ethnic composition. Still, the majority of people in Japan rarely question that theirs is an ethnically and culturally homogeneous nation. Over three decades ago, when kikoku-shijos' presence became conspicuous, Japanese society was even more ill-equipped than today to deal with the notion of diversity or how to accommodate that diversity within its institutions. In particular, Japan's highly centralized educational system was at a complete loss for what to do with children who had acquired cultural values and behavioral patterns different from those of their "home-grown" counterparts.[5]

In contrast, the United States has had a long history of immigration, and values (at least in principle) the multiethnic/multiracial nature of its population. Schools are expected to deal with students from various cultural backgrounds, and newcomers are given a chance to adapt into their host society. In such an environment, American children who return after a long absence from their home country may not be paid special attention to, for they might be assumed to not need the attention that is given to all newcomers who are unfamiliar with the U.S. social system.

Another factor that contributed to the intensity of the kikoku-shijo phenomenon is the Japanese fascination with things "Western," especially the English language, which coexists with the conviction that the essence of Japaneseness can only be grasped by "real" Japanese. History proves that Japan has always maintained a complex balance between nationalistic pride and desire for westernization, and this is arguably reflected in the polarized treatment kikoku-shijos receive in their home country. Kikoku-shijos can at times be looked down upon as undesirable outsiders, while at others they are elevated as models to emulate. Being Japanese by nationality and descent, kikoku-shijos do not benefit from the same level of sympathy foreigners enjoy when they step out of bounds of Japanese commonsense. However, by virtue of their life experience overseas, kikoku-shijos can also claim a quasiforeigner status that so many Japanese envy. This ambiguous positioning within Japanese society can thus be both a curse and a blessing for kikoku-shijos.

APPLYING A "TCK PERSPECTIVE" TO THE ANALYSIS OF THE KAIGAI/ KIKOKU-SHIJO EXPERIENCE

While TCKs often feel liberated when they learn of the existence of a label for people like themselves, *kikoku-shijo* is a label that many Japanese returnee children (including those who are now adults) find constricting and mismatched with their own experience.

The most serious problem with current kikoku-shijo stereotypes is their emphasis on language (mainly English) proficiency and intercultural communication skills. In order to "validate" the experiences of as many children as possible, however, we would argue that we need to focus instead on how these children have learned to view the world around them.

Most children who experience international mobility acquire a (literally) "global positioning system" and learn to locate themselves in relation to other cultures and societies in a way that cannot easily be achieved by children who never left their home country. This ability can be acquired regardless of how much exposure the child had to the host society's culture or how much of the local language he or she learned while overseas.

While not all TCKs return to their home (passport) country, kikoku-shijos are, in that sense, TCKs who are offered the chance to refamiliarize themselves with the society and culture their parents came from. Not only does this double process of departure and return strengthen their ability to navigate through various social systems, it also presents them with the unique opportunity to become an "insider/outsider" in more than one country.

Conceptualized in this manner, the kaigai/kikoku-shijo experience can indeed become a tremendous asset, but only if handled carefully. Parents have a heavy responsibility in this process, and should be concerned first and foremost by the emotional stability of their children, rather than by their own nebulous yearning for an "internationalized" offspring. In fact, I believe that children are better off *not* being regarded as international but feeling an insider in their own country, rather than the other way around.

It is clear that "cross-pollination," or learning from different approaches to the same phenomenon, can be extremely fruitful. On one hand, the study (and general perception) of kaigai/kikoku-shijos would greatly benefit from such a shift in focus. On the other hand, the study of third culture kids should also take into consideration the societal factors unique to each country of return, and how these can produce tremendous variations in the experience of those children.

Tribute

~~~~~~

Remembering David C. Pollock

by Betty Lou Pollock

O UR DAUGHTER, MICHELLE POLLOCK BOWER, likened her father to a great spreading oak tree, having deep roots and spreading branches. How apt a picture. His roots rested deeply in the soil of faith and hope. David endured massive storms while providing rest, shade, and enabling for many; his networking resembled not only a root system to sustain him but to connect others who became more effective for their interrelatedness to him and others. David was a catalyst and connector; he was always pleased to foster growth and development in others. Branches do not thrive and grow expansive without strong roots.

Many have asked how David became interested in *third culture kids (TCKs)*. It was largely due to his exposure to internationals, international students and missionary kids, some of whom were also TCKs. Dave realized that "someone should do something for these people"—that is, to help them ameliorate the challenges and enhance the benefits of their mobile childhoods. Words of a Dutch diplomat years later underlined this. He said that the benefits (of being a TCK) are social; the challenges are personal. Yes, and if the personal challenges are addressed, people grow freer to use their talents and knowledge.

David was equally at home behind a lectern in a Singaporean suit or running his chain saw in jeans frayed at the cuffs. He was comfortable in so many places in the world striving for cultural balance and assisting others in achieving that as well. Dave was a lifelong learner and was always proud of our family learning new things, even when we were separated due to his travels and life work. He loved teaching to make a positive difference.

David never believed it was a bad thing for parents to live and work and raise children cross-culturally. He did believe that preparation, intervention, and care could promote fewer shocks or trauma and greater health on all levels for entire families. He used to say that when TCKs were in charge of the world leadership, different decisions would be made, because he understood the heart and minds of those who know that humanness is universal. Can he know that Barack Obama was elected to lead the USA in 2008? Or that he has gathered around himself some highly skilled and bright TCKs? Does he know how much he is missed?

In April, 2004, David collapsed in the middle of presenting his TCK Profile to a group of teachers at the American International School in Vienna. He died nine days later, on April 11. Over many years and since his death, I have heard from countless TCKs who tell me how much David's work changed their lives. We still feel the expanse, the spreading branches of that oak tree.

Notes

CHAPTER 1

1. Carolyn D. Smith, *The Absentee American* (New York: Alethia Publications, 1994).
2. Brian Knowlton, "Americans Abroad Get an Advocacy Group in Congress," *International Herald Tribune*, March 11, 2007.
3. Graeme Hugo, "An Australian Diaspora?" *International Migration* 44 (1), 2006, 105–33.
4. Ted Ward, "The MKs' advantage: Three Cultural Contexts," in *Understanding and Nurturing the Missionary Family*, edited by Pam Echerd and Alice Arathoon (Pasadena, CA: William Carey Library, 1989), 57.

CHAPTER 2

1. Definition of TCK by David C. Pollock in *The TCK Profile* seminar material, Interaction, Inc., 1989, 1.
2. Global Nomads International is an organization formed by Norma McCaig in 1986 for TCKs of every background and nationality.
3. Families in Global Transition is an organization that sponsors an annual conference for those living and working with globally mobile families of all sectors. See *www.figt.org*.
4. Ruth Hill Useem, "Third Culture Kids: Focus of Major Study," *Newslinks*, Newspaper of the International School Services 12, 3 (January 1993), 1.
5. Ruth Hill Useem, "Third Cultural Factors in Educational Change," in *Cultural Factors in School Learning*, edited by Cole Brembeck and Walker Hill (Lexington, MA: Lexington Books, 1973), 122.
6. Ruth Hill Useem, "Third Culture Kids," *Newslinks*, 1.
7. Norma McCaig preferred to call those who grew up outside the parental culture(s) because of a career choice *global nomads*.
8. Dr. Ruth Hill Useem in a personal letter to David C. Pollock, February 1994.

9. Momo Kano Podolsky, "Kaigai-Shijo Socialization in Toronto," *IJJS*, Number 3, 11. See appendix B for a more detailed discussion on kaigai-shijos.

10. Ximena Vidal, "Third Culture Kids: A Binding Term for a Boundless Identity" (Senior Essay, April 10, 2000).

11. From the video *Global Nomads: Cultural Bridges for the Future*, coproduced by Alice Wu and Lewis Clark in conjunction with Cornell University.

CHAPTER 3

1. Brice Royer, owner of *TCKID.com*, in a personal e-mail to Ruth E. Van Reken, September 28, 2008. Used with permission.

2. Personal conversation with Ruth E. Van Reken, December 22, 2008.

CHAPTER 4

1. Alex Graham James, "Uniquely Me," in *Scamps, Scholars, and Saints*, edited by Jill Dyer and Roger Dyer (Kingswood, SA, Australia: MK Merimna, 1993), 234.

2. Hans Christian Andersen, *The Ugly Duckling*, adapted and illustrated by Jerry Pinkney (New York: Morrow Junior Books, William Morrow Publishing Co., 1999).

3. Paul G. Hiebert, *Cultural Anthropology*, 2nd ed. (Grand Rapids, MI: Baker Book House, 1983), 28–29.

4. Ibid., 25.

5. Gary Weaver, "The American Cultural Tapestry," *eJournal USA*, June 2006. *http://usinfo.state.gov/journals/itsv/0606/ijse/weaver.htm*.

6. Ibid.

7. Ibid.

8. From the musical *Fiddler on the Roof*. Book by Joseph Stein, music by Jerry Bock, lyrics by Sheldon Harnick, based on Sholom Aleichem's stories, *Fiddler on the Roof*, 4th Limelight Edition (New York: Crown Publishers, 1994), 29.

9. Figure 4-2 is adapted from a figure by Norma McCaig.

10. Ruth Hill Useem, "Third Cultural Factors in Educational Change," in *Cultural Factors in School Learning*, edited by Cole Brembeck and Walker Hill (Lexington, MA: Lexington Books, 1973), 126.

11. Helen Fail, "Some of the Outcomes of International Schooling" (Master's thesis, Brookes University, Oxford, England, 1995), 76.

12. John Denver, "Leaving on a Jet Plane," ©1967.

13. Joseph McDonald, e-mail communication, October 1995. Used by permission.

14. Personal correspondence from a TCK to David C. Pollock, November 1995. Used by permission.

15. Mary Edwards Wertsch, *Military Brats* (1991: reprint, Putnam Valley, NY: Aletheia Publications, 1996), 6.

16. This article by Crystal Chappell appeared in the Spring/Summer 1998 issue of the *Bastard Quarterly*. Copyright 1998 by Crystal Chappell.

17. Paulette M. Bethel and Ruth E. Van Reken, "Third culture kids and curriculum issues in the international school system: recognizing (and dealing effectively with) the hidden diversity of third culture kids (TCKs) in the classroom." Paper presented at "A conversation on educational achievements globally," Comparative and International Education Society Annual Conference, March 12–16, 2003, New Orleans, Louisiana.

18. Barbara H. Knuckles, in a personal e-mail to Ruth E. Van Reken, September 25, 2008. Used with permission.

CHAPTER 5

1. Sara Mansfield Tabor, *Of Many Lands: Journal of a Traveling Childhood* (Washington, DC: Foreign Service Youth Foundation, 1997), 1.

2. Paul Seaman, *Paper Airplanes in the Himalayas: The Unfinished Path Home* (Notre Dame, IN: Cross Cultural Publications, 1997), 7–8.

3. *Merriam-Webster's Collegiate Dictionary*, 11th ed., (Springfield, MA: Merriam-Webster, Inc., 2003).

4. Frances J. White, "Some Reflections on the Separation Phenomenon Idiosyncratic to the Experience of Missionaries and Their Children," *Journal of Psychology and Theology* 11, no. 3 (Fall 1983), 181–88.

5. Elisabeth Kübler-Ross, *On Death and Dying* (New York: Touchstone Books, 1997).

6. Mary Edwards Wertsch, *Military Brats* (1991: reprint, Putnam Valley, NY: Aletheia Publications, 1996).

7. Sharon Willmer, in a personal letter to David C. Pollock, 1984.

8. *Merriam-Webster's Collegiate Dictionary*, 11th ed. (Springfield, MA: Merriam-Webster, Inc., 2003).

9. John Bowlby, *Attachment and Loss: Attachment*, Vol. 1 (New York: Basic Books, 1969, 1982).

CHAPTER 6

1. Rachel Miller Schaetti, "Great Advantages," in *Notes from a Traveling Childhood*, edited by Karen Curnow McCluskey (Washington, DC: Foreign Youth Service Publication, 1994), 49.
2. From *http://en.wikipedia.org/wiki/Henry_Luce*.
3. Fareed Zakaria, "The Power of Personality," *Newsweek*, December 24, 2007.
4. Ibid.
5. Joseph McDonald, e-mail message on www.mknet.org, October 1995. Used with permission.
6. Jean Fritz, *Homesick: My Own Story* (New York: Bantam Doubleday Dell Publishing Group, 1984), 148–50.
7. Steve Eisinger, "The Validity of the 'Third Culture Kid' Definition for Returned Turkish Migrant Children" (research report submitted to The Ministry of Culture in the country of Turkey, August 31, 1994), 16.
8. Pico Iyer, "The Empire Writes Back," *Time*, February 8, 1992.
9. Ibid. Italics ours.

CHAPTER 7

1. Norma M. McCaig, "Understanding Global Nomads," *Strangers at Home* (New York: Aletheia Press, 1996), 101.

CHAPTER 8

1. Andrew Atkins, "Behavioral Strings to which MKs Dance," *Evangelical Missions Quarterly* (July 1989), 239–43.
2. Nancy Ackley Ruth, "What the World Needs Now . . . Global Skills," seminar presented at Families in Global Transition, Houston, Texas, March 6–8, 2008.
3. Nilly Venezia, "Ethics of Intercultural Education and Training," paper presented at SIETAR Europa Congress 2007, April 24–29, 2007, Sofia, Bulgaria.
4. Jeannine Heny, "Learning and Using a Second Language," in *Language: Introductory Readings*, 5th ed., edited by Virginia Clark, Paul A. Eschholz, and Alfred F. Rosa (New York: St. Martin's Press, 1994), 186.

CHAPTER 9

1.   Ruth E. Van Reken, response from original research survey on ATCKs, 1986. See Appendix A.
2.   Paul Seaman, *Paper Airplanes in the Himalayas: The Unfinished Path Home* (Notre Dame, IN: Cross Cultural Publications, 1997), 8.

CHAPTER 10

1.   Ruth E. Van Reken, original research survey on ATCKs, 1986. See Appendix A.
2.   Ard A. Louis, in an e-mail on MK issues, August 1996. Used by permission.
3.   From an e-mail on MK issues, August 1996. Used with permission.
4.   Mary Edwards Wertsch, *Military Brats* (1991: reprint, Putnam Valley, NY: Aletheia Publications, 1996), 263–65.
5.   Van Reken, original research.
6.   Hugh Missildine, *Your Inner Child of the Past* (New York: Simon and Schuster, 1963), 245–46.

CHAPTER 11

1.   Sophia Morton, "Let Us Possess One World," *Third Culture Kids: The Experience of Growing Up Among Worlds*, 1st ed. by David C. Pollock and Ruth E. Van Reken (Boston /London: Nicholas Brealey Publishing/Intercultural Press, 1999, 2001), 307–12.
2.   Sharon Willmer, "Personhood, Forgiveness, and Comfort," in *Compendium of the ICMK: New Directions in Mission: Implications for MKs*, edited by Beth Tetzel and Patricia Mortenson (West Brattleboro, VT: ICMK) 103–18.
3.   Ruth Hill Useem and Ann Baker Cottrell, "TCKs Experience Prolonged Adolescence," *Newslinks*, 13, no. 1 (September 1993), 1.
4.   "When Is a Child an Adolescent?" from *www.4troubledteens.com/adolescence.html*.
5.   Judith Gjoen, in a personal letter to David C. Pollock, November 1995.

CHAPTER 12

1. Poem by Alex Graham James. Used with permission.
2. Elisabeth Kübler Ross, *On Death and Dying* (New York: Touchstone Books, 1997).

CHAPTER 13

1. Robin Pascoe, *Raising Global Nomads: Parenting Abroad in an On-Demand World* (Vancouver, BC: Expatriate Press, 2006), 30.
2. Leslie Andrews, "The Measurement of Adult MKs' Well-being," *Evangelical Missions Quarterly* (October 1995), 418–26.
3. Shirley Torstrick, seminar handout. Used with permission.
4. From "Phoenix Rising: A Question of Cultural Identity" by Barbara Schaetti (*www.transition-dynamics.com/phoenix.html*).

CHAPTER 14

1. Anne P. Copeland, *Global Baby: Tips to Keep You and Your Infant Smiling Before, During and After Your International Move* (Boston: The Interchange Institute, 2004).
2. Ibid.
3. From a personal conversation with Ruth E. Van Reken, July 1997.

CHAPTER 15

1. Pico Iyer, "Living in the Transit Lounge," in *Unrooted Childhoods: Memoirs of Growing Up Global*, edited by Faith Eidse and Nina Sichel (Yarmouth, ME and London: Nicholas Brealey Publishing, 2004), 9.
2. Brian Hill, "The Educational Needs of the Children of Expatriates," in *Compendium of the ICMK: Manila*, edited by Beth A. Tetzel and Patricia Mortenson (Brattleboro, VT, 1986), 340.
3. Helen Fail, "Some of the Outcomes of International Schooling" (Master's thesis, Oxford Brookes University, June 1995), 8.
4. Jill Dyer and Roger Dyer, *What Makes Aussie Kids Tick?* (Kingswood, SA, Australia: MK Merimna, 1989), 139–40.
5. Helen Fail, "Some of the Outcomes of International Schooling."
6. Personal correspondence to David C. Pollock by Barbara F. Schaetti, Transition Dynamics, October 1998.
7. From Ruth E. Van Reken, research on 300 adult missionary kids, 1986. See Appendix A.

8. Leslie Andrews, "The Measurement of Adult MKs' Well-Being," *Evangelical Missions Quarterly*, Vol. 31, no. 4 (October 1995), 418–26.
9. John Useem, Ruth Hill Useem, Ann Baker Cottrell, and Kathleen Jordan, "TCKs Four Times More Likely to Earn Bachelor's Degrees" *Newlinks* 12, no. 5 (May 1993), 1.

CHAPTER 16

1. Read by Hendrik Verrijssen at the Procter & Gamble International Transferees, Inc. (PGITI) Conference, April 24, 2007, Cincinnati, OH. Used by permission.
2. Ted Ward, *Living Overseas: A Book of Preparations* (New York: Free Press, 1984).
3. Peter Gosling and Anne Huscroft, *How to Be a Global Grandparent: Living with the Separation* (Oakham, Rutland, UK: Zodiac Publishing, 2009).

CHAPTER 17

1. Faith Eidse and Nina Sichel, Eds., *Unrooted Childhoods: Memoirs of Growing Up Global* (Yarmouth, ME and London: Nicholas Brealey Publishing, 2004), 195.
2. Esther Schubert, "Keeping Third-Culture Kids Emotionally Healthy: Depression and Suicide Among Missionary Kids" in *ICMK Compendium: New Directions for Missions: Implications for MK,* edited by Beth A. Tetzel and Patricia Mortenson (Brattleboro, VT, 1986).
3. Barbara F. Schaetti, "A Most Excellent Journey," from *Raising Global Nomads: Parenting Abroad in an On-Demand World* by Robin Pascoe. (Vancouver, BC: Expatriate Press Limited, 2006), 214.
4. Robin Pascoe, *Homeward Bound: A Spouse's Guide to Repatriation* (Vancouver, BC: Expatriate Press Limited, 2002).
5. Craig Storti, *The Art of Coming Home* (Yarmouth, ME: Intercultural Press, 1997).
6. Conversation between Ruth E. Van Reken and Rosalea Cameron, author of "Missionary Kids: Why They Are; Why They Are What They Are; What Next" (Queensland, Australia: Cypress Trust, 2006). Used with permission.

CHAPTER 18

1. "A Most Excellent Journey" by Barbara Schaetti, Ph.D., in *Raising Global Nomads: Parenting Abroad in an On-Demand World* by Robin Pascoe (Vancouver, BC: Expatriate Press, 2006), 207–20.

2. Beverly Roman, Newsletter, BR Anchor Publishing, *http://www.branchor. com*, September 2008.
3. Mel Mandell and Lindsey Biel, "Global Repatriation," *Solutions* (February 1994), 23–26.
4. From the *ExpatExpert.com*/AMJ Campbell International Relocation "Family Matters!" Survey.
5. Ibid.
6. Ibid.
7. Ibid.
8. Beverly Roman, Newsletter, BR Anchor Publishing, *http://www.branchor. com*, September 2008.

CHAPTER 19

1. Brice Royer, developer of *www.TCKID.com*, in a personal e-mail to Ruth E. Van Reken, September 2008. Used with permission.
2. John Bowlby, *Attachment and Loss: Attachment*, Vol. 1 (New York: Basic Books, 1969, 1982).

APPENDIX B

1. Gunei Sato, *Kaigai Kikokushijo Kyouiku no Saikouchiku* (The Reconstruction of Kaigai/Kikoku-Shijo Education), (Tamagawa Daigaku Shuppan: 1997), 54.
2. Ibid., 206–40.
3. Ibid., 225.
4. Kakehashi, an association formed by parents of returnee students in the Kansai region, conducts an extensive survey of schools that are willing to admit children upon their return to Japan. Their findings are published in an annual directory, complemented by in-depth analyses of educational trends regarding the treatment of kikoku-shijos in the Japanese school system.
5. Momo Kano Podolsky, "Internationally Mobile Children: The Japanese Kikoku-Shijo Experience Reconsidered," *Contemporary Society Bulletin*, 2008: 49–69. Kyoto Women's University.

Resources for TCKs, ATCKs, and their Families

Organizations/Website Resources

AramcoBrats
www.aramco-brats.com
For Aramco TCKs who grew up in Saudi Arabia.

Around the World in a Lifetime (AWAL)/Foreign Service Youth Foundation
www.fsyf.org
Organization for United States foreign service teens.

British Expat
www.britishexpat.com
Full-featured site for expatriate Brits.

CanuckAbroad
www.canuckabroad.com
Caters to the Canadian expatriate, but provides information and resources—including a forum—that are equally useful for U.S. and other expatriates.

Expat Weekly Telegraph
www.telegraph.co.uk/expat
An online section of the *Weekly Telegraph* (U.K.) newspaper dedicated to expatriate living, with resources, news, articles, and information.

Expat Women
www.expatwomen.com

A free website helping expatriate women from all nationalities in any country in the world share experiences and advice, and find resources for living in a foreign country.

Expatica
www.expatica.com

This Netherlands-based website provides useful resources for those living and working in the Netherlands, Germany, France, Spain, and Belgium. It also publishes an online newsletter and hosts conferences on expat-related topics.

Families in Global Transition
www.figt.org

Hosts a yearly international conference on topics related to global family living.

Global Education Explorer
www.Globaleducationexplorer.com

A web-based tool that enables companies and families to learn about curricula in other countries, educational assessments, and customs surrounding schooling so that they are informed before making this all-important life change.

Hobsons
www.hobsons.com

Enables the preparation, recruitment, management, and advancement of students.

Interaction International
www.interactionintl.org

Organization founded by David C. Pollock. "The voice for third culture kids and internationally mobile families."

The Interchange Institute
www.interchangeinstitute.org

Offers training for educators, human resources personnel, and others in matters related to cross-cultural living.

Mu Kappa
www.mukappa.org

A fraternal association for missionary kids.

Overseas Brats
www.overseasbrats.com
Group for military kids.

School Choice International
www.schoolchoiceintl.com
Helps families with a child with special needs, for whom an overseas move is particularly difficult, both emotionally and educationally.

TCKid.com
www.TCKid.com
Founded by Brice Royer. Resource-rich interactive website for adult TCKs and CCKs.

Transitions Abroad
www.transitionsabroad.com/listings/living/resources/
    expatriatewebsites.shtml#global
A list of website addresses for expats of all countries.

Publications

Among Worlds
www.interactionintl.org/amongworlds.asp
A quarterly magazine for adult TCKs.

BR Anchor Publishing
www.branchor.com
Publisher of books for families on the move, including workbooks for young children.

Expatriate Expert
www.expatexpert.com
Website for Robin Pascoe, author of *A Moveable Marriage*, *Homeward Bound*, and *Raising Global Nomads*.

The Interchange Institute
www.interchangeinstitute.org

Publisher of books on the U.S. educational system for expats, moving with babies, and other resources.

Nicholas Brealey/Intercultural Press
www.nicholasbrealey.com

Get your favorite books here, including *Intercultural Marriage: Promises and Pitfalls* by Dugan Romano, *Unrooted Childhoods: Memoirs of Growing Up Global* by Faith Eidse and Nina Sichel, and *The Art of Coming Home* by Craig Storti.

Index